BIOLOGY OF MEMORY

CONTRIBUTORS

G. G. ARAKELOV

D. E. BROADBENT

J. BUREŠ

O. BUREŠOVÁ

KAO LIANG CHOW

L. GERBRANDT

HOLGER HYDÉN

ALLAN L. JACOBSON

V. Ph. KONOVALOV

I. KUPFERMANN

M. LAUFER

JAMES V. McCONNELL

SHARON McDONALD

JAMES L. McGAUGH

ARTHUR W. MELTON

BRENDA MILNER

BENNET B. MURDOCK, JR.

P. B. NEVELSKY

A. PAKULA

H. PINSKER

A. H. RIESEN

MARK R. ROSENZWEIG

HAROLD SALIVE

JAY M. SCHLECHTER

T. P. SEMYONOVA

TSUYOSHI SHIGEHISA

E. N. SOKOLOV

PHYLLIS SPEAR

D. N. SPINELLI

ENDEL TULVING

M. VERZEANO

O. S. VINOGRADOVA

NANCY C. WAUGH

BIOLOGY OF MEMORY

EDITED BY

KARL H. PRIBRAM

DEPARMENTS OF PSYCHIATRY AND PSYCHOLOGY
STANFORD UNIVERSITY
STANFORD, CALIFORNIA

DONALD E. BROADBENT

M. R. C. APPLIED PSYCHOLOGY UNIT
CAMBRIDGE, ENGLAND

1970

ACADEMIC PRESS   New York and London

QP406
P75

ACADEMIC PRESS, INC.
111 Fifth Avenue, New York, New York 10003

United Kingdom Edition published by
ACADEMIC PRESS, INC. (LONDON) LTD.
Berkeley Square House, London W1X 6BA

LIBRARY OF CONGRESS CATALOG CARD NUMBER: 77-84157

PRINTED IN THE UNITED STATES OF AMERICA

CONTENTS

v

Part III.   **Chemical Transfer**

Part IV.   **Neuronal Plasticity**

Part V.   **Realizing the Models**

LIST OF CONTRIBUTORS

Numbers in parentheses indicate the pages on which the authors' contributions begin.

G. G. ARAKELOV, Department of Neuropsychology, Moscow State University, Moscow, USSR (175)

DONALD E. BROADBENT, M.R.C. Applied Psychology Unit, Cambridge, England (15)

J. BUREŠ, Institute of Physiology, Prague, Czechoslovakia (223)

O. BUREŠOVÁ, Institute of Physiology, Prague, Czechoslovakia (223)

KAO LIANG CHOW, Division of Neurology, Stanford University School of Medicine, Stanford, California (273)

L. GERBRANDT,* Institute of Physiology, Prague, Czechoslovakia (223)

HOLGER HYDÉN, Institute of Neurobiology, Faculty of Medicine, University of Göteborg, Göteborg, Sweden (101)

ALLAN L. JACOBSON,† University of California, Los Angeles, California (123)

V. Ph. KONOVALOV, Department of Memory Problems, Academy Center for Biological Research, Puschino-on-the-Oka, USSR (191)

I. KUPFERMANN, Department of Physiology and Biophysics, and Department of Psychiatry, New York University Medical School, New York, New York (163)

M. LAUFER,‡ Department of Biophysics and Nuclear Medicine, University of California, Los Angeles, California (239)

JAMES V. McCONNELL, Mental Health Research Institute, University of Michigan, Ann Arbor, Michigan (129)

SHARON McDONALD, Department of Biophysics and Nuclear Medicine, University of California, Los Angeles, California (239)

JAMES L. McGAUGH, Department of Psychobiology, University of California, Irvine, California (51)

* Present address: Neuropsychology Laboratory, Veterans Administration Hospital, West Haven, Connecticut.
† Present address: Department of Psychology, San Francisco State College, San Francisco, California.
‡ Present address: Fellow of the Instituto Venezolano de Investigaciones Cientificas, Caracas, Venezuela.

ARTHUR W. MELTON, University of Michigan, Ann Arbor, Michigan (3)

BRENDA MILNER, Montreal Neurological Institute, McGill University, Montreal, Canada (29)

BENNET B. MURDOCK, JR., University of Toronto, Toronto, Ontario (11)

P. B. NEVELSKY, Kharkov University, Kharkov, USSR (21)

A. PAKULA, Department of Neuropsychology, Moscow State University, Moscow, USSR (175)

H. PINSKER, Department of Physiology and Biophysics, and Department of Psychiatry, New York University Medical School, New York, New York (163)

A. H. RIESEN, University of California, Riverside, California (87)

MARK R. ROSENZWEIG, University of California, Berkeley, California (69)

HAROLD SALIVE, Mental Health Research Institute, University of Michigan, Ann Arbor, Michigan (129)

JAY M. SCHLECHTER, University of California, Los Angeles, California (123)

T. P. SEMYONOVA, Department of Memory Problems, Academy Center for Biological Research, Puschino-on-the-Oka, USSR (191)

TSUYOSHI SHIGEHISA, Mental Health Research Institute, University of Michigan, Ann Arbor, Michigan (129)

E. N. SOKOLOV, Department of Neuropsychology, Moscow State University, Moscow, USSR (175)

PHYLLIS SPEAR, Department of Biophysics and Nuclear Medicine, University of California, Los Angeles, California (239)

D. N. SPINELLI, Stanford University, Stanford, California (293)

ENDEL TULVING, University of Toronto, Toronto, Ontario (7)

M. VERZEANO,* Department of Biophysics and Nuclear Medicine, University of California, Los Angeles, California (239)

O. S. VINOGRADOVA, Department of Memory Problems, Academy Center for Biological Research, Puschino-on-the-Oka, USSR (191)

NANCY C. WAUGH, Harvard Medical School, Boston, Massachusetts (63)

* Present address: Department of Psychobiology, University of California, Irvine, California.

PREFACE

As recently as in midcentury, biologists and psychologists alike despaired of coming to grips with the problem of how we organize our experience into the lasting structures that influence subsequent behavior. The scientific climate has changed radically during the 1960's—a frontal attack on the problem of memory organization has been mounted. Computer scientists, mathematicians, behavioral psychologists, neuropsychologists, neurophysiologists, biophysicists, and biochemists have each in their own way found it possible to work effectively on the nature of memory. Some start with introspections and externalize these into programs meant to simulate subjective experience. Others begin with observed behavior and analyze the time course of the effectiveness of events that determine that behavior. Still others record the electrical and chemical changes produced in the brain as evidence that a record is being organized by this critical anatomical unit.

The enigma of memory has thus finally been engaged and work is underway. One might therefore best view this volume as pages from a diary describing a scientific journey of discovery. As such, it makes a fascinating tale.

The contributions are presented according to topic. An analysis of the issues is given in the beginning chapters and the final chapters deal with some attempts at realizing memory models in hardware and wetware. In between is detailed much of the meager and hard-won biological evidence that is available today—that plastic changes can and do occur within the organism as a consequence of experience.

The XVIII International Congress of Psychology, held in Moscow in August 1966, was notable for its outstanding program of symposia organized by Alexander Romanovitch Luria. Among these, two were devoted to the topic of the memory trace. Luria and the chairmen of these gatherings decided that the topic was of sufficient general interest and the presentations of sufficient merit to warrant publication. This decision was implemented and supplemented in the following way. For one or another reason some who were invited were unable to attend the Moscow meetings. Manuscripts were solicited and obtained from these absentees. Further, a few cogent contributions were presented at the Fiftieth Anniversary Convention of the American Psychological Association held in Washington,

D.C. in 1967 and these were solicited. All in all, the volume therefore represents the thinking and research on memory current in the latter part of the 1960's.

We hope the reader will come away sharing our enthusiasm for this vista of a research area.

KARL H. PRIBRAM
DONALD E. BROADBENT

BIOLOGY OF MEMORY

Part I

ANALYZING THE ISSUES

SHORT- AND LONG-TERM POSTPERCEPTUAL MEMORY: DICHOTOMY OR CONTINUUM?

ARTHUR W. MELTON

University of Michigan
Ann Arbor, Michigan

Novel stimulus information, which is known to have been responded to (perceived), suffers a rapid decrease in recallability over the first 30 sec. filled with rehearsal-preventing activity. With increased duration or frequency of the original presentation, short-term memory (STM) for such novel information shows marked improvement, with perfect recognition and complete recall after very long periods of time as the limit (LTM). In spite of this apparent continuity of STM and LTM, some behavior theorists assume that two mechanisms with different characteristics are involved in STM and LTM; others assume that the processes involved in STM are qualitatively the same as those involved in LTM.

Currently it seems unlikely that any set of experimental observations will persuade continuum proponents to accept a dichotomy interpretation of STM or vice versa. The reason for the intransigence of the continuum theorist may, however, be readily identified. They expect the principles of the interference theory of long-term forgetting, which are rooted in the assumptions of contemporary S-R association theory, to be applicable to short-term forgetting and remembering. To grant an exception in STM would place severe limitations on the application of S-R theory to perceptual, discriminative, and categorizing responses. In particular, the point at issue seems to be the role of the stimulus in determining excitatory and inhibitory processes, and even more specifically, the role of stimulus similarity in the production of interference or inhibition in recall or both.

At the level of observation, the S-R theory of forgetting, as developed in the context of LTM, specifies that the amounts of retroactive interference (RI) and proactive interference (PI) are positively correlated with the similarity of the to-be-remembered unit (TBRU) and the interpolated activity (RI) or prior activity (PI). At the level of theory, these observed effects (and their vagaries) are traced to similarity of the *stimulus* terms in the two (or more) S-R paradigms

3

involved in the perception and retrieval of two (or more) differentiated but mutually incompatible responses.

Theories that assume a special STM mechanism or process seek, at the observational level, to deny the importance of the similarity of the TBRU and the prior or interpolated activity. Instead, the loss of information from STM is attributed either to the passage of time and the autonomous decay processes correlated with time (Brown, 1958; Broadbent, 1963), or to the number of perceptual acts subsequent to the perception of the TBRU (Waugh & Norman, 1965). Both of these theories identify the period of time following the perception of the TBRU as the locus of the processes that produce decrement in recall; neither theory has given particular attention to the effect of prior activities (PI) on STM, and when such effects are considered, it must be assumed that, following Conrad (1960), they are interpreted as a consequence of the forgetting of the TBRU, not as a cause of such forgetting.

The evidence that persuades the S-R association theorist to remain intransigent regarding STM processes is of two kinds. The first shows that short-term forgetting is very imperfectly correlated, if at all, with either time or the number of dissimilar perceptual responses when the similarity of prior activity and the TBRU is minimal, as it is on the very first trial of an experiment. Data from the first trial of an experiment by Noyd (1965) show that the recall of 2-, 3-, and 5-noun TBRUs after 4 sec. of digit reading have the expected differences attributable to length of TBRU, but there is no further reduction in recall after an additional 4 or 20 sec. of digit reading. Although the 4-sec. interval in this experiment may be too long to provide a proper test of the recency effect attributed by Waugh and Norman (1965) to "primary" memory, it is noteworthy that a strongly bowed serial-position curve for correct responses is present in recall after 4, 8, and 24 sec., although slightly reduced at the 24-sec. interval as compared with the 4-sec. interval.

The second persuasive line of evidence relates to the presence and amount of proactive interference in STM. Keppel and Underwood (1962) and Loess (1964) have demonstrated that PI builds up rapidly over the first few trials of an experiment in which the successive TBRUs are drawn from the same category of elements (consonants). Wickens, Born and Allen (1963) have confirmed this finding and have shown that release from this accumulated PI occurs when one shifts to a different category of elements in constructing the TBRU. Loess (1965) has again confirmed the build-up of PI over successive strings of words drawn from the same semantic category (e.g., "animal" words) and has again obtained release from PI by shifting to a different semantic category.

The data to be reported extend this evidence for PI as a major factor in short-term forgetting and its dependence on similarity. The data of Noyd (1965) provide evidence that the amount of forgetting of a 2-, 3-, or 5-word unit is greatest when the preceding unit has the same length. Intrusion errors (words from the preceding stimulus unit) are likewise maximal in frequency when the preceding unit and the TBRU have the same length. There is a high correlation of the serial position of occurrence of an intrusion and its serial position in its source. This correlation is maximal when the TBRU and the preceding stimulus units have the same length, but it is present even when there are wide discrepancies in length. Finally, other studies that use only 3-word stimuli or only 5-word stimuli confirm the strong correlation of serial positions in the case of intrusions and show that the PI in recall (and the overt intrusions) varies in the expected orderly fashion as one manipulates the degree of learning (number of repetitions or retention interval or both) of the prior stimulus unit and the degree of learning of the TBRU.

The position is taken that PI is a major factor in STM and that it occurs as a consequence of activity prior to the presentation of the initial element of the TBRU only to the extent that such prior activity and the TBRU are similar. Some portion of this inhibitory effect of the similar prior activity is attributable to active reproductive interference, as evidenced by the overt occurrence of words appropriate to prior stimulus units. The occurrence of PI and of such overt intrusions is interpretable in S-R association theory as a coding of TBRUs by the category of the elements of which they are composed, by a length category, and by a serial-position category, as well as by contextual cues common to the entire experimental situation. Such coding is reflected in the functional, implicit stimuli involved in retrieval of information that has been stored in memory, and such functional stimulus similarity is responsible for the inhibition or interference in STM as well as in LTM.

REFERENCES

Broadbent, D. E. Flow of information within the organism. *Journal of Verbal Learning and Verbal Behavior,* 1963, **2**, 34-39.

Brown, J. Some tests of the decay theory of immediate memory.*Quarterly Journal of Experimental Psychology,* 1958, **10**, 12-21.

Conrad, R. Serial order intrusions in immediate memory. *British Journal of Psychology,* 1960, **51**, 45-48.

Keppel, G., & Underwood, B. J. Proactive inhibition in short-term retention of single items. *Journal of Verbal Learning and Verbal Behavior,* 1962, **1**, 153-161.

Loess, H. Proactive inhibition in short-term memory. *Journal of Verbal Learning and Verbal Behavior,* 1964, **3**, 362-368.

Loess, H. Proactive inhibition and word category in short-term memory. Paper presented at meetings of the Midwestern Psychological Association, Chicago, May 1965.

Noyd, D. E. Proactive and intrastimulus interference in short-term memory for two-, three-, and five-word stimuli. Paper presented at meetings of the Western Psychological Association, Honolulu, June 1965.

Waugh, N. C., & Norman, D. A. Primary memory. *Psychological Review,* 1965, **72**, 89-104.

Wickens, D. D., Born, D. G., & Allen, C. K. Proactive inhibition and item similarity in short-term memory. *Journal of Verbal Learning and Verbal Behavior,* 1963, **2**, 440-445.

SHORT- AND LONG-TERM MEMORY: DIFFERENT RETRIEVAL MECHANISMS[1]

ENDEL TULVING

University of Toronto
Toronto, Ontario

The dichotomy between short-term memory (STM) and long-term memory (LTM) probably reflects a somewhat optimistic oversimplification of an extremely complex situation, but it has been with us, in one form or another, at least as long as memory has been studied in the laboratory. Recently the distinction has become the focus of considerable theoretical interest and even controversy. As shown by most papers presented at this symposium, the question of primary interest has to do with the nature of mechanisms or processes underlying the two types of memory. Are these mechanisms or processes similar or different?

The nature of underlying processes can be inferred only from the relations among observable variables. The processes are assumed to be identical, or at least similar, when experimentally manipulable variables or operations have identical effects on observable performance, and different when the effects are different. Since sufficient evidence has been presented at this symposium and since other evidence is available in the literature to show that a number of variables do produce different effects on recall at different retention intervals, it seems to be necessary to conclude that STM and LTM involve at least partially nonoverlapping mechanisms. In other words, the dualistic position seems to be easier to reconcile with experimental facts than the continuity position.

If we accept the dualistic position, we can ask further questions about the distinction between STM and LTM. One such question that sooner or later will have to be asked has to do with the *locus* of the distinction in the sequence of events constituting an act of memory. There are three such events: input of information into the memory store, storage of information (i.e., maintenance of the information in the store), and retrieval of information from the store (Mel-

[1]The preparation of this paper has been supported by the National Science Foundation, Grant No. GB 3710.

ton, 1963). The question, then, is the following: Do the differences between STM and LTM mechanisms reflect differences in input, storage, or retrieval?

Usually the distinction between STM and LTM is made in terms of storage processes. A number of theorists have proposed that separate stores exist for STM and LTM [e.g., Broadbent (1958), Glanzer & Cunitz (1966), Waugh & Norman (1965)]. The STM store is assumed to have strictly limited capacity, with all of the incoming information regularly being displaced by subsequent inputs or simply decaying unless rehearsed, while the LTM store is thought to have much greater capacity for holding information selectively received through the short- term store.

The major weakness of the conception of STM and LTM in terms of separate storage mechanisms lies in its failure to specify the processes responsible for getting the information out of either type of store. Frequently the assumption is made that whatever information exists in either store can be retrieved, by searching through the store, as long as the information exists in the store, but this is clearly an untenable assumption. Recall performance does not only depend on the information *available* in the store, but also on *accessibility* of that information (Tulving & Pearlstone, 1966). Accessibility of stored information is determined by retrieval cues available to the subject at the time of attempted recall. It is possible to think of the function of retrieval cues as that of guiding the search through the store, but the conception of guided search is quite different from one of unguided or probabilistic search.

Given the necessity of postulation of retrieval cues as an important component of the recall process, the identification of STM and LTM with different storage systems loses much of its heuristic usefulness. It seems somewhat more reasonable to explore the view that STM and LTM involve different retrieval processes rather than different storage systems. According to this view, all information that is to be retrieved at a later time, regardless of when it will be retrieved, is stored in one and the same store. Retrieval from this unitary store occurs as a consequence of availability of retrieval cues which bridge the gap between the present environmental demands and the information stored in memory on an earlier occasion. Unless at least one retrieval cue exists for a given unit of information, the unit cannot be retrieved.

What events constitute retrieval cues that provide access to the information about to-be-remembered items in the memory store? In general, the nature of effective retrieval cues is determined by the coding of input material at the time of input. When a to-be-remembered unit is stored, some ancillary information about it is also stored with it. The storage of this ancillary information represents what is referred to as "coding." When some of this ancillary information (or the "code" of the to-be-remembered unit) is available at the time of attempted recall, the code serves as a retrieval cue. The effectiveness of retrieval cues thus depends, among other things, upon coding operations that have taken place at input and the availability of information about these coding operations at output. Conversely, of course, coding of to-be-remembered units at input facilitates recall only if the ancillary information is more readily accessible at output than are the to-be-remembered units as such.

One type of ancillary information stored with each to-be-remembered unit at the time of input consists of "time tags" (Yntema & Trask, 1963). Such temporal coding provides specific temporal retrieval cues that affect the recall of to-be-remembered units over short periods of time in case of homogeneous series of input events, and perhaps over longer periods of time in case of nonhomogeneous series (cf., von Restorff, 1933). Another type of ancillary information stored at input has to do with semantic and associative features of to-be-remembered units determined by the pre-experimental experiences of the subject (e.g., Tulving & Pearlstone, 1966). Retrieval cues resulting from such semantic coding are effective over much longer intervals than those provided by temporal coding and thus can be thought of as providing the major access route to stored information following longer retention intervals.

Even though we cannot specify the exact nature of different kinds of effective retrieval cues very precisely at the present time, the general conception of the somewhat arbitrary dichotomy between STM and LTM in terms of different kinds of retrieval processes seems to be promising. The ideas I have tried to summarize here have fruitfully guided our own research and thinking at Toronto. We have done a series of experiments in which we have studied the role, function, and nature of retrieval cues of various types, and the results have been most encouraging. The conceptual distinction between STM and LTM in terms of differences in retrieval mechanisms, in my opinion, has a distinct advantage over the dual storage conception in that it forces the theorist to do some hard thinking about retrieval processes as such. A theory of memory is incomplete, or perhaps not even a theory, until it specifies how the information available in the memory store becomes accessible at the time of recall.

REFERENCES

Broadbent, D. E. *Perception and Communication.* New York: Macmillan (Pergamon), 1958.
Glanzer, M., & Cunitz, A. R. Two storage mechanisms in free recall. *Journal of Verbal Learning and Verbal Behavior,* 1966, **5**, 351-360.
Melton, A. W. Implications of short-term memory for a general theory of memory. *Journal of Verbal Learning and Verbal Behavior,* 1963, **2**, 1-21.
Tulving, E., & Pearlstone, Z. Availability versus accessibility of information in memory for words. *Journal of Verbal Learning and Verbal Behavior,* 1966, **5**, 381-391.
von Restorff, H. Uber die Wirkung von Bereichsbildungen im Spurenfeld. *Psychologische Forschung,* 1933, **18**, 299-342.
Waugh, N. C., & Norman, D. A. Primary memory. *Psychological Review,* 1965, **72**, 89-104.
Yntema, D. B., & Trask, F. P. Recall as a search process. *Journal of Verbal Learning and Verbal Behavior,* 1963, **2**, 65-74.

SHORT- AND LONG-TERM MEMORY FOR ASSOCIATIONS

BENNET B. MURDOCK, JR.

University of Toronto
Toronto, Ontario

The formation, retention, and utilization of associations have long been topics of considerable interest to students of memory. Studies of the learning and retention of lists of paired associates have provided the experimental psychologist with one technique for studying associative phenomena, and findings from these studies provide a major source of data on long-term memory. Recently techniques have been developed to study forgetting of single pairs over much briefer periods of time, and already there is much information about short-term memory. The question naturally arises as to whether it is necessary to postulate different processes (either in storage or retrieval) for long- and short-term memory.

There is at least some reason to think that, with paired associates, a dichotomous model may be unnecessary. The nature of the intratrial forgetting of single paired associates is such that, immediately after presentation, probability of correct recall of any given pair drops rapidly as the next few pairs are presented. However, forgetting levels off at some asymptotic value greater than zero. In one study (Murdock, 1963) it was found that the asymptote varied regularly with experimental conditions in a way that one would expect from knowledge of intertrial effects; namely, the asymptotic value increased with study time and repetition. The argument was advanced that, in typical list-learning studies, intratrial forgetting regularly occurs but is not detected by the typical experimental arrangements. With repetition the asymptote of this forgetting becomes progressively higher, until eventually the subject reaches whatever performance criterion is specified by the experimenter. What is generally referred to as "learning" is essentially increased resistance to intratrial forgetting.

This general point of view suggests then that perhaps processes occurring within a single trial can be extended to longer periods of time to account for typical list-learning effects. Further evidence along this line came from a later study (Murdock, 1967) where first-trial performance on lists ranging in length from 9 to 100 pairs was predictable from knowledge of asymptotic performance on 6-pair lists obtained by a simple probe-type test. Further, a fluctuation model was suggested which postulated two states of memory but no distinction between short- and long-term processes.

Evidence in favor of a dichotomy seems to come from studies showing differential similarity effects in short- and long-term memory. For instance, semantic similarity has been shown to affect long- but not short-term memory (Baddeley & Dale, 1966) whereas acoustic similarity affects short- but not long-term memory (Bruce & Murdock, 1968). However, there is evidence of a rather different sort that would suggest acoustic effects in long-term memory. The "tip of the tongue" phenomenon (Brown & McNeill, 1966) seems to show quite clearly that, in generic recall of items in the long-term store, similarity in sound to the target item does occur and in fact seems to be somewhat more common than similarity in meaning (224 SS words compared to 95 SM words).

Short-term memory is often studied as a *Ding an sich.* However, from an information-processing point of view it is only part of the system and other components must be involved. For instance, sufficient information to output (vocalize) words must be stored as part of the permanent long-term store. Show an individual a pictorial representation of a common object and he can name it. These "output subroutines" are acquired early in life and must result in something like the formation of a neural "dictionary" (Brown & McNeill, 1966, p. 333). Access to this stored information must be by a variety of routes; many stimuli can elicit the same response. Just as a computer stores content and address, so it may be that the contents (*what* is stored) of this neural dictionary are the output subroutines necessary to articulate words whereas the locations (*where* it is stored) are specified in terms of semantic information which function as retrieval cues (Tulving & Osler, 1968).

According to this view, then, one would expect to find both articulatory and semantic similarity effects in long-term memory. Semantic factors would guide or direct the search, and they specify the address of the requisite information. For various reasons the contents of the specified location may not be completely legible, resulting in a tentative response which is similar or identical in some features but clearly not complete. The "tip of the tongue" effect then represents a case of degraded articulatory information, but the retrieval cues unambiguously designate the desired location. The other case surely exists too; the content is clear but the address is too vague.

There does seem to be some evidence for the operation of articulatory cues in short-term memory. Hintzman (1967) has found that confusion errors for visually presented nonsense syllables reflected more the articulatory than the auditory similarities. Murray (1965) has found that degree or intensity of vocalization has a facilitating effect on short-term recall. Levy and Murdock (1968) found acoustic-similarity effects but no effects due to delayed auditory feedback; the most promising interpretation seemed to be in terms of loss of articulatory cues.

Human memory is of sufficient complexity so that undoubtedly many processes must be involved. It is therefore unrealistic to hope that any single-process model would be very adequate. What is suggested here then is simply that the assumption of continuity between short- and long-term memory may still be tenable. Phenomena occurring over short time periods do seem to have some predictive value for longer-term effects. One component of long-term memory must be the articulatory subroutines to produce the actual verbalizations of adult human beings, and perhaps semantic information may designate the specific addresses.

REFERENCES

Baddeley, A. D., & Dale, H. C. The effect of semantic similarity on retroactive interference in long- and short- term memory. *Journal of Verbal Learning and Verbal Behavior,* 1966, 5, 417-420.

Brown, R., & McNeill, D. The "tip of the tongue" phenomenon. *Journal of Verbal Learning and Verbal Behavior,* 1966, 5, 325-337.

Bruce, D., & Murdock, B. B., Jr. Acoustic similarity effects in short- and long-term memory. *Journal of Verbal Learning and Verbal Behavior,* 1968, 7, 627-631.

Hintzman, D. L. Articulatory coding in short-term memory. *Journal of Verbal Learning and Verbal Behavior,* 1967, 6, 312-316.

Levy, B. A., & Murdock, B. B., Jr. The effects of delayed auditory feedback and intra-list similarity in short-term memory. *Journal of Verbal Learning and Verbal Behavior,* 1968, 7, 887-894.

Murdock, B. B.. Jr. Short-term memory and paired-associate learning. *Journal of Verbal Learning and Verbal Behavior,* 1963, 2, 320-328.

Murdock, B. B., Jr. A fixed-point model for short-term memory. *Journal of Mathematical Psychology,* 1967, 4, 501-506.

Murray, D. J. Vocalization-at-presentation and immediate recall, with varying presentation-rates. *Quarterly Journal of Experimental Psychology,* 1965, 17, 47-56.

Tulving, E., & Osler, S. Effectiveness of retrieval cues in memory for words. *Journal of Experimental Psychology,* 1968, 77, 593-601.

RECENT ANALYSES OF SHORT-TERM MEMORY

DONALD E. BROADBENT

M. R. C. Applied Psychology Unit
Cambridge, England

A proper desire for parsimony makes many investigators wish to explain all forms of memory by a single mechanism. Forgetting of well-learned material is now usually explained as due to the subsequent learning of other interfering material, the stimulus formerly appropriate to response *A* now producing response B. Those investigators who wish to preserve the economical view of a single mechanism for a long- and short-term memory would also like to argue that forgetting in short-term memory is of the same type. An opposing view is that forgetting in short-term memory is a quite different kind; that when one has just looked up a telephone number, one is retaining it only by continuous rehearsal, that is, by somehow devoting to the preservation of the telephone number the mechanisms which are normally used in perception. Any interfering activity which is demanded of one, such as answering a question, dropping and picking up the telephone directory, or something of than sort may prevent rehearsal and so cause forgetting the number. On this view, once material has been well learned, it is preserved in a different mechanism and the importance of distracting activities is changed. Both these theories in fact require forgetting to be preceded by some form of interference. Even the person who believes in two mechanisms, such as myself, needs some sort of interfering activity to fully load the rehearsal mechanism, if forgetting in short-term memory is to appear. Arguments about the need for two mechanisms rather than one must therefore hinge upon the precise nature of the interfering activity that is needed for forgetting.

In long-term memory, it is known to be the nature of the interfering activity which produces forgetting, as might be expected if the cause of the forgetting is the learning of new associations between items which become incompatible with old ones. Clearly, if one learns a telephone number and subsequently learns the Russian language, there is very little similarity between the material in the two cases, and so learning Russian should not cause one to forget one's own telephone numbers. It is however plausible that learning Russian might cause one to forget Greek, in so far as there are similarities between the two languages, and

15

one must suppress one's early learning in order to succeed with Russian. It has been argued however, by myself among others, that in short-term memory it is not so much the nature of the intervening activity, but simply its occurrence that matters: Whatever distracts attention and prevents rehearsal may produce inefficiency in short-term memory. Some evidence has been presented by Conrad and by myself that the same interfering activity produces more serious effects on short-term memory when it is performed slowly than when it is performed fast, and this was assumed to indicate a decay of short-term memory resulting purely from time and therefore rather different from the forgetting produced by interference in long-term memory. However, the effects are very slight, and difficult to reproduce: Some evidence has been presented by Waugh and Norman (1965) that the effect of time hardly matters compared with the sheer number of events that have intervened between learning something and being asked to recall it.

It is perhaps better therefore to concentrate not so much upon the time taken by the intervening activity, as upon the similarity between it and the material originally learned. As has already been argued, it is possible to produce forgetting in short-term memory by means of activities which bear no obvious similarity to the material one is trying to remember. In the experiment of Waugh and Norman, it is even necessary, in order to produce consistent relationships, to count as an item the blank intervals which occur at certain points in the sequence of events between presentation and recall. This certainly supports one's intuitive feeling that picking up the telephone directory is as likely to produce the forgetting of the telephone number as is some other intruding activity more similar in content to the telephone number itself. From the point of view of drawing distinctions between short- and long-term memory, the difference in the effects of similarity is just as good as a difference in the effect of the time taken by the intervening activity; and it is therefore of interest to examine this question.

Unfortunately for those who, like myself, support the two mechanisms theory, Wickelgren (1965) has shown that acoustic similarity between something that has been learned and other material that is subsequently presented will increase the amount of forgetting of the first items. Thus for example one might be given the three letters BCD to remember and then subsequently told to copy out six other letters before reproducing the first three. If the intervening copied letters were PTPVVT, one is very likely to forget the original letters. If however the intervening letters were FLFMML, one has much less trouble in remembering the earlier items (Dale, 1964). Similarity does definitely play a part in short-term memory, and to that extent there is a resemblance to long-term memory.

In long-term memory, however, it is not only the sounds of items which are being remembered that are important but also their meanings. Much recent research in memory has involved the transfer of learning through mediated associations in meanings, and it is quite well established that similarity in meaning between two words, even though they sound quite different, may be important in determining the efficiency of long-term memory. Baddeley (1964) has examined the effect of varying semantic similarity of material presented in short-term memory and finds quite different results. If for example one presents a sequence of five words "broad, great, large, wide, big," one can compare performance with a sequence such as "hot, old, strong, foul, deep." In the first case, each item is accompanied by other items of similar meaning, while in the second case the meanings of the items are different. In short-term memory there is very little difference in the efficiency of performance with the two types of lists, although a similar technique employed with acoustic similarity showed the same effect as had been found by Wickelgren. In short-term memory, therefore, semantic similarity does not seem to be nearly as important as acoustic similarity in producing interference. There is a difference in the two processes, although it is not the difference which I originally expected.

It is perhaps fair to argue that this difference reflects some corresponding difference in the organization of memory for retrieval in the two cases. Material that has only recently been received seems to be classified by sensory properties such as sound, while that which is better established is organized by meaning. In either case, when one comes to recall particular items, they have to be distinguished from the intervening ones, and this is hardest when those intervening items are more similar along the particular dimensions that are of primary importance for the particular form of memory in use. Such a view makes a distinction between learning the nature of items, and being able to retrieve them and produce them properly on the appropriate occasion: a distinction which is now widely held by a number of theorists, including many who do not draw a distinction between long- and short-term memory. Indeed, the extent to which one may get different results by requiring people to learn serial lists or paired associates on the one hand, and simply to reproduce items by free recall on the other, suggests that there is indeed a distinction between the learning of response items and memory for the circumstances under which a particular response is appropriate. Many experiments on short-term memory use a vocabulary of possible responses which is already well established, such as letters, numbers, or words. Even in the rare cases where nonsense syllables are used, these are made up of letters which are themselves familiar, and it has been shown by Melton (1963) that in some ways a single nonsense syllable of three letters behaves rather like three words that are already known. In retrieving material which has been selected from a known vocabulary of this sort, a good deal obviously depends upon the preferences among the various items which the learner has before he does any learning at all: his "response bias" in favor of some alternatives rather than others. Dale, for example, has recently conducted a study on memory (unpublished) for lists of items in which each item was the name of an English county. The names of some counties are remembered better than the names of others. Other groups of subjects were however simply asked to produce as many counties as they could think of, without particularly having to learn a special list. The counties which were best remembered were those which were given by a high proportion of people who had done no learning at all and were merely asked to think of the counties. I have little doubt that similar results could be found for states of the U.S.A. or departments of the French Republic. There are probably too few republics in the U.S.S.R. to show this effect, since I imagine that most Soviet citizens know the complete list whereas most English people will forget one or two counties on any particular occasion, although they would probably recognize the names were they suggested to them.

It is clear from Dale's results therefore that recall of the names of English counties is being affected by a response bias in favor of the names of some counties rather than others, which exists even before any learning whatever has taken place. Similar biases may well exist between the various numbers, letters, words, and so on. In the case of numbers for example it has been shown by Baddeley that subjects of the type we use in our experiments tend to produce the digits zero, one, or two especially frequently if they are asked to continue sequences of digits; and correspondingly, they find these digits easier to reproduce when they are given a number of digits to write down from a tachistoscopic presentation. In perceptual experiments, there have recently been advances of technique which have allowed a proper correction for such biases. The traditional guessing correction is undoubtedly inadequate, in the perceptual case, since it is quite clear that the easier perception of probable rather than improbable words is not due simply to the random guessing of probable words whenever nothing at all has really been perceived. A more complex theory is necessary, in which neural activity is viewed as analogous to a statistical decision: But in the perceptual case, such a theory can adequately separate response bias and the basic efficiency of the senses. Using such methods of analysis, it has now been possible to make much more reliable psychophysical measurements than were previously possible, since individual differences in response bias are responsible for a good deal of the unreliability of traditional sensory thresholds.

Several laboratories have shown that similar methods of analysis can be applied to memory experiments, and it immediately becomes of interest to know whether the deterioration produced in memory by interfering activity is due to a genuine change in memory itself, or rather to some temporary change in response bias. J. D. Ingleby has carried out a study (unpublished) in which subjects were asked to recall lists of numbers, each of which was presented at an interval of 10 or 20 sec. following a previous list. In such a situation, it is of course known that instrusions tend to occur from one list into the next list, so that mistakes at any position in the list are especially likely to be of a particular digit which would have been correct at that particular position in the previous list. Ingleby found that the presence of a particular digit at a particular position in the previous list produced a response bias in favor of that digit, this bias becoming less as the time interval between lists increased. If we take the other parameter from a decision theory analysis, which in perceptual experiments corresponds to sensory efficiency, and in this case may be regarded as memory efficiency, correctness of association, or something of that sort, then the presence of a particular item in a previous list actually increased the value of this parameter rather than decreasing it. Thus it seems clear that these methods of analysis discriminate different features of the recall process: The temporary change in response bias shown in Ingleby's experiment is not necessarily a drop in the true efficiency of memory, nor is either parameter necessarily identical with the changes that occur in memories that have been well established and have been present for some time. This type of analysis is as yet at an early stage, but it is to be hoped that it will, in time to come, allow a better resolution of the theoretical differences between those who believe in two mechanisms of memory and those who hold only one.

REFERENCES

Baddeley, A. D. *Nature,* 1964, **204** 1116-1117.
Dale, H. C. A. *Nature,*1964, **203**, 1408.
Melton, A. W. *Journal of Verbal Learning and Verbal Behavior,* 1963, **2**, 1-21.
Waugh, N. C., & Norman, D. A. *Psychological Review,* 1965, **72**, 89-104.
Wickelgren, W. A. *Journal of Verbal Learning and Verbal Behavior,* 1965, **4**, 53-61.

COMPARATIVE INVESTIGATION OF THE SHORT- AND LONG-TERM MEMORY SPAN

P. B. NEVELSKY
Kharkov University
Kharkov, USSR

By memory span we shall mean the number of items a subject can recall per one trial or on the average per one trial. When the material to be memorized is perceived for a short time and is recalled fully and immediately, the number of the recalled items makes up the short-term memory span. The short-term memory span reflects the capacity of immediate retention. Unlike it, the long-term memory span reflects the capacity not only of retention, but also of gradual storage of information, and shows what a man can memorize in addition to what he has already memorized, what he can add to the information he has already assimilated. When memorizing some material exceeding the short-term memory span, the first recall is usually incomplete, and for complete and faultless recall it is necessary to perceive and repeat the information to be memorized more than once. In the latter case, the memory span corresponds to the number of items which are contained in the material to be memorized divided by the number of rehearsals.

According to Miller's (1956) data in the experiments where binary figures, decimal figures, letters of the English alphabet, and monosyllabic English words were to be memorized, the short-term (immediate) memory span was equal to 9,8,7, and 5 symbols, i.e., 7 ± 2; the length of the alphabet of these symbols was equal to 2,10,26, and 1000 symbols, respectively, which corresponds to 1, 3.3, 4.7, and 10 bits of information for each symbol or 9, 26, 33, and 50 bits in the whole sequence of the symbols to be memorized, making up the short-term memory span.

When the information per symbol was changed by 10 times, the short-term memory span in terms of symbols changed by 1.8 times, and the memory span in terms of bits—5.5 times. The short-term memory span proved to come more closely to the invariant when it was measured by the number of symbols and not by bits of information that were contained in these symbols.

In the experiments carried out by us previously (Nevelsky, 1965), in which random sequences of symbols (three-figure numbers) selected in various sets of experiments from alphabets of various lengths (2, 8, 64, 512) were to be memorized, the information per symbol amounted to 1, 3, 6, or 9 bits. Eight symbols containing 1 bit each were memorized in most cases after the first time, and the memory span for such symbols amounted to 8 symbols or 8 bits. To memorize 36 such symbols the subjects required 3.4 rehearsals on the average, and the memory span amounted to 11 symbols or 11 bits. When 8 or 12 symbols containing 3 bits each were memorized, the memory span was equal to 3 symbols or 9 bits. When 6, 8, or 12 symbols containing 6 bits each were memorized, the memory span amounted to 2-2½ symbols or 13-15 bits, and when 8 symbols containing 9 bits each were memorized, the subjects recalled 1.7 symbols or 16 bits on the average for each rehearsal.

It means that when the amount of information per symbol changes by 9 times, the long-term memory span changes in terms of symbols by 6.5 times, and the memory span in terms of bits by only 1.8 times.

In the experiments of S. V. Bocharova (see Nevelsky, 1965) where the alphabet of symbols did not change and was equal to 900, and the average information per symbol decreased (at the expense of changing the probability of the occurrence of symbols) by 7 times, the memory span in terms of symbols increased also by 7 times, and the memory span in terms of bits almost did not change.

These experiments have shown that, as distinct from the short-term memory, the long-term memory span comes more closely to the invariant if it is measured by bits, and not by the number of symbols.

The other results of the experiments carried out (Nevelsky, 1965) may be summarized as follows:

1. The long-term memory span in per cent ratio of the recalled material to the represented one showed dependence upon the total uncertainty of the material to be memorized and decreased when the length of the sequence of the symbols to be memorized increased and when the information per one symbol increased.

2. The long-term memory span in terms of symbols showed almost no change when the sequence length of the symbols to be memorized changed and it was inversely dependent on the average information per symbol, or the entropy of the ensemble of probabilities.

3. The long-term memory span in bits showed almost no change when the sequence length of the symbols to be memorized and the average information per symbol changed, and it increased only to some extent when the nominal information per symbol increased, which depends on the length of the symbol alphabet, on their variety.

Thus, it turned out that behind the notion of the amount of information there are at least three parameters: uncertainty, probability, and variety, which are for man such agents of reality that they in different ways affect memory span and, consequently, teaching and self-teaching.

Hence it follows: (*a*) After one rehearsal, a man can recall a greater part of the material to be memorized if this material contains less information: It makes no difference whether it contains fewer symbols or less information per symbol, (b) a man can recall more symbols if the occurrence of these symbols has different probability, if some symbols emerge more often, and others, on the contrary, more rarely; (c) a man can recall more information if the rated information per symbol is larger, i.e., the alphabet the symbols were chosen from is larger.

The task of the comparative investigation of the memory span (Nevelsky, 1967) was to observe how the transition from short-term memory to long-term memory takes place in the experiments with the same material and the same subject when the sequence length of the symbols to be memorized increases gradually and how the memory span characteristics change when the material with different information saturation is memorized.

Ebbinghaus (1885) memorized 7 meaningless syllables after the first trial, but to memorize sequences of 12, 16, 24, and 36 syllables he required 17, 30, 44, and 55 rehearsals, respectively. Thus his short-term memory span was equal to seven syllables, and his long-term memory span was only .5-.7. As Woodworth (1938) stated, 8 figures can be memorized after the first time, but one requires three rehearsals to memorize 9 figures. In this case the short-term memory span is equal to 8, and the long-term memory span to 3 figures (9:3). Hence it could be assumed that the memory span should decrease when a transition from short-term to long-term memory takes place. However, experiments with meaningful material have shown that the memory span does not decrease when the length of the list increases (Nevelsky, 1965). As meaningful material contains less information than meaningless, i.e., more random material, it was interesting to check how the long-term memory span would differ from the short-term memory span if meaningless material with a small amount of information was represented.

We also raised the problem of observing how the memory span (short- and long-term) would change if the information for each symbol changed greatly.

To achieve this end, it was necessary to select uniform symbols with very large and very small amounts of information per symbol (Nevelsky, 1967). Specially arranged meaningless words served as such symbols, which consisted of three syllables and six letters, the consonants occupying the even places and the vowels the odd ones, with the stress falling on the last syllable, for example: tinolu.

The words and the sequences of words were drawn up by means of a table of random syllables. Each of these syllables included one of the 20 consonants and one of the 5 vowels and occurred with a probability equal to .01. In the first set of experiments, each syllable in a word varied. In the second set only the last syllable varied. In the third and fourth sets only sequences of two words were selected. The occurrence of each of them was determined by means of a table of random binary sequences with the probabilities of .5 and .5 (third set) and .9 and .1 (fourth set). The subjects (10 university students) were presented sequences of from 2 to 15 words for memorization. The order of applying the sets and the sequences of different lengths was determined according to the random figures table[1] (see Table I).

TABLE I

Characteristics of the Material to Be Memorized

Indices	Sets of experiments			
	1	2	3	4
Length of the alphabet of symbols	1000000	100	2	2
Rated information per symbols (in bits)	19.93	6.64	1.00	1.00
Probabilities of the occurrence of symbols	.000001	.01	.5	.9 and .1
Individual information per symbol (in bits)	19.93	6.64	1.00	.15 and 3.32
Average information per symbol (in bits)	20 (19.93)	7 (6.64)	1 (1.00)	.5 (0.47)

It should be noted that the decrease of the information per symbol in the second set as compared with the first and in the third as compared with the second was achieved by means of decreasing the length of the alphabet of symbols, and the decrease of the information per symbol in the fourth set as compared with the third was achieved by means of changing the occurrence probabilities of the symbols of the same alphabet.

The average indices of the memory span in symbols and in bits are given in Figs. 1 and 2. As may be seen from the comparison of these figures, when the memory span is measured by the number of symbols, the weak point is the short-term memory, and when the memory span is measured by the number of bits, the weak point is the long-term memory; the weak point for the short-term memory is the number of symbols, and for the long-term memory the number of bits.

In spite of the considerable change in the amount of information per symbol, the number of symbols in short-term memory span continued to remain close to the invariant. If we assume that the short-term memory span is the number of symbols which the subjects recalled from the very first on the average in more

[1] Larisa M. Ioselevich took part in carrying out the experiments.

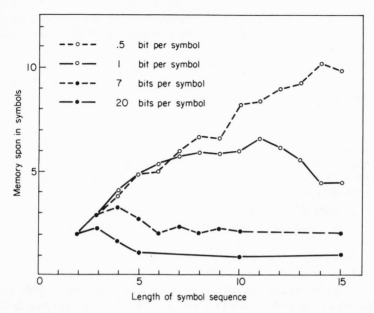

FIG. 1. Dependence of the memory span on the length of symbol sequence and the information per symbol.

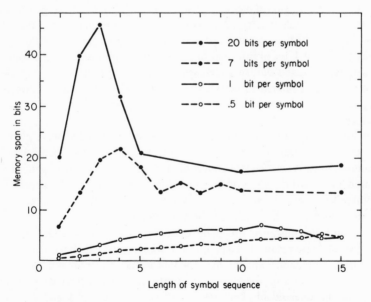

FIG. 2. Dependence of the memory span (in bits) on the length of symbol sequence and the information per symbol.

than 90% of trials, then the short-term memory span in various sets was equal to 2, 3, 5, and 5 symbols or 40, 20, 5, and 2.5 bits, respectively. When the information per symbol was changed by 40 times, the short-term memory span in symbols changed 2.5 times, and the memory span in bits by 16 times. If, however, we assume that the short-term memory span is the number of symbols which the subjects recalled from the very first on the average in more than 50% of trials, then the short-term memory span in various sets was equal to 3, 4, 8, and 12 symbols or 60, 27, 8, and 6 bits, respectively, whereas the short-term memory span in symbols changed by 4 times, and the memory span in bits changed by 10 times. Although the memory span in symbols varied within rather broad limits (broader than 7 ± 2), it still remained closer to the invariant than the memory span in bits.

When 15 symbols were memorized, the information per symbol being equal to 20, 7, 1, or .5 bits, the long-term memory span amounted to .9, 2, 4.4, and 9.8 symbols or 18, 13, 4.4, and 4.6 bits. When the information per symbol was changed by 40 times, the long-term memory span in symbols changed by 11 times, and the memory span in bits by 4 times. The complete transition to long-term memory, when not a single subject could recall the whole list from the very first, took place in the first set (20 bits per symbol) when five symbols were represented, in the second set (7 bits) when 8 symbols were represented, in the third set (1 bit) when 14 symbols were represented. In the fourth set (.5 bit), the subjects memorized 15 symbols in 40% of trials from the very first, and the transition to the long-term memory was not complete here, although the average number of rehearsals was equal to two. As there remained some uncertainty concerning the further behavior of the memory span curves for the symbols containing .5 and 1 bit of information, additional experiments in the fourth and third sets were carried out, in which sequences of 30 symbols were represented. The memory span proved to be 9.6 and 4.8 symbols or 4.5 and 4.8 bits, respectively; i.e., it remained at approximately the same level as when 15 symbols were memorized.

The memory span in bits (Fig. 2) when 15 and 30 symbols were memorized was equal to the memory span when as many symbols were memorized, each containing .5 bit. As was shown above, the memory span in bits depends only on the rated information per symbol and on the length of the alphabet symbols, and symbols in these two sets were selected from alphabets of equal lengths.

While considering the results of the experiments, we must take into account an important circumstance which introduces an essential amendment into the evaluation of these results and also into the conclusions which were made on the ground of the previous experiments. The fact is that recurrent symbols occurred in the lists of words of the third and fourth set. The recurrence of the same symbols is the unavoidable consequence of small uncertainty and great redundancy. In accordance with the thesis which is being developed in Soviet psychology about the role of classification of various ways of semantic, logical processing of the material to be memorized (which is also reflected in G.A. Miller's (1956) "unitization" hypothesis), recurrent symbols in the process of memorization are united into larger symbols or chunks of information. If the short-term memory span is measured not by the number of objectively represented symbols but by the number of symbols the subject operates upon in memorization, by the number of the operative units of memory, the short-term memory span in this case will be still closer to the invariant. At the same time the long-term memory span also becomes closer to the invariant if it is measured not by the objectively represented symbols, but by the operative units of memory, i.e., by the larger symbols which are formed in the process of memorization. Hence it follows that if Miller's hypothesis concerning the independence in memory of the amount of information in the material to be memorized refers only to short-term memory and cannot be extended to long-term memory, his "unitization" hypothesis also becomes apparent in the long-term memory.

The unitization of the material to be memorized in chunks decreases the number of the items to be memorized, thus increasing the amount of information in such a generalized symbol, but without increasing the amount of information in the objective symbols and in the whole material to be memorized. In this connection, the memorization is considerably facilitated, which leads to an increase of the memory span. This may be whàt Miller meant when he attached great importance to the fact that the memory span depends on the number of symbols or chunks and not on the amount of information

It should be noted that the change of the memory span when the amount of information per symbol changes to some extent refers not only to the long-term memory span, but also to the short-term memory span. The short-term memory span is only relatively (as compared to the change of information per symbol) independent of the amount of information. In accordance with the fundamental tenets of the Soviet psychology of memory, there are good reasons to believe that the memory span is a function of the activity: processing the material to be memorized, classifying it, and making up operative units of memory. More favorable conditions for such activity arise in the course of long-term and not short-term memorization, and when there is a small amount of information per symbol. We must think that the amount of information affects the memory span not in itself, but through man's activity applied to a certain structure of the material to be memorized, which, in its turn, depends on the amount of information. It may be supposed that in the memorization of the two lists equal in their length and amount of information, but different in the structural peculiarities of the material to be memorized, the memory span will be larger where there is more redundancy, and consequently, the conditions for processing the information are more favorable, and that redundancy determines the memory span to a greater degree than the amount of information does.

Thus, the short-term memory span is limited by the number of symbols and by the number of operative units, and not limited by the number of bits and long-term memory is limited by the number of operative units and not by the number of symbols.

In connection with the problems of ensuring a symbiosis of man and machine, it is important to know the influence on human memory of the characteristics of the operative units, i.e., the symbols a man operates upon and the objective symbols which both a man and a machine can operate upon.

REFERENCES

Ebbinghaus, H. *Über das Gedächtnis: Untersuchungen zur experimentellen Psychologie.* Leipzig: 1885.

Miller, G. A. Human memory and the storage of information. *IRE (Institute of Radio Engineers) Transactions on Information Theory*, 1956, **IT-2**, No. 3, 129-137.

Nevelsky, P. B. The capacity of memory and quantity of information. In P. I, Zinchenko, V. P. Zinchenko, & B. F. Lomov (Eds.), *Problems of engineering psychology*, Vol. 3. Leningrad: 1965. Pp. 19-118.

Nevelsky, P. B. Investigation of the capacity of short and long-lasting memory. In B. F. Lomov (Ed.), *Problems in engineering psychology*. Moscow: Nauka, 1967.

Woodworth, R. S. *Experimental psychology*. New York: Holt, 1938.

MEMORY AND THE MEDIAL TEMPORAL REGIONS OF THE BRAIN

BRENDA MILNER

Montreal Neurological Institute
McGill University, Montreal, Canada

The purpose of this chapter is to describe some effects of temporal-lobe lesions in man that are hard to reconcile with any unitary-process theory of memory. It is now well-established that bilateral lesions of the hippocampus and parahippocampal gyrus, on the medial aspect of man's temporal lobes, cause a severe, lasting, and generalized memory disorder, unaccompanied by other intellectual change. Patients with these lesions show no loss of previously acquired knowledge or skill; nor do they have any perceptual difficulty. The immediate registration of new information appears to take place normally, provided the information does not exceed the span of immediate memory. Yet these patients seem largely incapable of adding new information to the long-term store. Unilateral lesions, even when they include the lateral temporal cortex, result in far milder defects, but these still fall within the domain of memory. They are specifically related to the nature of the stimulus material and vary with the side of the lesion. Neither in the bilateral nor in the unilateral cases could the pattern of breakdown have been predicted with confidence solely on the basis of work with normal subjects.

In the discussion that follows, the material-specific memory disorders resulting from unilateral lesions will first be considered, before passing to a more extensive analysis of the amnesic syndrome seen after bilateral lesions in the hippocampal zone. Taken as a whole, the data point to the critical role of medial temporal-lobe structures in the consolidation phase of human learning.

MATERIAL-SPECIFIC MEMORY LOSSES AFTER UNILATERAL ANTERIOR TEMPORAL LOBECTOMY

The study of patients undergoing unilateral temporal lobectomy for the relief of epilepsy has by now yielded abundant proof of a complementary specialization of the two temporal lobes of man with respect to memory. If we compare the effects on memory of left and right temporal lobectomies, we find that the most significant variable is the verbal or nonverbal character of the material to be retained. Thus left temporal lobectomy, in the dominant hemisphere for speech, selectively impairs verbal memory (Meyer & Yates, 1955; Milner, 1958), regardless of whether the material to be retained is heard or read (Blakemore & Falconer, 1967; Milner, 1967), and regardless of how retention is tested (Milner, 1958; Milner & Kimura, 1964; Milner & Teuber, 1968). A corresponding removal from the right, nondominant hemisphere leaves verbal memory intact but impairs the recognition and recall of complex visual and auditory patterns to which a name cannot readily be assigned (Kimura, 1963; Prisko, 1963; Milner, 1968; Shankweiler, 1966; Warrington & James, 1967). Right temporal lobectomy also retards the learning of stylus mazes, whether visually or proprioceptively guided (Corkin, 1965; Milner, 1965). On all these nonverbal tasks, the performance of patients with left temporal-lobe lesions is indistinguishable from that of normal control subjects.

The experiments on which these conclusions are based have been reported at length in the papers cited above and will not be reviewed here. Instead, I shall describe some ongoing work of Mr. Philip Corsi designed to bring out the role of the hippocampal lesion in the material-specific memory disorders.

Verbal Memory Defect after Left Hippocampal Excision

Because unilateral temporal lobectomy typically includes the amygdala and parts of the hippocampus and parahippocampal gyrus as well as the lateral neocortex, the question naturally arises as to whether the severity of the deficit is related to the degree of damage to these medial structures. In the case of right temporal lobectomy, we have known for some time that the postoperative deficit in maze learning is contingent upon removal of the hippocampus (Corkin, 1965; Milner, 1965), and we have hints that the same is true for the deficit in recognition of unfamiliar photographed faces (Milner, 1968), although not for the recall or recognition of nonsense figures or complex geometric designs. Corsi has now set out to investigate the problem systematically, beginning with an analysis of the verbal memory defect produced by left temporal lobectomy.

The question can only be approached indirectly because all removals involve the neocortex, although some spare the hippocampus. Corsi has, however, been able to subdivide his subjects into four groups, matched for mean extent of lateral removal but differing with respect to the amount of hippocampus excised. To do this, he has used a classification suggested by Dr. Theodore Rasmussen and illustrated in Fig. 1.

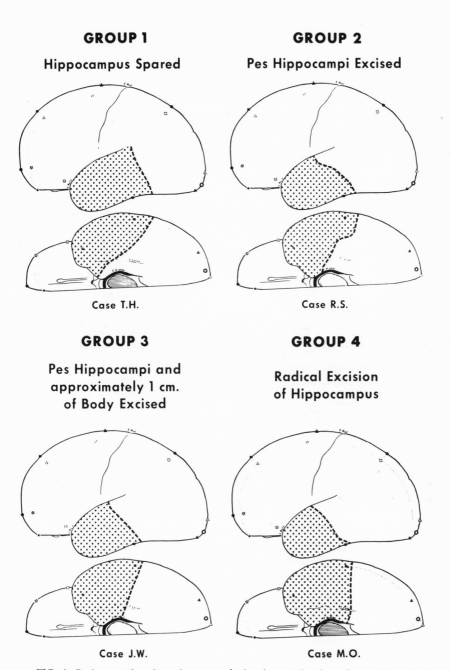

FIG. 1. Brain maps based on the surgeon's drawings at the time of operation, showing representative left temporal lobectomies in four groups of patients, classed according to the extent of hippocampal destruction (lateral surface above, medial surface below; stippled area indicates extent of cortical excision).

Recall of Consonant Trigrams

Up to now the verbal memory task on which Corsi has amassed the most data is a slightly simplified version of the Peterson & Peterson (1959) technique, in which the subject has to recall a consonant trigram after a short interval occupied with counting backwards from a given number. Peterson and Peterson found that normal performance on this kind of task deteriorates rapidly with increasing time interval. As would be predicted from the performance of such patients on other verbal memory tasks, Corsi's left temporal-lobe group as a whole showed an abnormally rapid decline in their accuracy of recall. Of greater interest, however, is the result shown in Fig. 2, where the degree of impairment after left temporal lobectomy becomes progressively greater as we pass from the group with the hippocampus minimally invaded to the group with this structure radically excised.

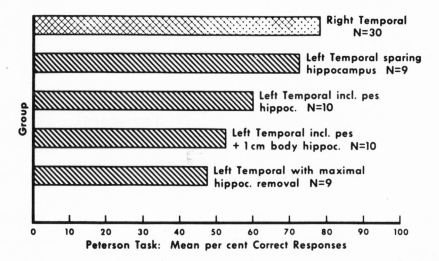

FIG. 2. Verbal memory defect after left temporal lobectomy as related to medial extent of temporal-lobe resection. These results from the Peterson task show the progressive reduction in the number of consonant trigrams recalled with increasing damage to the left hippocampus. No impairment is seen after right temporal lobectomy (Corsi, 1969).

No impairment is seen on the Peterson test after right temporal lobectomy, regardless of whether or not the hippocampus is spared. Yet, with a formally similar task requiring the subject to reproduce the position of a cross on a line after some seconds of distracting activity (Posner, 1966), Corsi is obtaining a defect after right hippocampal removal but not after left. These experiments taken together implicate the hippocampus and neighboring medial temporal region in the holding of simple information in the face of distraction.

Hebb's Recurring Digits Task

In this next experiment, strings of unrelated digits, exceeding by one digit the subject's immediate memory span, are presented for immediate recall. Unknown to the subject, the same sequence recurs every third trial, the intervening series occurring only once. Under these conditions, as Hebb (1961) has shown and Melton (1963) has confirmed, normal subjects demonstrate cumulative learning of the recurring sequence, despite the interpolated interfering activity. Hebb takes this finding as proof of the early establishment of a structural trace. Corsi is now exploring the effects of a left hippocampal lesion on this learning process.

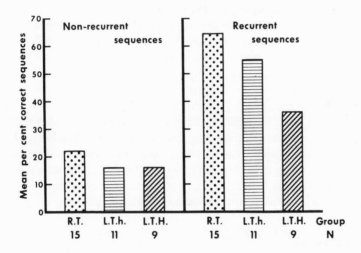

FIG. 3. Hebb Digits Task: Preliminary results of Corsi, showing impaired learning of the recurring sequence after left hippocampectomy. H. M., the patient with bilateral hippocampal resection, shows still more marked impairment (R. T. – right temporal; LT.h – left temporal, small hippocampal removal; Lt.H–left temporal, large hippocampal removal).

To date, he has examined 15 patients after right lobectomy and 20 after left. As would be expected, the left temporal group is inferior to the right on this verbal memory task. If the left temporal patients are then subdivided into two subgroups, according to the extent of hippocampal removal, the two subgroups do not differ from each other in the recall of the nonrecurring sequences, both showing a mild impairment (Fig. 3). The subgroup with extensive hippocampal destruction shows, however, significantly greater impairment in the recall of the recurring sequence. This finding implicates the left medial temporal region in the consolidation process of verbal learning, and thus provides a link with the global learning disability observed after bilateral lesions in this critical zone.

THE AMNESIC SYNDROME PRODUCED BY BILATERAL
MEDIAL-TEMPORAL-LOBE LESIONS

The mild, specific memory changes seen after unilateral temporal-lobe lesions interfere little, if at all, with the daily life of the patient, because they do not affect the recall of events. In Montreal, we first encountered a grave amnesic syndrome after left temporal lobectomy in a patient, P.B., who harbored an additional, but preoperatively unsuspected lesion in the hippocampal region of the opposite hemisphere (Penfield & Milner, 1958). This case is instructive on several counts. First, because the unilateral temporal lobectomy was carried out in two stages, five years apart, and the memory disorder only appeared after the second operation, at which time the uncus, amygdala, hippocampus, and hippocampal gyrus alone were excised. Second, because the patient died twelve years later of a massive pulmonary embolism, and on section of the brain Dr. Gordon Mathieson found the right hippocampus to be shrunken and pale and to have lost its normal structure. On the left (which was the side of the operation), approximately 22 mm. of the posterior hippocampus remained. Since histological examination failed to reveal any significant abnormality in other parts of the brain, we feel confident in attributing this patient's amnesia to bilateral damage to the hippocampal region. Lastly, this patient, who was a civil engineer, also merits attention because he was of superior intelligence, and despite his amnesia, was still able to repeat 9 digits forwards and 7 back without error and to solve difficult mental arithmetic problems quickly and accurately.

The Critical Lesion

At the Montreal Neurological Institute, persistent amnesia after unilateral temporal lobectomy has been seen only in patients with electrographic or radiological evidence of damage to the opposite temporal lobe. In view of the long series of cases in which radical excision of the hippocampal region of one hemisphere has been carried out with only material-specific memory deficits resulting, we have concluded that a bilateral lesion is necessary for the occurrence of a lasting amnesic syndrome.

The first direct proof of the importance of the hippocampal lesions in this memory disorder came from Dr. William Scoville, who in 1954 reported a grave loss of recent memory as a sequel to bilateral medial temporal-lobe resection in one psychotic patient and one patient with intractable seizures. These operations had been radical ones, undertaken only when more conservative forms of treatment had failed. The removals were said to extend posteriorly along the mesial aspect of the temporal lobes for a distance of about 8 cm. from the temporal tips, destroying bilaterally the anterior two-thirds of the hippocampus and hippocampal gyrus, as well as the uncus and amygdala, but sparing the lateral neocortex. Thus they differ from the temporal lobectomies described earlier in this chapter both in being bilateral and in being limited to the medial structures. Figure 4 illustrates the most radical removal described by Dr. Scoville.

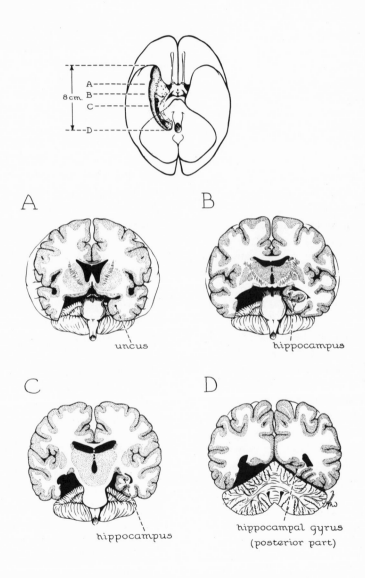

FIG. 4. Diagrammatic cross sections of the human brain, showing the extent of removal in Dr. Scoville's bilateral medial temporal-lobe resections (Milner, 1959).

This medial temporal-lobe operation had been devised by Scoville as a possible treatment for long-standing psychosis, in the hope that it would alleviate some of the symptoms of the illness without producing the undesirable side-effects of a frontal lobotomy. Thirty such operations, of varying extent, had been performed in seriously disturbed patients, before the postoperative amnesia of the epileptic patient, H.M., disclosed the risk to memory in this procedure. Subsequently Scoville & Milner (1957) examined eight of the psychotic patients who were well enough to cooperate in formal testing. They discovered some generalized memory loss in all cases in which the hippocampal region had been invaded bilaterally, but no deficit after removals limited to the uncus and amygdala.

The Clinical Picture

The memory loss in the cases of bilateral hippocampal excision resembles that described by Penfield and Milner, except that it is even more severe. There is continuous anterograde and some retrograde amnesia, but no confabulation and no intellectual decline. Like P.B., these patients show normal memory span, but an inability to recall material in excess of the span (Drachman & Arbit, 1968; Zangwill, 1943).

Much of our present rather detailed knowledge of this memory disorder is based on an intensive study of H.M., the one nonpsychotic patient in Scoville's series, whom we have been able to follow for 15 years (Corkin, 1968; Milner, 1962; 1966; Milner, Corkin, & Teuber, 1968; Wickelgren, 1968). This young man, a motor-winder by trade, had had generalized seizures since the age of 16, which, despite heavy medication had increased in frequency and severity until, by the age of 27, he was no longer able to work. Because of his desperate condition, Dr. Scoville carried out a radical bilateral medial temporal-lobe resection on August 25, 1953. The patient was drowsy for the first few postoperative days, but then, as he became more alert, a severe memory impairment became apparent, which has persisted with only slight improvement to the present day.

Unlike Terzian & Dalle Ore's (1955) patient with a complete bilateral temporal lobectomy, H.M. has shown no significant personality change. Like his father, he has always been rather placid, but has occasional outbursts of irritability. His intelligence as measured by standard tests is actually higher now than before the operation, the Wechsler I.Q. of 118 obtained in 1962 comparing favorably with that of 104 reported in 1953. This paradoxical finding may be due to the fact that he is having far fewer seizures than before. He shows normal recall for events from his early life, except for an ill-defined period of retrograde amnesia covering one or two years just before the operation. The central feature of his amnesia continues to be a failure in long-term retention for most ongoing events. This forgetfulness applies to the surroundings of the house where he has lived for the past six years, and to those neighbors who have been visiting the house regularly during this period. He has not yet learned their names and does not recognize them if he meets them in the street. He has, however, succeeded in retaining a few constant features of his immediate environment, such as the lay-out of the rooms in the house.

Analysis of the Defect

On formal testing of this patient, 20 months after the operation, it was clear that forgetting occurred the instant his focus of attention shifted, but in the absence of distraction his capacity for sustained attention was remarkable. Thus, he was able to retain the number 584 for at least 15 minutes, by continuously working out elaborate mnemonic schemes. When asked how he had been able to retain the number for so long, he replied:

"It's easy. You just remember 8. You see, 5, 8, and 4 add to 17. You remember 8, subtract it from 17 and it leaves 9. Divide 9 in half and you get 5 and 4, and there you are: 584. Easy."

A minute or so later, H.M. was unable to recall either the number 584 or any of the associated complex train of thought; in fact, he did not know that he had been given a number to remember because, in the meantime, the examiner had introduced a new topic. Observations such as this one suggest that the only way the patient can hold on to new information is by constant verbal rehearsal. One gets some idea of what such a state must be like from H.M.'s own comments, repeated at intervals during a recent examination. Between tests, he would suddenly look up and say, rather anxiously:

"Right now, I'm wondering. Have I done or said anything amiss? You see, at this moment everything looks clear to me, but what happened just before? That's what worries me. It's like waking from a dream; I just don't remember."

Delayed Comparison and Delayed Matching Tasks

Drachman & Ommaya (1964) have suggested that forgetting occurs in amnesic patients when the memorandum attains the level of complexity at which it overloads the immediate memory system, but that less complex material can be held indefinitely, provided no interfering activity supervenes. This formulation applies well to the memorization of material that is either intrinsically verbal or can be adequately verbalized, such as numbers, sequences of turns in a maze, or prose passages. We have seen, however, that for H.M. verbal rehearsal plays a key role in the holding process. In contrast, some nonverbal stimuli that one would not ordinarily term complex appear to be forgotten by him within about 30 seconds, whereas normal subjects can remember them for much longer intervals.

Prisko (1963) was the first to demonstrate H.M.'s rapid forgetting of such simple perceptual material, and her findings have since been confirmed and extended by Sidman, Stoddard & Mohr (1968). Prisko used the "compound stimuli" method invented by Konorski (1959) for work with animals and later

adapted by Stepien & Sierpinski (1960) for experiments with man. In this procedure, two stimuli in the same sense modality are presented in succession, separated by a short interval; the subject must then say whether the two stimuli were
the same or different. This means that he must retain an impression of the first
stimulus in order to compare the second one with it. The various pairs of stimuli
are chosen so that they can easily be discriminated when one follows the other
without delay. Task difficulty may be increased by increasing the intratrial
interval, or by introducing a distraction before the second stimulus is presented.

Prisko used five different sets of stimuli, each set constituting a separate task;
three tasks were visual and two auditory. The stimuli used were: clicks, tones,
light flashes, shades of red, and nonsense patterns. At least five values were
assigned to each variable, to prevent as far as possible the use of verbal mediation
to bridge the delay. Despite this precaution, normal subjects averaged only 1
error in 12 trials even with an intratrial interval of 60 sec. plus distraction.

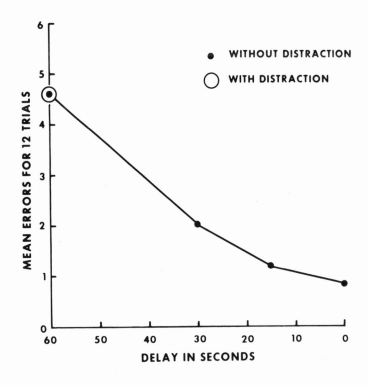

FIG. 5. Effect of bilateral medial temporal-lobe resection on delayed paired comparison.
Mean error scores of patient H.M., for five tasks, as a function of intratrial interval (Prisko,
1963).

Figure 5 summarizes the results for H.M. (averaged over the five tasks), as related to intratrial interval. The scores are the mean number of errors in twelve trials, so that six represents chance performance. At zero delay, H.M. discriminates normally, averaging only one error. But with increasing delay his performance deteriorates sharply, so that at 60-sec. intratrial interval his scores are approaching the chance level.

The steep rise in H.M.'s error curve over such a short time scale was unexpected, as was the fact that his performance was equally impaired, at the 60-sec. interval, with and without distraction. These results imply that the role of distraction in anterograde amnesia is to prevent verbal rehearsal and that with nonverbal material performance deteriorates rapidly with mere lapse of time.

Recently, Sidman, Stoddard & Mohr (1968) have confirmed these findings, using a delayed matching-to-sample technique that permitted the plotting of discrimination gradients. In the nonverbal form of the test, H.M. was required to indicate which of 8 ellipses matched a sample ellipse. With zero intratrial delay, he chose correctly most of the time, showing a normal discrimination of axis ratios, but he made no correct matches with delays greater than 5 sec., although his choices were still related to the sample. When the delay was increased to 32 sec., the sample ceased to exert any control over his choice. Normal subjects (including children from 9 to 12 years old) show accurate matching for delays of 40 sec. or longer.

With the verbal version of this task, which involved the matching of trigrams, H.M. had no difficulty with delays of 40 sec., which was the longest interval sampled. As with other verbal memory tasks, he succeeded only by constant rehearsal: his lips could be seen moving throughout the delay interval.

These two studies highlight the contrast between H.M.'s unimpaired immediate registration of new information, and his failure to store this information beyond the immediate present. They are consonant with the view that distinguishes between a primary memory process and an overlapping secondary process by which the long-term storage of information is achieved (Waugh & Norman, 1965). The typical "short-term" memory experiment, which measures retention after intervals varying from a few seconds to several minutes, must call upon both these processes (Kintsch & Buschke, 1969; Wickelgren, 1968).

Residual Learning Capacities of H.M.

H.M.'s failure on delayed matching and delayed comparison tasks, which assess memory after a single presentation, does not rule out the possibility that he might be capable of some learning with intensive practice, or indeed that certain kinds of learning might take place at a normal rate. Accordingly, we have sampled a wide variety of learning tasks both verbal and nonverbal, including paired-associate learning as well as tests embodying a continuous recognition procedure. With a few exceptions, to be discussed below, we found little or no evidence of learning within the limited time available for testing. The three learning studies reported here are chosen to illustrate the patient's residual capacities.

Maze Learning

In 1960, I first tried to train H.M. on the stylus-maze task shown in Fig. 6. The circles represent metal bolt heads that provide visible "stepping-stones." The subject has to learn the one correct path leading from the lower left-hand to the upper right-hand corner of the array. This path, shown by the winding black line, is of course invisible to the subject, but every time his stylus touches a bolthead that is not on the correct path, an error counter clicks loudly, informing him of his mistake. He thus proceeds by trial and error, with the counter as his guide.

This task is not difficult for normal subjects, who reach the criterion of 3 successive errorless runs in about 20 trials. It can also be mastered by patients with unilateral cortical lesions. H.M., in contrast, failed to show any progress in

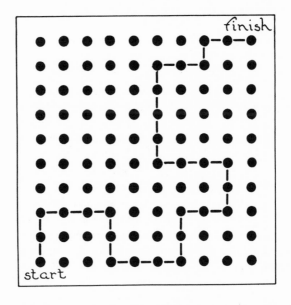

FIG. 6. Plan of visually guided stylus maze. The black circles represent metal bolt heads on a wooden base. The subject must discover and remember the correct route, indicated here by a black line (Milner, 1962).

215 trials spread over 3 days. Training was carried out in blocks of 25 trials, and, as can be seen from Fig. 7, there was no consistent improvement even within a single block of trials. At the end of the 3 days, H.M. was still "having a little debate with himself" about which way to turn at the first choice-point.

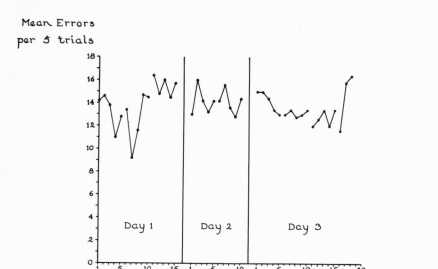

FIG. 7. Maze-learning curve for H.M. He failed to reduce his error score in 215 trials spread over 3 days (Milner, 1962).

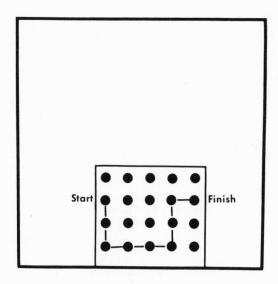

FIG. 8. Shortened form of the visual stylus maze. The large maze has been shielded from view, except for the short section of the path exposed through the aperture (Milner, Corkin, & Teuber, 1968).

In retrospect, H.M.'s failure is less surprising than it seemed to us at the time. This maze has 28 choice-points, so that, even with recoding, the sequence of turns to be remembered cannot be encompassed within the span of immediate memory. This means that experience obtained in the later part of the maze will interfere with rehearsal of the first part. Hence H.M., who seems to rely entirely on verbal rehearsal to bridge a delay, must approach each new trial as a fresh problem. We therefore decided, in 1966, to retest the patient on a much shorter version of the maze, in which the total number of turns to be remembered would fall within his immediate memory span.

Figure 8 shows the shortened form of the maze, obtained by covering the rest of the apparatus with a board. H.M. now had to learn the very simple route indicated by the black line. He was again trained in blocks of 25 trials, 4 times a day, and he eventually reached the criterion of 3 successive errorless runs, but only after 155 trials and 256 errors (Fig. 9, solid line).

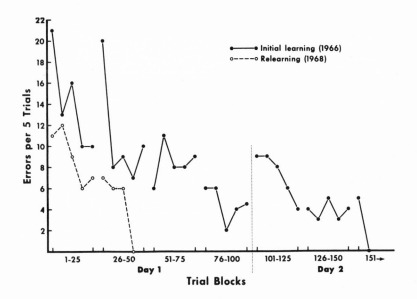

FIG. 9. Learning and retention curves for H.M. on the shortened version of the maze.

This relative success gave us the opportunity to test retention of a habit that had been learned to a strict criterion. We were able first to show extensive savings up to one week after the initial training (Milner, Corkin & Teuber, 1968). What was more impressive, however, was the amount of savings shown on re-learning this short maze two years later (Fig. 9, dotted line). H.M. then reached criterion in 39 trials with only 69 errors, although he did not remember the previous training sessions. He was, however, still quite unable to learn a maze just two choice-points longer than this short path. This failure is yet another instance of the amnesic patient's inability to retain sequences that slightly exceed his immediate memory span.

The fact that H.M. showed 75 per cent retention of a habit learned two years previously is consistent with the view that the main defect produced by hippocampal lesions is a defect in acquisition (Gross, 1968); but we cannot conclude that H.M.'s retention is normal, because many of our patients with unilateral lesions (considered here as control subjects) show nearly perfect retention of the 28 choice-point maze one year after learning it.

Mirror Drawing – A Motor-Learning Task

The maze results illustrate the extreme slowness of H.M.'s learning in most laboratory situations, as well as in real life. An exception appears to be the domain of motor skill. In 1960, at the time that he was failing to learn the original maze, he was trained on a mirror-drawing task, in which he had to draw a pencil line around the outline of a five-pointed star, keeping within the double lines (Fig. 10). He could not observe his hand or the star by direct vision, but only as reflected in a mirror.

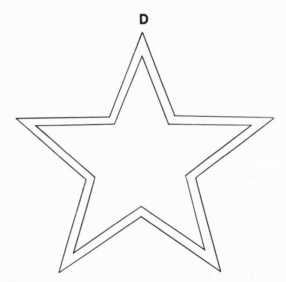

FIG. 10. Star pattern used in the mirror-drawing task. Starting at the point D, the subject must learn to trace the outline with a pencil, keeping between the lines. Crossing a line constitutes an error (Milner, 1962).

This task is initially difficult for normal subjects, but they improve with practice. Figure 11 shows the results for H.M. He has a normal learning curve

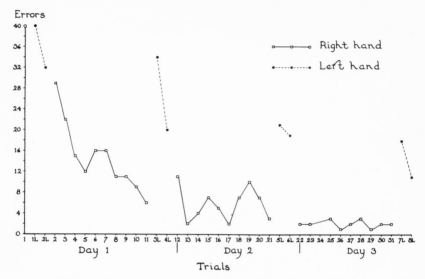

FIG. 11. Mirror-drawing learning curve for H.M. (Milner, 1962).

over a 3-day period, beginning each new session at the level he had attained at the end of the previous day's training. On the other hand, he was totally unaware that he had done the task before; this was learning without any sense of familiarity (Milner, 1962).

These results, which are in marked contrast to the results for maze learning, led us to postulate that the acquisition of motor skills takes place independently of the hippocampal system. Since then, Corkin (1968) has trained H.M. on a variety of manual tracking and coordination tasks, on which he showed significant improvement from session to session and from day to day, although his initial performance tended to be inferior to that of control subjects of his age. This dissociation, in an amnesic patient, between the acquisition of motor skill and most other kinds of learning is consistent with experiments in normal subjects that suggest qualitative differences between kinesthetic memory and memory for words or for visual location (Bilodeau, Sulzer & Levy, 1962; Posner, 1966; Posner & Konick, 1966; Williams, Beaver, Spence & Rundell, 1969).

Recognition of Incomplete Figures – A Perceptual-Learning Task?

The final experiment to be reported derives from a study by Warrington and Weiskrantz (1968) showing that amnesic patients can learn to recognize fragmented drawings of common objects and words, and that they show good retention 4 weeks later, although they do not remember doing the task before. It seemed worthwhile to explore H.M.'s capacities with a similar task, to ascertain whether he too might be capable of this simple perceptual learning.

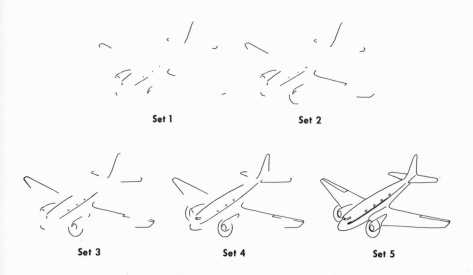

Set 1   Set 2

Set 3   Set 4   Set 5

FIG. 12. Sample item from the Incomplete-Pictures task (Gollin, 1960).

The test material is based on the sets of incomplete drawings of objects and animals first devised by Gollin (1960). The material consists of 20 realistic line drawings, each of which can be presented in a series, graded in difficulty from 1 (the most sketchy outline) to 5 (the complete, easily recognizable picture). Figure 12 shows a typical item: a sketchy drawing of an aeroplane, which becomes progressively more complete, from its first presentation in Set 1 to its final presentation in Set 5.

The subject is shown all the most incomplete drawings first (Set 1), one at a time. He is allowed to look at each drawing for about 1 sec. and is encouraged to guess what it might be. Set 2 is then presented in the same way, but in a different order, so that the subject cannot anticipate which drawing will be coming next. This procedure is continued through successively easier sets of cards, until all 20 drawings have been correctly identified. Failure to name, or misnaming, constitutes an error. The entire test is given again, one hour later, without forewarning.

H.M. was given this test twice, as described above. He was then retested 4 months later, to discover how much he had retained of his previous learning. The results are shown graphically in Fig. 13, where H.M.'s performance is compared with the mean performance of 7 normal control subjects of his own age.

H.M. made fewer errors than the control subjects on first exposure to the task, a finding that is consistent with his superior performance on many other perceptual tests. On retesting, one hour later, he reduced his error score by 48 %, although he had already forgotten that he had seen the pictures before. The control group showed even greater improvement, but one can argue that this is a very different learning task for normal subjects, who can rely on verbal memory as a guide, than it is for an amnesic patient. Once the normal subject has identified a picture, the name of that object is facilitated, so that when it is presented in its most sketchy version for a second time, only an hour later, he is ready to sample from the correct population of names. If the items of Set 1 resembled each other closely, then this verbal recall might be a disadvantage. In fact, the drawings are quite dissimilar, so that normal subjects must be aided by knowing the possibilities beforehand, and this could account for them making fewer errors than H.M. at the second testing.

What is most striking, however, in these results is the high degree of retention shown by H.M. on reexposure to the task after a 4-month interval. These findings are consistent with the observations of Warrington and Weiskrantz, and are unusual in showing stable learning in a severely amnesic patient after only two training sessions, and despite the interfering effect of looking at 20 different drawings, one after another. Puzzling as these results are, we must bear in mind that the Gollin pictures in their complete form would be identified promptly by a very young child. This means that when H.M. learns to recognize these draw-

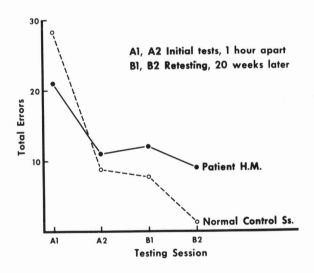

FIG. 13. Gollin Incomplete-Pictures test: graph showing H.M.'s performance on initial testing and on retesting 4 months later, in comparison with the mean performance of 7 male control subjects of his age.

ings with fewer and fewer cues, he is demonstrating a lowered threshold of arousal for a long-term memory rather than the acquisition of new information. It remains to be seen whether more complex forms of perceptual learning, like some forms of motor learning, can proceed normally in patients with such lesions.

COMMENT

This review has brought together clinical and experimental data implicating the medial temporal-lobe regions of man in the acquisition of long-term memory. We are far from any precise understanding of the underlying mechanisms, but at the level of behavioral analysis certain conclusions seem inescapable. The sharp discontinuity between the amnesic patients' normal performance on tests of immediate memory and their almost total failure to retain material that exceeds the span must surely mean that more than one process is involved in normal memory. The bilateral medial temporal-lobe lesion appears to disturb selectively an essential transition process, or process of consolidation, by which some of the evanescent information in primary memory acquires an enduring representation in the brain.

It seems clear that the hippocampus itself is not the site of the structural changes corresponding to long-term memory. Such learning must involve the neocortex primarily, and we have seen, from the study of patients with unilateral removals, that different material-specific memory disorders result from left and right temporal-lobe lesions. In these disorders, as in the global amnesias, the effect of the hippocampal lesion is to reduce the patient's capacity to hold quite simple information in the face of an interfering activity that claims his attention.

These observations can be made consistent with theories that attribute to the hippocampus a role in the inhibition of interference from new sensory input (Grastyan & Karmos, 1962; Douglas & Pribram, 1968; Douglas, 1969), but only if it is realized that patients with hippocampal lesions are not abnormally distractible in the behavioral sense. In this respect they differ markedly from patients (and animals) with frontal-lobe lesions (Grueninger & Pribram, 1969). Nor are they abnormally perseverative when working on problems that do not require the long-term storage of new information. For example, they have no difficulty with card sorting tests that require frequent changes of method for their solution, whereas patients with frontal-lobe lesions may be unable to suppress their preferred response tendencies. The perseveration of certain stereotyped responses shown by amnesic patients in learning situations and in daily life may therefore be secondary to the memory defect rather than its cause.

ACKNOWLEDGMENTS

This work was supported by the Medical Research Council of Canada through Grant M2624 to Brenda Milner. The follow-up studies of H.M. were made possible through United States Public Health Grant M5774A to Brenda Milner and by grants from the John A. Hartford Foundation and the National Institutes of Health (MHO5673) to H. -L. Teuber, and by United States Public Health Service Grant FR88 to M.I.T. Clinical Research Center. I thank Dr. William B. Scoville for the continuing opportunity to study this patient.

REFERENCES

Bilodeau, E. A., Sulzer, J. L., & Levy, C. M. Theory and data on the interrelationships of three factors of memory. *Psychological Monographs*, 1962, **76**, No. 20.

Blakemore, C. B., & Falconer, M. A. Long-term effects of anterior temporal lobectomy on certain cognitive functions. *Journal of Neurology, Neurosurgery, and Psychiatry*, 1967, **30**, 364-367.

Corkin, S. Tactually-guided maze-learning in man: Effects of unilateral cortical excisions and bilateral hippocampal lesions. *Neuropsychologia*, 1965, **3**, 339-351.

Corkin, S. Acquisition of motor skill after bilateral medial temporal-lobe excision. *Neuropsychologia*, 1968, **6**, 255-266.

Corsi, P. M. Verbal memory impairment after unilateral hippocampal excisions. Paper presented at the 40th Annual Meeting of the Eastern Psychological Association, Philadelphia, April 1969.

Douglas, R. J. The hippocampus and behavior. *Psychological Bulletin*, 1967, **67**, 416-422.

Douglas, R. J., & Pribram, K. H. Learning and limbic lesions. *Neuropsychologia*, 1966, **4**, 197-220.

Drachman, D. A., & Arbit, J. Memory and the hippocampal complex. *Archives of Neurology*, 1966, **15**, 52-61.

Drachman, D. A., & Ommaya, A. K. Memory and the hippocampal complex. *Archives of Neurology*, 1964, **10**, 411-425.

Gollin, E. S. Developmental studies of visual recognition of incomplete objects. *Perceptual Motor Skills*, 1960, **11**, 289-298.

Grastyan, E., & Karmos, G. The influence of hippocampal lesions on simple and delayed instrumental conditioned reflexes. In *Physiologie de l'hippocampe* Paris: Centre National de la Recherche Scientifique, 1962, Pp. 225-234.

Gross, C. G. Effects of hippocampal lesions on memory in rats. In H. E. Rosvold (Chm.), *Functions of the hippocampus in learning and memory*. Symposium presented at the meeting of the American Psychological Association, San Francisco, 1968.

Grueninger, W. E., & Pribram, K. H. Effects of spatial and nonspatial distractors on performance latency of monkeys with frontal lesions. *Journal of Comparative Physiology and Psychology*, 1969, **68**, 203-209.

Hebb, D. O. Distinctive features of learning in the higher animal. In J. F. Delafresnaye (Ed.), *Brain mechanisms and learning*. London & New York: Oxford University Press, 1961, Pp. 37-51.

Kimura, D. Right temporal-lobe damage. *Archives of Neurology*, 1963, **8**, 264-271.

Kintsch, W., & Buschke, H. Homophones and synonyms in short-term memory. *Journal of Experimental Psychology*, 1969, **80**, 403-407.

Konorski, J. A new method of physiological investigation of recent memory in animals. *Bulletin de l'Académie Polonaise des Sciences,* 1959, **7**, 115-117.

Melton, A. W. Implications of short-term memory for a general theory of memory. *Journal of Verbal Learning and Verbal Behavior,* 1963, **2**, 1-21.

Meyer, V., & Yates, A. J. Intellectual changes following temporal lobectomy for psychomotor epilepsy. *Journal of Neurology, Neurosurgery, and Psychiatry*, 1955, **18**, 44-52.

Milner, B. Psychological defects produced by temporal-lobe excision. *Research Publication of the Association for Research on Nervous and Mental Disorders*, 1958, **36**, 244-257.

Milner, B. The memory defect in bilateral hippocampal lesions. *Psychiatric Research Reports*, 1959, **11**, 43-52.

Milner, B. Les troubles de la memoire accompagnant des lesions hippocampiques bilaterales. In *Physiologie de l'hippocampe*. Paris: C. N. R. S., 1962. Pp. 257-272. [English translation in P. M. Milner and S. Glickman (Eds.), *Cognitive processes and the brain*. Princeton: Van Nostrand, 1965, Pp. 97-111.]

Milner, B. Visually-guided maze learning in man: Effects of bilateral hippocampal, bilateral frontal, and unilateral cerebral lesions. *Neuropsychologia*, 1965, **3**, 317-338.

Milner, B. Amnesia following operation on the temporal lobes. In C. W. M. Whitty and O. L. Zangwill (Eds.), *Amnesia*. London: Butterworths, 1966, Pp. 109-133.

Milner, B. Brain mechanisms suggested by studies of temporal lobes. In F. L. Darley (Ed.), *Brain mechanisms underlying speech and language*. New York: Grune & Stratton, 1967. Pp. 122-145.

Milner, B. Visual recognition and recall after right temporal-lobe excisions in man. *Neuropsychologia*, 1968, **6**, 191-210.

Milner, B., Corkin, S., & Teuber, H. -L. Further analysis of the hippocampal anmesic syndrome. *Neuropsychologia*, 1968, **6**, 267-282.

Milner, B., & Kimura, D. Dissociable visual learning defects after unilateral temporal lobectomy in man. Paper presented at 35th Annual Meeting of the Eastern Psychological Association, Philadelphia, April 1964.

Milner, B., & Teuber, H. -L. Alteration of perception and memory in man: Reflections on methods. In L. Weiskrantz (Ed.), *Analysis of behavioral change*. New York: Harper & Rowe, 1968. Pp. 268-375.

Penfield, W., & Milner, B. Memory deficit produced by bilateral lesions in the hippocampal zone. *American Medical Association Archives of Neurology and Psychiatry*, 1958, **79**, 475-497.

Peterson, L. R., & Peterson, M. S. Short-term retention of individual verbal items. *Journal of Experimental Psychology*, 1959, **58**, 193-198.

Posner, M. I. Components of skilled performance. *Science*, 1966, **152**, 1712-1718.

Posner, M. I., & Konick, A. F. Short-term retention of visual and kinesthetic information. *Organizational Behavior and Human Performance*, 1966, **1**, 71-86.

Prisko, L. *Short-term memory in focal cerebral damage*. Unpublished Ph.D. thesis, McGill University, 1963.

Scoville, W. B. The limbic lobe in man. *Journal of Neurosurgery*, 1954, **11**, 64-66.

Scoville, W. B., & Milner, B. Loss of recent memory after bilateral hippocampal lesions. *Journal of Neurology, Neurosurgery, and Psychiatry*, 1957, **20**, 11-21.

Shankweiler, D. Defects in recognition and reproduction of familiar tunes after unilateral temporal lobectomy. Paper presented at 37th Annual Meeting of the Eastern Psychological Association, New York, April 1966.

Sidman, M., Stoddard, L. T., & Mohr, J. P. Some additional quantitative observations of immediate memory in a patient with bilateral hippocampal lesions. *Neuropsychologia*, 1968, **6**, 245-254.

Stepien, L., & Sierpinski, S. The effect of focal lesions of the brain upon auditory and visual recent memory in man. *Journal of Neurology, Neurosurgery, and Psychiatry*, 1960, **23**, 334-340.

Terzian, H., & Dalle Ore, G. Syndrome of Kluver and Bucy reproduced in many by bilateral removal of the temporal lobes. *Neurology*, 1955, **5**, 373-380.

Warrington, E., & James, M. An experimental investigation of facial recognition in patients with unilateral cerebral lesions. *Cortex*, 1967, **3**, 317-326.

Warrington, E., & Weiskrantz, l. New method of testing long-term retention with special reference to amnesic patients. *Nature*, 1968, **217**, 972-974.

Waugh, N., & Norman, D. A. Primary memory. *Psychological Review*, 1965, **72**, 89-104.

Wickelgren, W. A. Sparing of short-term memory in an amnesic patient: Implications for strength theory of memory. *Neuropsychologia*, 1968, **6**, 235-244.

Williams, H. L., Beaver, W. S., Spence, M. T., & Rundell, O. H. Digital and kinesthetic memory with interpolated information processing. *Journal of Experimental Psychology*, 1969, **80**, 530-536.

Zangwill, O. L. Clinical tests of memory impairment. *Proceedings of the Royal Society of Medicine*, 1943, **36**, 576-580.

MEMORY STORAGE PROCESSES[1]

JAMES L. McGAUGH
Department of Psychobiolgoy
University of California
Irvine, California

The findings of recent research strongly suggest that our ability to remember is due to at least two processes. One process is assumed to be of relatively short duration—sufficient to allow precise recall of events for a few seconds or minutes after their occurrence—and the other process is assumed to underlie long-term memory. Although the view that there are two kinds of memory processes has existed in one form or another for a number of years (e.g., Hebb, 1949; Broadbent, 1958, 1967), it has only recently been the focus of intense experimental investigation.

An alternative view, and one that is also supported by some experimental findings, considers memory storage as a single process with short- and long-term memory but different ends of a continuum (e.g., Melton, 1963, 1967). For the most part, discussions by the proponents of the two views have relied almost exclusively upon findings from studies of human memory. This paper does not detail either the arguments or the evidence since they are well represented by the other participants in this symposium. Rather, this paper presents some of the findings of studies of memory storage in laboratory animals which bear on the question of the relationship between short- and long-term memory storage processes.

There are several ways in which short- and long-term memory processes might be related. First, as just indicated, they might be but different ends of a single continuum. Second, short- and long-term memory might be based upon two separate and completely independent processes. Sensory stimulation or identical processes might trigger the two memory processes simultaneously. Third, short-term memory processes might be different from long-term processes but neces-

[1]This research was supported by Research Grants MH 10261 and MH 12526 from the National Institute of Mental Health.

sary for the establishment of long-term memory. This is the view originally proposed by Hebb (1949) and the one that is generally preferred by proponents of a dual-trace theory of memory. Fourth, long-term memory processes might be different from but subject to the influences of short-term memory processes. According to this latter view, short-term memory would not be necessary for the development of long-term memory.

It is of course difficult to obtain data providing either a clear acceptance or a clear rejection of any of these alternatives. And it would seem to be an impossible task for data obtained solely from studies of human memory. For example, the fact that short- and long-term memory are both influenced by associative interference does not necessarily mean that but one process underlies both types of memory as has been suggested (Melton, 1963). It is equally possible that short- and long-term memory are based on two processes, each subject to associational influences.

THE SHORT-TERM RETENTION "PARADOX"

Proponents of a dual-trace hypothesis have generally assumed that the short-term trace declines fairly rapidly following its initiation and that the decline is due either to interference or autonomous decay. Findings of delayed response studies in infrahumans are analogous to those obtained in studies of humans' memory for digits following a single presentation. With these tasks, performance does decline quickly over short intervals of time. However, it is also well known that, under a variety of circumstances in mice, monkeys and men, retention may increase over short intervals of time. The beneficial effect of distribution of practice on learning is one of the oldest and most robust findings of experimental research on memory. Such "inverse forgetting" (e.g., Crawford, Hunt, & Peak, 1966), or reminiscence, whether short- or long-term, has not yet been systematically considered by most contemporary theories of memory. One interpretation of "inverse forgetting," which might be accepted by theorists of either persuasion, is that the time interval between the initial trial and a retention trial given a few seconds or minutes later allows opportunity for consolidation or fixation of the memory trace. If this were the general case, however, the rapid decline of short-term memory found in studies such as those discussed by Professors Broadbent and Melton and those found in typical studies of delayed response in infrahumans would not be expected. The paradox awaits resolution. It will no doubt be resolved after we have achieved a clearer understanding of the experimental conditions under which the two phenomena are obtained, or perhaps more optimistically, when we have developed better theories of memory than those currently available. The analysis of this phenomenon by Peterson (1966) strongly suggests that the paradox can be resolved only by assuming that more than one process is involved: a short-term process and a longer term process which is influenced by the former.

Although recent studies of memory in infrahumans do not settle these issues, they do provide rather compelling evidence in support of either the third or fourth alternatives listed above; that is, that long-term memory processes are different from, but subject to, the influence of short-term memory processes. At the very least, the findings, like those of Peterson (1966), cast serious doubt on the validity of the single-trace hypothesis.

GROWTH OF SHORT-TERM MEMORY

In spite of this "paradox" I have tended to accept the more or less conventional view that "inverse forgetting" is due to consolidation resulting from the activity of a short-term memory trace. Results of some recent experiments have, however, required us to reconsider this whole interpretation (McGaugh, 1966, 1968). First, our findings indicate that, in mice, retention, as indicated by the animals' performance, *increases* over short intervals of time following training. The experimental condition we have used is quite simple. Mice are placed, one at a time, on a small metal platform which is attached to the outside wall of a box. The mice receive a single shock as they step from the platform through a small hole into the darkened interior of the box. As Fig. 1 shows, most mice step through the hole within 10 sec. on the first trial. If the mice are replaced on the platform within 5 sec., they re-enter without hesitation and receive another shock. If the second trial is delayed, the step-through latencies increase as the retention interval is increased. The asymptote lies somewhere between 2 min. and 1 hr. Retention remains at a high level for 24 hrs. and declines slightly at 48 hrs. That the increase in latency on the second trial is due to memory and not simply to some general effect of the shock is seen by the fact that the latencies do not show comparable increases if the first shock is delivered in a different apparatus.

It is tempting to interpret these findings as providing a direct behavioral measure of consolidation. Other evidence indicates that this is not the case however. We and others (e.g., Kopp, Bohdanecky, & Jarvik, 1966) have found that a single electroconvulsive shock treatment can produce retrograde amnesia when administered at intervals up to several hours after a single training trial on the step-through apparatus, whereas, as just indicated, retention performance reaches an asymptote in less than an hour. For example, mice in several groups were given a single training trial followed by a single electroconvulsive shock

(ECS) administered at one of the several retention intervals used for the simple retention study just cited (that is, 5 sec., 30 sec., 2 min., 1 hr., 24 hrs). They were then given a single retention test trial 24 hrs. later. The results are shown in Fig. 2. At each interval examined, the performance of the mice given an ECS and retention test 24 hrs. later was inferior to that of mice given only a retention

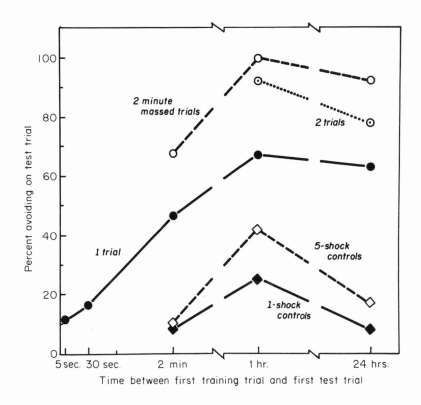

FIG. 1. Retention of inhibitory avoidance (step-through task) as a function of time and number of training trials given during the first 2 min. of training. Retention (that is, percentage of mice showing avoidance response on retention test) after a single trial increases with increase in the interval between the training and test trials (middle curve). Retention is enhanced by repetition of trials. The two lower curves show that the retention performance is not due to a nonspecific effect of foot shock; animals in the groups represented by the lower curves were given foot shocks in a different apparatus and then tested on the step-through apparatus at one of the times indicated.

test at the particular interval. For example, at the 1 hr. interval, 66% of the retention subjects avoided entering the box; avoidance was found with only 30%

of the animals given an ECS 1 hr. after the first trial. ECS does not impair subsequent retention, however, if it is administered 8 or more hours after a training trial. If it is assumed that ECS disrupts memory consolidation processes without affecting consolidated traces (e.g., Glickman, 1961), then these findings suggest that even when 1 hr. lapses between a single training trial and a single retention trial, performance on the retention trial is based at least in part upon temporary memory processes.

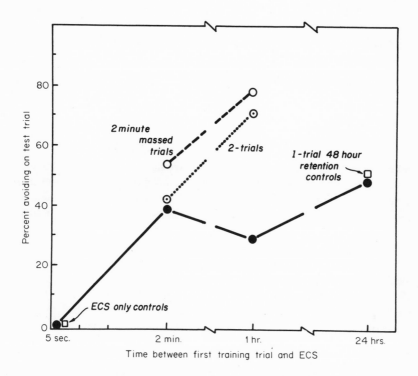

FIG. 2. The effect of electroshock (8 mA, 800 msec) on retention of an inhibitory avoidance response. The lower curve shows that the effect of electroshock decreased as the time between a single training trial and the electroshock given 1 hr. after training was attenuated by increasing the number of training trials during the first 2 min. of training. The retention trials were given 24 hrs. after training for all groups except for the 48-hr. controls. As may be seen, the performance (50%) of this control group was poorer than that (63%) of the 24-hr. retention group shown in Fig. 1. Thus for all groups given electroshock, with the exception of the 24-hr. group, performance on the 24-hr. retention test was lower than that of controls on the 24-hr. retention test. The controls were given electroshock only and received no foot shock.

Typically, in experiments using treatments producing amnesia, retention is measured 20 hrs. or longer after the training and treatment. In recent experiments (e.g., Geller & Jarvik, 1968), retention tests have been given within the first few hours after the treatments. The evidence from such studies indicates that the animals' retention of the response is high after treatment but declines within a few hours. Experiments from my laboratory (McGaugh & Landfield, 1969) suggest that these effects are due to a decay to short-term memory and not to nonspecific effects of ECS; that is, the ECS appears to prevent consolidation without destroying a short-term memory process. Similar effects have been obtained with protein synthesis inhibitors (Agranoff, 1967) and other amnesic treatments (e.g., Albert, 1966).

THE EFFECT OF REPETITION

The findings discussed above suggest that the increase in short-term memory following a single trial is time-dependent. We have also examined the effect of repeated training trials on the development of short- and long-term memory. Several groups of mice were given massed training trials on the step-through avoidance task during a 2-min. period. Most mice received either four or five trials. Mice in other groups were given two training trials separated by a 2-min. interval. All mice were then given a single retention test either 1 hr. or 24 hrs. later. The results of these groups were compared with those of mice given only a single training trial (see Fig. 1). Performance is clearly enhanced by increasing the number of training trials given during the first 2-min. interval. On the last training trial, 68% of the massed training trial group remained on the small platform for over 30 sec. This criterion was attained by only 47% of the mice given only a single training trial followed by the retention test trial 2 min. later. The additional massed trials filling the interval had a significant enhancing effect on the subjects' performance. Control experiments indicated that, if the shocks were administered in a separate apparatus, they did not have comparable effects upon step-through latencies. Increasing the number of training trials also affected performance on the delayed retention tests. At both the 1- and the 24-hr. intervals, the mice given massed training trials were superior to those given only two trials, and the mice on the two-trial groups were superior to those given only a single trial.

These results are, of course, not surprising, and they are not critical for either a dual-trace or a single-trace theory of memory. The important question concerns the *basis* of the effect of repetition on performance. Which processes—short-term memory, long-term memory, or both—are enhanced by repetition? In an attempt to answer this question, groups of mice were given a single ECS immediately after receiving either two trials separated by 2 min. or massed trials for a 2-min. period. They were then given a single-retention trial 24 hrs. later (see Fig. 2). Other groups received similar training but received the ECS treatment 1 hr. after the training. For both the two-trial and massed-trial groups, retention was poorest in the group given the ECS treatment immediately after the last training trial. Further, for both ECS treatment intervals (either immediately or 1 hr. after the original training), the percent of subjects avoiding on the retention test was highest in groups given the 2 minutes of massed training trials.

Under these particular experimental conditions, repetition appears to enhance both short-term memory, as reflected in enhanced performance at the end of 2 min., and long-term memory, as reflected in enhancement of delayed retention performance and attenuation of ECS effects on retention. It seems clear that acquisition of the avoidance response during the 2 minutes of massed training trials is not based solely upon the consolidation or development of a durable memory process. Comparable effects have been obtained in other studies of the effects of ECS on memory (e.g., Thompson & Dean, 1955).

As I suggested earlier, repetition seems to affect both short- and long-term memory processes. And both processes appear to be time-dependent as well as event-dependent. For both processes, within limits, retention can be improved by increasing either the retention interval or the number of training trials given during the interval.

DRUG EFFECTS ON MEMORY

In other research we, as well as other investigators, have attempted to influence learning and memory by administering drugs affecting central nervous system activity. Briefly, the findings indicate that several drugs (e.g., strychnine, nicotine, picrotoxin, pentylenetetrazol) facilitate learning when administered either shortly before or shortly after training (McGaugh & Petrinovich, 1965; McGaugh, 1968; Bovet, Bignami, & Robustelli, 1963; Oliverio, 1968).

The results of recent studies on the effect of strychnine sulphate on learning are shown in Figs. 3 and 4. In one study (Fig. 3) mice received either saline or one of several doses of strychnine each day immediately after training trials on a visual discrimination learning task. Posttraining injections were used in order to influence consolidation processes without directly influencing the performance on either the training or subsequent testing. Training was continued until all animals reached a criterion of nine out of ten correct responses. As Fig. 3 shows, errors in learning varied with the drug dose. Best learning was obtained in groups given either low or high doses.

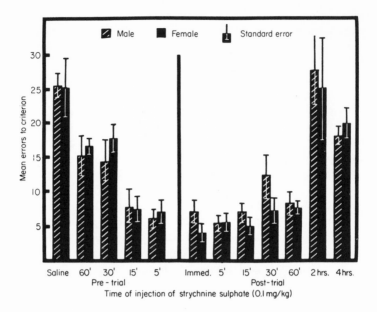

FIG. 3. The effect of post-training administration of strychnine sulphate on visual discrimination learning in mice. Mice in each group ($N = 6$ per group) received either saline or strychnine in one of the doses indicated each day immediately after the last of three massed training trials. All animals were trained to a criterion of nine out of ten correct responses. (From McGaugh & Krivanek, 1969.)

Another study investigated the effect of varying the time of drug administration. With pretrial injections, degree of facilitation increased as the time between the injection and training was decreased. With posttraining injections, degree of facilitation decreased as the interval between training and injection was increased. These findings are consistent with evidence from ECS studies that the lability of long-term memory storage processes decreases with time following training. Thus, conclusions about memory storage processes based on facilitation of learning are similar to those based on interference with learning.

Other investigators (Agranoff, 1967; Barondes & Cohen, 1968) have reported that the drugs, puromycin and acetoxycycloheximide (inhibitors of protein synthesis), impair memory storage without affecting short-term memory which is required for the acquisition of a response over a series of massed trials. These results, considered together, suggest that drugs can influence memory by acting either on short-term memory processes or on processes involved in the consolidation of durable traces. Other evidence from work by Deutsch (1969) indicates that drugs can also affect memory retrieval processes. The findings of differential effects of drugs on memory at various intervals following training provide additional support for a distinction between short- and long-term memory.

CONCLUSIONS

The findings of these recent studies of memory in mice have not, of course, provided final answers to questions concerning the relationship between short- and long-term memory. The findings do indicate that, at least for the conditions investigated, one must assume that at least two kinds of processes underlie subjects' ability to remember experiences. And, it appears that each process is both time-dependent and event-dependent. It is not yet clear whether short-term memory processes are necessary for long-term memory consolidation or whether the processes are in fact parallel but independent. Other findings, including those obtained by Milner in her studies of memory in human patients with bilateral

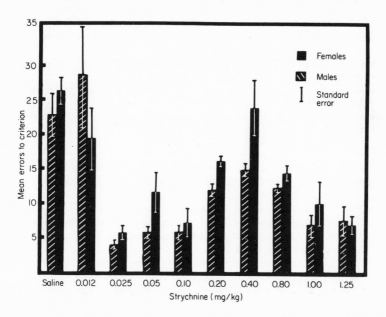

FIG. 4. The effect of time of administration of strychnine sulphate on visual discrimination learning in mice. The procedures used were similar to those of the dose-response study (see Fig. 3). Mice (N = 6 per group) received an injection of strychnine sulphate (or saline) each day at one of the times indicated—either prior to or following the three training trials.

temporal lobe lesions, suggest that under some circumstances the two memory processes can be *quite* independent (Milner, 1966). Although there is some reason to doubt that short- and long-term memory processes are in fact completely independent, this possibility cannot be excluded on the basis of currently available evidence. It is an intriguing possibility, however, and should be given serious consideration in subsequent research.

REFERENCES

Agranoff, B. W. Agents that block memory, In G. C. Quarton, T. Melnechuk, & F. O. Schmidt (Eds.), *The neurosciences,* New York: Rockefeller Univ. Press, 1967 Pp.756-764.

Albert, D. J. The effects of polarizing currents on the consolidation of learning. *Neuropsychologia,* 1966, 4, 65-77.

Barondes, S. H., & Cohen, H. D. Memory impairment after subcutaneous injection of acetoxycycloheximide. *Science,* 1968, **160**, 556-557.

Bovet, D., Bignami, G., & Robustelli, F. Action de la nicotine sur le conditionnement a la reaction d'evitement chez le Rat. *Comptes Rendus Hebdomadaires des Seances de l'Academie des Sciences,* 1963, **256**, 778-780.

Broadbent, D. E. *Perception and communication.* New York: Macmillan (Pergamon), 1958.

Broadbent, D. E. Distinctions among various types of memory, In D. P. Kimble (Ed.), *Organization of recall.* Palo Alto; Calif.: Sciences & Behavior Books, 1967. Pp.63-111.

Crawford, J., Hunt, E., & Peak, G. Inverse forgetting in short-term memory. *Journal of Experimental Psychology,* 1966,□, 415-422.

Deutsch, J. A. The physiological basis of memory. *Annual Review of Psychology,* 1969, **20**, 85-104.

Geller, A., & Jarvik, M. E. Time relations of ECS-induced amnesia. *Psychonomic Science,* 1968, **12**, 169-170.

Glickman, S. E. Perseverative neural processes and consolidation of the memory trace. *Psychological Bulletin,* 1961, **58**, 218-238.

Hebb, D. O. *The organization of behavior.* New York: Wiley, 1949.

Kopp, R., Bohdanecky, Z., & Jarvik, M. E. Long temporal gradient of retrograde amnesia for a well-discriminated stimulus. *Science,* 1966, **153**, 1547-1549.

McGaugh, J. L. Time-dependent processes in memory storage. *Science,* 1966, **153**, 1351-1358.

McGaugh, J. L. A multi-trace view of memory storage processes. Paper presented at the *International Symposium on Recent Advances in Learning and Retention,* University of Sassari and Academia Nazionale dei Lincei, Rome, May 1967. *Academia Nazionale Dei Lincei,* 1968, **365**, 13-26.

McGaugh, J. L., & Krivanek, J. Strychnine effects on discrimination learning in mice: Effects of dose and time of administration. 1969, in preparation.

McGaugh, J. L., & Landfield, P. The development of amnesia following ECS. 1969, in preparation.

McGaugh, J. L., & Petrinovich, L. F. Effects of drugs on learning and memory. *International Review of Neurobiology,* 1965, 8, 139-196.

Melton, A. W. Implications of short-term memory for a general theory of memory. *Journal of Verbal Learning and Verbal Behavior,* 1963, 2, 1-21.

Melton, A. W. Relations between short-term memory, long-term memory and learning, In D. P. Kimble, (Ed.), *Organization of recall.* Palo Alto, Calif.: Science & Behavior Books, 1967. Pp.24-62.

Milner, B. Amnesia following operation on the temporal lobes. In C. W. M. Whitty & O. L. Zangwill (Eds.), *Amnesia.* New York: Appleton-Century-Crofts, 1966. Pp.109-133.

Oliverio, A. Effects of Nicotine and Strychnine on transfer of avoidance learning in the mouse. *Life Sciences*, 1968, 7, 1163-1167.

Peterson, L. R. Short-term verbal memory and learning. *Psychological Review,* 1966, 73, 193-207.

Thompson, R., Dean, W. A further study on the retroactive effects of ECS. *Journal of Comparative and Physiological Psychology,* 1955, 48, 488-491.

PRIMARY AND SECONDARY MEMORY
IN SHORT-TERM RETENTION[1]

NANCY C. WAUGH

Harvard Medical School
Boston, Massachusetts

I should like to begin by describing briefly a dual-trace model for short-term memory that Dr. Donald Norman and I have developed over the past two years in an effort to tie together a variety of experimental results. I shall then try to summarize what I consider to be some of the major points put forth by the principal speakers and attempt to show you why I believe that they are consistent with this particular model.

The model is meant to describe the serial retention of well-defined verbal items, such as digits, letters or words, occurring in homogeneous lists. We assume, first of all, that every serial item that one perceives enters into a temporary storage system from which it can be retrieved immediately as long as one's attention is not diverted. This temporary store, which we have called primary memory, is limited to the most recent few items attended to. Their physiological traces apparently do not decay autonomously in time; but they are completely disrupted by the traces of items perceived later on—or by subsequent shifts of attention, if you will. Primary memory thereby spans a fixed number of recent events, rather than a fixed interval of time. Naturally if events occur in a rapid series, they will remain in primary memory for only a short while; but this does not mean that primary and short-term memory are the same thing.

For we have also had to assume that a serial item can be transferred more or less automatically from primary memory into a much larger and more stable store, called secondary memory. Sometimes transition may occur immediately, and sometimes it may not occur at all before the item is displaced from primary memory. In general, however, the longer an item remains in primary memory, the likelier it is to have been copied into secondary memory and to be temporarily available in both stores. An item retained over a short interval, therefore,

[1]This work was supported by research grant MH 08119-03 from the National Institute of Health, U. S. Public Health Service.

may be retained in either primary or secondary memory or in both. The traces of items stored in secondary memory do not seem to decay in time, nor do they appear to be disrupted by subsequent items as such, at least over intervals of a few minutes.

Retrieval from secondary memory is another matter: Evidently not every item that is stored there can be recalled. The likelihood that such an item will be recalled seems to decrease with the number of similar items that were stored in secondary memory at about the same time. An item in primary memory, on the other hand, does not seem to be interfered with by similar items presented earlier in a series. Of course it will be highly vulnerable to interference from items that follow it—not because these later items resemble it but simply because they are new. Short-term memory is therefore affected by associative interference, we believe, only to the extent that it includes secondary memory.

Let me now turn to some of the issues raised by the principal speakers. Dr. Broadbent has pointed out that an item retained over a short interval can be interfered with by acoustically similar items that occurred in the same list. It can also be interfered with by an item that occurred in the same serial position on a list presented earlier. It is well known, of course, that similar effects can be observed in long-term retention. Dr. Broadbent, himself a dual theorist, wonders whether associative interference may not actually affect response biases, rather than memory traces themselves, over short intervals of time. Dr. Melton has described what happens when a subject tries to retain a short list embedded in a series of similar lists—lists of more or less the same length, made up of items from more or less the same semantic category. A list that occurs late in such a series is likelier to be forgotten or misremembered after even a short delay than is the very first list in the series. Dr. Melton argues that, since proactive interference of this sort can also be shown to affect long-term memory, it is perhaps gratuitous to assume that two separate mechanisms underlie retention over short and long intervals of time.

The point I should like to reemphasize, however, is that a single item or a short list recalled a few seconds after its initial presentation may have been retrieved from either primary or secondary memory. The longer the retention interval, of course, the likelier is an item to be retrieved from secondary memory, and the more obviously will it then be affected by associative interference. I think that this does indeed appear to be the case in various studies reported in the recent literature. My real point, I suppose, is that just because short- and long-term retention are affected in similar ways by the same experimental variables, it is not necessary to conclude that there is only one storage system underlying short-term retention. The experimental evidence in favor of two such systems is, I think, rather strong.

The results reported by Dr. Nevelsky are, in my opinion, nicely consistent with the primary-secondary memory hypothesis. He defines the long-term memory span as the number of items in a list divided by the number of trials taken to memorize the entire list in serial order—that is, as the average number of new items acquired per trial. The size of this span depends on the statistical properties of the list, ranging from less than one nonsense word per trial when all the words in a list are different to over ten per trial when a list contains only two different words, one of which occurs very frequently and the other, very seldom. The results of some recent experiments that Dr. Norman and I have done suggest that a completely redundant item—one that the subject knew would occur when it did—does not displace anything from primary memory. Nor does an item repeated in immediate succession do so, except on its first occurrence in a string of repetitions: A string of this sort seems to function as a perfectly predictable sequence. The capacity of primary memory would actually appear to be limited, therefore, not to a fixed number of items but to a fixed number of runs of identical or of completely redundant items. On the assumption that it takes one trial for a subject to learn Dr. Nevelsky's 3-syllable nonsense words as well-integrated verbal units, I have translated his long-term spans into the average number of new runs acquired on each trial beyond the first. In the case of the larger vocabularies, this number seems to range from about 2.7 to 3.8 runs of syllables per trial; while in the case of the binary vocabularies, it ranges from about 2.6 to 3.0 runs of words per trial. This result suggests, then, that on each successive trial with a long list, a person can transfer to secondary memory the contents of one primary memory span. The size of this span, and therefore the size of the long-term span, would appear to be most nearly constant when measured in runs of items, rather than in items as such or in bits of information.

Dr. Milner's discussion of amnesia in temporal lobe patients I find very interesting indeed. Apparently the hippocampus serves a vital function in the retention of verbal information, so that lesions in the speech-dominant temporal lobe often produce measurable defects in verbal memory. I am especially fascinated by the case of patient H. M., who had both temporal lobes removed. Here is a person who can recall three digits immediately but not after a delay of 15 sec. He can utter a normal sentence, but 5 min. later he cannot remember ever having said it. He has, in other words, primary but no secondary memory. Yet he can still learn new motor skills, and he can remember verbal information that he acquired before his operation. This fact suggests to me that perhaps we will have to entertain the possibility of still another storage system, the repository of traces so well entrenched that they can be revived automatically without an intervening process of verbal search. Whether by consolidation then, we mean the copying of a trace from primary into secondary memory or from secondary into tertiary memory (if there indeed exists such a store) is not at all clear to me at the moment.

This brings me finally to Dr. McGaugh's remarks. Apparently a sequence of events contiguous in time—such as a response followed by a noxious stimulus—initiates a process in the central nervous system which takes several seconds for its completion. If the pattern of electrical activity in the cerebral cortex is disrupted during this critical interval, an animal loses his memory for the events that triggered the process. If the ECS occurs after the process has terminated, on the other hand, he will remember those events. These results are consistent with the idea that the pattern of neural impulses initiated by a recent event can be translated into some kind of structural change that is impervious to the effects of ECS. One is tempted, naturally, to try to equate primary memory with postperceptual neural activity and secondary (or possibly tertiary) memory with structural changes. There are so many obvious differences, however, between avoidance conditioning in the infrahuman organism and verbal retention in man that it would probably be unwise to pursue the analogy any further at this point, even though it may appear to be a very reasonable one.

Part II
MEMORY MICROSTRUCTURES

EVIDENCE FOR ANATOMICAL AND CHEMICAL CHANGES IN THE BRAIN DURING PRIMARY LEARNING[1]

MARK R. ROSENZWEIG

University of California
Berkeley, California

INTRODUCTION

In this paper I will attempt to show that measurable anatomical and chemical changes may occur in the brain in response to complex experience. Before presenting the evidence, I would like to examine some of the difficulties that have beset the search for such material correlates of learning. To show some of the current viewpoints on this question, let me quote a little of the discussion at a conference on *The Anatomy of Memory* (Kimble, 1965) that took place in the fall of 1963; some of the participants at that conference are members of this symposium.

KRUGER: Ideas concerning morphological changes in the brain which might be related to experience or the behavioral repertory of organisms have been considered with great favor but poor experimental support since the period that might be called antiquity, in terms of scientific history. If any structural changes could be demonstrated in the brain of adult organisms, these might be relevant to the increased informational capacity or learning of that organism . . . (p. 88).

SPERRY: I have a point that concerns your initial assumptions. From the standpoint of development, it is recognized that growth itself lays down an extremely efficient neural network, and there is a real question as to whether the learning and memory modifications imposed later involve any morphological change in the original network; these latter could

[1] This paper was prepared for the Moscow Congress while the author held a one-year research professorship in the Miller Institute for the Basic Research in Science, University of California, Berkeley, 1965-1966. The investigation was supported in part by Research Grant MH 7903-03 from National Institute of Mental Health and by Research Grant GB-5537 from National Science Foundation; it also received support from the United States Atomic Energy Commission. The experiments reported here were done in collaboration with Drs. Edward L. Bennett, Marian C. Diamond, and David Krech. Since the summer of 1966 this research has continued in collaboration with Drs. Bennett and Diamond.

conceivably involve only changes in physiological resistance and conductance . . . or various endogenous properties of the neurons and glia. So I don't think that you should start out with the assumption that one needs some kind of growth or degeneration . . . .

KRUGER: Absolutely. I couldn't agree with you more strongly. I would only say if, in the adult nervous system, we could demonstrate something which would be suggestive of growth, it might be considered.

ECCLES: I agree with Dr. Sperry in this respect, in that I favor growth just of bigger and better synapses that are already there, not growth of new connections. This is the kind of structural change that I would imagine is possible, rather than growth of extended axons from one place to another.

LEVINE: I think it was Voltaire who said, "I place a high premium on ignorance." I am not sure that I am completely surprised by the fact that growth could occur.

PRIBRAM: It's a good point. It is certainly true, though, that for the last 100 years most people who have tried to demonstrate that growth takes place in the adult nervous system have come up with negative results. (p. 97).[2]

Having heard this discussion, let us now consider briefly two points that emerge from it, both revealing barriers to research in this field. One obvious barrier is the point made by Pribram—that negative results have piled up during the last century in the attempt to find growth with learning in the adult brain. Certainly previous failures should not be disregarded, lest one repeat them, but neither should they be taken as an absolute bar to further attempts. Indeed, such failures may be turned to account if scrutiny of them can suggest deficiencies in the techniques or experimental designs that had been brought to bear on the problem. The failures, insofar as they can be taken at face value, only show routes that did not lead to the goal; they do not demonstrate that the goal does not exist.

The second barrier is concentration on typical adult learning in most attempts to find brain correlates of training. The reason for using adult subjects is the desire to distinguish possible changes induced by learning from changes that occur with normal growth. But this concern has needlessly led workers to concentrate on typical adult learning, ignoring what seems to me to be the most accessible route toward our goal. Typical adult learning involves a rapid recombination of units that have already been learned thoroughly. An example of such a task would be learning a sentence in a familiar language. One trial often suffices for permanent fixation of such material. In a case like this, the cerebral changes underlying the learning may be rapid physiological alterations at a relatively small number of scattered points in an existing and extensive neural network. Locating and specifying such changes would indeed be a formidable task and one whose accomplishment will, I believe, lie far in the future.

On the other hand, extensive and prolonged learning seems to be required for the original formation of complex perceptual and motor organizations in the

[2]This material is quoted from *The Anatomy of Memory*, D. Kimble (Ed.), 1965, by permission of the publisher, Science and Behavior Books, Inc., Palo Alto, California.

brain. This is what Hebb (1949) referred to as "primary learning." Granted that an elaborate and efficient neural network is laid down during growth, as Sperry has stressed, there is accumulating evidence that growth cannot occur in a vacuum and that for normal growth to occur, there must be normal opportunities for interaction between the organism and the environment. Consider, for example, the evidence of faulty development in the retina and visual centers in animals deprived of light (Riesen, 1960). Often primary learning is completed during infancy, but it may also occur during adulthood if it did not take place earlier. An example of deferred primary learning occurs when an individual blind from birth (or shortly thereafter) regains sight as an adult. Another example of primary learning occurring in an adult might be the learning of a new language. (Here I would want to stress mastery of the new language, from the basic sounds to conversational ability, and not just recombination of the phonemes of one's native language.) It seems to me that searching for the cerebral effects of extensive and prolonged learning is a feasible project, and I will largely confine myself to it in this paper.

EFFECTS OF DIFFERENTIAL EXPERIENCE ON BRAIN

Methods

Behavioral Procedures

In planning our own research, we benefited from earlier investigations demonstrating that the brain is quite stable in gross structure and composition, so that large changes were hardly to be expected. For this reason, we employed procedures that we hoped would *maximize* the cerebral effects of experience and that would *minimize* variability from extraneous sources.

In an attempt to maximize the effects of differential experience on the brain, we decided to put rats into two markedly different experimental situations, to start the animals at an early age when their brains might be most plastic, and to maintain them in these situations for a prolonged period. Rats are therefore assigned at weaning (about 25 days of age) and kept for 80 days in either an enriched environment—Environmental Complexity and Training (ECT)—or in an impoverished one—Impoverished Condition (IC). The enriched situation has these characteristics: The animals are housed in groups of ten to twelve in a large cage that is provided with "toys" such as ladders, wheels, boxes, platforms, etc. The toys are changed each day from a larger group. To enrich the rats' experience further we take them out each day for a half-hour exploratory session in a square field (90 x 90 cm.) with a pattern of barriers that is changed daily. After about 30 days in this permissive free-play environment, some formal training is given in a series of mazes. In the home cage, the animals have food and water *ad lib*. Thus these animals received a variety of experience from cage-mates, from their complex environment, and from trials in several apparatuses.

Each enriched-experience animal has a littermate assigned to the impoverished condition. Here animals live in individual cages that have solid side walls, so that an animal cannot see or touch another. These cages are placed in a separate, quiet, dimly lighted room, while the ECT cages are in a large, brightly lighted room with considerable incidental activity. The isolated rats have food and water *ad lib* and, like their enriched brothers, they are weighed about once a week.

Some of the difficulties with earlier investigations were the high background variability due to the use of heterogeneous subjects and the lack of proper control groups against which to evaluate possible effects. We attempted to overcome these difficulties by taking the following precautions: In any given experiment, animals of only one strain, age, and sex are used. (In most cases, they have been males.) All comparisons are made between littermates. The littermates are assigned randomly between the experimental conditions, so that no initial bias can enter. All brain analyses are carried out under code numbers that do not reveal the experimental treatment, so that no analytical bias can affect the results.

Brain Dissection

At the end of the behavioral phase of an experiment, the brains are removed and, in most cases, divided by gross dissection into five samples (see Fig. 1 in Rosenzweig, Krech, Bennett, & Diamond, 1962). With the aid of a small calibrated plastic T-square, a sample of the visual cortex is first circumscribed and then peeled off from the underlying white matter. Next, a sample of the somesthetic cortex is removed. The third sample is the remaining dorsal cortex. (In the rat, cortex can be separated from the white matter much more readily and accurately than is the case in the cat or dog or primate.) The fourth sample includes ventral cortex and associated tissues such as the hippocampus, the amygdaloid nuclei, and the corpus callosum; by weight, it is about two-thirds hippocampus. The fifth and final sample consists of all the rest of the brain after the cortex and associated tissues have been removed. This final sample includes not only the core of the cerebral hemispheres, but also the olfactory bulbs, the midbrain, the cerebellum, and the medulla. Each sample is weighed to .1 mg. and then stored at $-20°C$ for subsequent chemical analysis. Less than 10 min. elapses between decapitation and placing the last sample of a brain on dry ice.

Chemical Methods

The brain samples were analyzed colorimetrically for activity of acetylcholinesterase (AChE) and, in the later experiments, also for cholinesterase (ChE). For analysis of AChE, acetylthiocholine is the substrate and promethezine is used to inhibit ChE activity. For analysis of ChE, butyrylthiocholine is the substrate and AChE is inhibited with BW284C51. Analyses are made in duplicate, and two AChE values usually agree within 2%, and ChE values, within 3%. Enzyme activities are expressed in terms of millimicromoles of substrate hydrolyzed per minute.

Results

Anatomical Effects

The results demonstrate that the enriched-environment rats consistently develop greater weight of cerebral cortex than do their impoverished littermates, as Table I shows. Here all four cortical samples are pooled into total cortex for simplicity of exposition. This table is based on 141 littermate pairs of male rats

TABLE I

Effects of Enriched (ECT) or Impoverished (IC) Experience on Weight of Brain (mg)[a]

	Total cortex		Rest of brain		Total brain		Cortex/rest	
	ECT	IC	ECT	IC	ECT	IC	ECT	IC
Mean	698	671	940	950	1638	1621	.744	.707
S.D.	31	30	39	37	64	63	.027	.023
% diff., ECT–IC[b]	4.1		-1.1		1.1		5.3	
p	<.001		<.01		<.01		<.001	

[a]Based on 141 littermate pairs of male S_1 rats.
[b]100 (ECT mean minus IC mean)/IC mean.

of the S_1 strain; they were run in thirteen experiments conducted over a six-year period. Overall, the cortex of the enriched rats weighs 4% more than that of the restricted rats ($p < .001$), and four-fifths of the pairs show a difference in this direction. The standard deviation is small, being only about 4% of the mean. The rest of the brain is slightly but significantly lower in weight in the ECT rats than in their IC brothers. It is worth noting that differences in weight of the total brain are slight, so that we probably would not have noticed any effect if we had not analyzed separately the cortex and the rest of the brain. Several other strains of rats have also been used in such experiments, and they have yielded similar results.

Although the ECT animals are greater in cortical weight, they are about 8%

less in terminal body weight than the IC animals. If we were to express brain weight in terms of body weight or to correct for differences in body weight, this would only enlarge the effects that we have reported. A more enlightening procedure is to express the weight of one part of the brain in terms of another part. If we take the ratio of weight of total cortex to that of the rest of the brain, we obtain the results given at the right of Table I. The cortical/subcortical weight ratio is consistently greater for the enriched than for the restricted rats, 90% of the differences being in favor of the ECT member of a pair. Needless to say, this differential growth of brain is a highly significant effect ($p < .001$).

Not only does the cortex differ from the rest of the brain in its response to differential experience, but the regions of the cortex do not participate equally, as Table II demonstrates. With our standard ECT and IC situations, the occipital

TABLE II

Effects of Enriched (ECT) or Impoverished (IC) Experience on Weights of Cortical Regions (mg.)[a]

	Occipital		Somesthetic		Remaining dorsal		Ventral	
	ECT	IC	ECT	IC	ECT	IC	ECT	IC
Mean	65.0	61.2	51.4	50.5	283	270	299	289
S.D.	4.2	4.6	3.0	3.1	17	15	23	23
% diff., ECT−IC	6.1[b]		2.0		4.9[c]		3.3	
p	$< .001$		$< .01$		$< .001$		$< .001$	

[a]Based on 141 littermate pairs of male S_1 rats.

[b]Significantly greater than both somesthetic percentage effect ($p < .01$) and ventral effect ($p = .01$).

[c]Significantly greater than somesthetic percentage effect ($p < .05$).

region shows the largest changes, amounting to 6% ($p < .001$). The nearby somesthetic region shows the smallest differences, amounting to 2% ($p < .05$). The ECT-IC differences in the occipital region are significantly larger than those found in either the somesthetic or the ventral regions.[3]

The greater weight of the cortex of the stimulated rats reflects greater thickness, as we found in independent experiments (Diamond, Law, Rhodes, Lindner, Rosenzweig, Krech, & Bennett, 1966; Diamond, 1967). In these experiments we

[3] After this paper was written, we demonstrated that such percentage differences in wet weight of brain tissue are maintained when dry weights are taken.

made anatomical sections of the brains, rather than consuming the tissue for chemical analyses. Depth has been measured in a standard part of the occipital area. The results of four experiments (Table III) demonstrate that the cerebral cortex becomes significantly thicker in the enriched-experience rats than in their

TABLE III

Percentage Differences in Depth of Occipital Cortex between Brains of ECT and IC Littermate Rats[a]

Experiment No.	III	IV	VI	VII	Combined
Number of Pairs	3	9	9	11	32
% diff., ECT–IC	9.4	8.3	2.3	7.0	6.3

[a]From Diamond (1967), Table 1.

deprived littermates. The outermost layer of the cortex shows no change, so it has been excluded from these data. For the remaining layers, the overall result amounts to 6% ($p < .001$). Preliminary measures indicate that the hippocampus also becomes thicker as a consequence of enriched experience, so the whole gray bark of the brain grows thicker with enriched experience.

In one experiment we measured the diameter of capillaries in the cortex, and we found the average diameter to be greater in the enriched-experience animals than in their impoverished littermates. Other investigators (Opitz, 1951) have found that with acclimatization to high altitude, the cortical capillaries of the rat increase in diameter. Apparently, then, the anatomy of the cerebral vasculature can also respond adaptively to increased demand.

Biochemical Effects

After having seen these *anatomical* effects of differential experience, let us turn to *biochemical* effects. Much of our biochemical analysis has concerned the enzyme acetylcholinesterase (AChE). This enzyme is important at those central synapses where acetylcholine is the chemical transmitter that conveys messages from one neuron to the next. Enzymes are measured in terms of their activity; one can consider either the total activity in a tissue sample or the activity per unit of weight of the sample. The total activity of AChE was found to increase slightly but consistently in the enriched-experience animals, both in the cortex and in the rest of the brain (Table IV). Since the percentage increase in cortex was not much greater than that in the rest of the brain, the difference in ratio of cortex to rest of brain is not significant on this measure. In the cortex, the increase in enzymatic activity was less than the increase in tissue weight, so the activity per unit weight decreased in the ECT animals.

TABLE IV

Effects of Enriched (ECT) or Impoverished (IC) Experience on Total Activities
of Acetylcholinesterase and Cholinesterase in Brain[a]

	Total cortex		Rest of brain		Total brain		Cortex/rest	
	ECT	IC	ECT	IC	ECT	IC	ECT	IC
Total AChE activity[b]								
Mean	5971	5878	17,838	17,680	23,810	23,558	.335	.333
S.D.	335	297	775	865	977	1029	.018	.017
% diff., ECT–IC	1.6		0.9		1.1		0.6	
p	<.05		<.10		<.05		NS	
Total ChE activity[c]								
Mean	230	214	547	548	777	762	.421	.391
S.D.	13	14	26	24	34	31	.026	.026
% diff., ECT–IC	7.6		−0.2		2.0		7.8	
p	<.001		NS		<.001		<.001	

[a]Based on 98 littermate pairs of male S_1 rats.
[b]Expressed in millimicromoles acetylthiocholine hydrolyzed/min.
[c]Expressed in millimicromoles butyrylthiocholine hydrolyzed/min.

Now there are other enzymes in the brain that can also act on acetylcholine, although less specifically than does AChE. These other enzymes are known collectively as *cholinesterase* (ChE). In the rat, there is relatively little ChE activity, but we wanted to be certain that the effects we were measuring could not be attributed to ChE. Therefore, we measured ChE activity independently. These measures confirmed our early reports of AChE effects when the more and less specific enzymes had not been differentiated, since there is too little ChE activity in rat brain to affect the overall hydrolysis of acetylcholine. Unexpectedly, these new measures also showed that ChE activity was being modified by differential experience and according to its own pattern (see lower half of Table IV). Total ChE activity was up by 7.6% in the cortex of the ECT rats, while showing no change in the rest of the brain.

Let us summarize these effects by showing results for 98 littermate pairs of S_1 rats for whom we have both enzymatic measures (Fig. 1). The results are given in terms of percentage differences. Note that at the cortex, tissue weight and the total activity of both enzymes increase significantly, but with the percentage change in AChE lagging beyond that in tissue weight, while the percent-

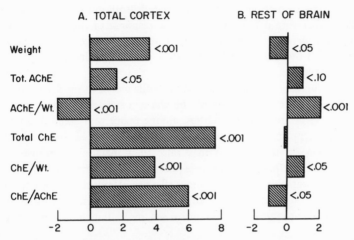

A. TOTAL CORTEX   B. REST OF BRAIN

Weight	<.001	<.05
Tot. AChE	<.05	<.10
AChE/Wt.	<.001	<.001
Total ChE	<.001	
ChE/Wt.	<.001	<.05
ChE/AChE	<.001	<.05

-2 0 2 4 6 8   -2 0 2

FIG. 1. Percentage differences, ECT minus IC, in nine experiments with S_1 rats (98 littermate pairs).

age change in ChE surpasses the change in weight. Note also that the cortex seems to be more responsive to the environmental influences than the rest of the brain.

In seeking to understand what these enzymatic changes might mean, it occurred to us that neurons contain chiefly AChE, while the glial cells contain chiefly the less specific enzyme ChE. The glia had long been regarded simply as structural members, supporting the neurons, but there have been many recent indications that glia may play an active role in the brain. It has also been known that the number of nerve cells, like the number of muscle cells, is fixed at birth or soon thereafter, but glia may multiply. We therefore sought to determine whether the increased bulk of cortex as a consequence of experience might be due, in part at least, to proliferation of glia. This sent us back to anatomy, now at a cellular level.

Histological Results

To test this possibility, we made counts of neurons and of glia in a specified region of the occipital cortex. In order to obtain a satisfactory degree of reliability in such counts, we devised a procedure in which photographic enlargements were made of the anatomical slides, and two anatomists made independent counts (Diamond *et al.*, 1966). The number of neurons within the region measured showed a slight but nonsignificant decrease for the ECT rats. Presumably this decrease in packing density occurred because the number of neurons is fixed, and they are forced somewhat further apart as the cortex expands. The glia, on the contrary, were 14% ($p < .01$) more numerous in ECT than in IC, and the ratio of glia to neurons then also increased. Both our chemical and anatomical findings therefore demonstrate that one response of the brain to heightened environmental demands is a proliferation of glia. This conclusion has recently been supported by Altman and Das (1964) at M.I.T., using a different measure of glial proliferation.

What the increase in the number of glia cells means in the functioning of the brain is not clear, since the role of the glia is a subject of active research and controversy. Here are two possibilities, among many that could be advanced: If the glia help to nourish the neurons, as has been suggested, then increasing the functional load on the neurons may raise their metabolic turnover and thus require more glial support. Again, it is possible that the branches of the neurons ramify more complexly during learning. (We are attempting to test this in some experiments in progress and have some positive preliminary results.) Since the glia form the sheaths around neural processes, more branching may require more glia.

Results of Variant Experiments

The standard ECT-IC experiments have been varied in a number of ways in attempts to determine which aspects of the ECT and IC situations are important in producing the cerebral effects and which contribute little or nothing. To summarize briefly, we can state that the extra-cage environment is of no appreciable importance. Placing the environmental complexity (EC) cage in the quiet, dim isolation room or placing IC cages in the bright, active room with ECT cages does not affect the usual pattern of results. Also, the few daily training trials given to the ECT animals can be omitted with no measurable effect. Impoverishment but not isolation is required for the IC effect, since two animals placed in an IC cage show brain values identical to those of single animals (Krech, Rosenzweig, & Bennett, 1966). Four rats per IC cage, however, show differences from single rats, and in the ECT direction. Both social grouping and cage furniture appear to contribute to the ECT-IC differences. [More recently, we have found that only 2 hr. per day of enriched environment over a 30-day period suffice to produce the ECT-IC brain differences (Rosenzweig, Love, & Bennett, 1968).]

FURTHER TESTS OF HYPOTHESIS

Granting that the brain responds anatomically and chemically to the differential environments, we still need to test further the hypothesis that learning is responsible for these cerebral effects. As we have stated previously, "We wish to make clear that finding these changes in the brain consequent upon experience does not prove that they have anything to do with storage of memory. The demonstration of such changes merely helps to establish the fact that the brain is responsive to environmental pressure—a fact demanded by physiological theories of learning and memory" (Bennett, Diamond, Krech, & Rosenzweig, 1964). For this reason, we are pursuing three lines of research which I will list and then discuss:

(a) We are continuing to test alternative hypotheses in order to determine whether variables other than experience—such as differential handling or locomotion or stress—can account for any major part of the cerebral effects.

(b) We are determining to what extent the adult brain shows similar changes to those we have seen in the younger animal.

(c) We are conducting experiments in which only intensive formal training differentiates the experimental and control groups.

Alternative Hypotheses

As to the first point, we have been concerned with alternative hypotheses ever since our initial publications on this research (Krech, Rosenzweig, & Bennett, 1960; Rosenzweig *et al.*, 1961). It was apparent from the start that the IC animals received less handling and engaged in less locomotor activity than their ECT littermates, and both early handling and locomotion have been shown to have some physiological effects. Futhermore, the fact of isolation by itself has been shown to produce physiological effects in some strains of rats. Time will not permit me to describe the experiments that we have done to test for possible effects of handling, locomotion, or isolation. Let me simply state that manipulation of none of these variables was able to reproduce the cerebral effects that we obtained when we varied environmental stimulation (Bennett *et al.*, 1964; Krech *et al.*, 1966; Rosenzweig, Love, & Bennett, 1968). I would like, however, to describe some previously unpublished experiments done to test possible effects of stress and of adrenal involvement.

Can Stress Account for the Brain Effects?

Five experiments were run in 1959-1960 to test directly whether stress due to unavoidable shock could produce cerebral effects similar to those of our differential environments. These experiments employed rats of five different strains (S_1, K, RCH, RDH, S_3), each of which had previously shown ECT-IC effects (Krech *et al.*, 1960). The first two of these experiments each lasted two weeks, and the last three, each four weeks. We had already found (Zolman & Morimoto, 1965) and have since abundantly confirmed (Rosenzweig, 1968) that a few weeks are sufficient to produce EC-IC cerebral differences similar to the usual ECT-IC pattern. The shock subjects received intermittent unavoidable electrical shock in daily 12-min. sessions; the shocks were delivered through the floor bars of a special experimental box. During the shock sessions, littermate controls were placed in similar experimental enclosures but with no shock and in a different room. Thus the controls received neither shock nor stimulation from the shocked animals.

In all five experiments, employing a total of 42 littermate pairs, the terminal body weight was lower in the shocked than in the control rats; overall the difference amounted to 6% ($p < .01$). Adrenal weights were taken in the first four of these experiments and were found to be 6% greater in the shocked than in control animals, but this difference reached only the .10 level of significance. Since adrenal weight normally correlates closely with body weight (within a group of the same sex, age, strain, and treatment), the ratio of adrenal weight to total body weight was taken. The adrenal/body weight ratio was 14% greater ($p < .001$) in the shocked rats. In comparison, six other experiments showed no consistent difference in this ratio between ECT and IC littermates.

Although shock affected body weight and the adrenal/body weight ratio, it had little or no effect on brain measures. Among the four cortical regions, none yielded a significant shock-control difference, the occipital and somesthetic weights being slightly greater in the shocked rats, and weights of remaing dorsal and ventral areas being somewhat less in the shocked rats than in the controls. The ventral effect reached the .10 level, and the decrease of weight of total cortex of the shocked rats was significant ($p < .05$). The pattern of differences was clearly unlike that found between ECT and IC animals, where IC is lower in weight of all cortical sections and especially in the occipital region. AChE activity was analyzed in all but the second of these experiments; it showed no significant differences between shocked and control for any brain region. In total cortex, AChE/weight of the shocked animals was 1.1% below the control value, while IC typically exceeded ECT by several per cent on this measure. Thus stress had only slight effect on brain measures, and these did not follow the pattern induced either by environmental enrichment or environmental impoverishment; conversely stress affected the adrenal/body weight ratio, while environmental richness had no significant effect on this measure. We conclude that our ECT-IC cerebral differences cannot be attributed to differences in stress between the enriched and impoverished groups.

Tests of other alternative hypotheses to explain the cerebral effects are being carried out regularly as part of our research program.

Effects among Adult Rats

As to the second line of research, we noted at the start of this paper that the occurrence of effects in adult animals would be evidence that training, rather

TABLE V

Comparisons between Adult and Young Rats in Percentage Differences between Enriched and
Impoverished Groups on Several Brain Measures[a]

	Cortex					Rest of brain	Total brain	$\dfrac{\text{Cortex}}{\text{Rest}}$
	Occip-ital	Somes-thetic	Dorsal	Ventral	Total			
Weight								
Adult[b]	10.7***	4.1*	5.5***	3.5**	5.0***	1.2*	2.8***	3.7***
Young[c]	5.4***	1.5	4.8***	2.6**	3.6***	−1.1*	.9*	4.8***
Total AChE								
Adult	9.1***	4.5*	3.4*	1.4	2.7*	3.1**	3.0**	−.4
Young	1.7	.2	2.4**	1.2	1.6*	.9	1.1*	.6
AChE/wt.								
Adult	−1.6	.4	−1.4	−2.0	−2.1*	1.8	.2	−4.0**
Young	−3.6***	−1.5*	−2.3***	−1.3	−2.0***	2.0***	.2	−4.0***
Total ChE								
Adult	13.2***	4.5	6.0*	5.6**	6.4***	1.2	2.8**	5.1***
Young	10.2***	4.7***	8.3***	6.9***	7.6***	−.2	2.0***	7.8***
ChE/wt.								
Adult	2.6*	.5	1.1	1.9	1.3	.1	.1	1.2
Young	4.7***	3.4***	3.3***	4.4***	3.9***	1.0*	1.2**	3.0***
ChE/AChE								
Adult	4.2**	−.1	2.5	4.6*	3.7**	−1.7	−.1	5.5**
Young	8.6***	5.0***	5.6***	5.7***	6.0***	−1.1*	.9	7.2***

[a]Based on 33 pairs of adults and 98 pairs of young S_1 rats.

[b]Kept in ECT or IC from 105 to 185 days of age.

[c]Kept in ECT or IC from 25 to 105 days of age.

*$p < .05$,   **$p < .01$,   ***$p < .001$.

than normal processes of growth, was responsible for the observed cerebral
changes. For this reason we have done some experiments with animals kept
under colony conditions until 105 days of age (the age at which we usually
terminate our experiments) and then assigned for 80 days to the differential
environments. At 105 days the rat has been sexually mature for over a month,
and the growth of the brain, which never completely stops in the rat, has almost
leveled off. Between 25 and 105 days, cortical weight increases by more than
20% in rats maintained in colony conditions, and the weight of the rest of the

brain increases by 40%; between 105 and 185 days, cortical weight does not increase under colony conditions, and weight of the rest of the brain increases by only about 5%. With growth contributing very little between 105 and 185 days of age, can the differential environments still induce anatomical and chemical changes in the brain?

Our results indicate that, on most of our measures, the adult rat brain is just as capable of change as is the younger brain. Three replication experiments were done with adults, run from 105 to 185 days of age, and the results can be compared with those of nine experiments with younger animals, run from 25 to 105 days of age. Table V compares percentage differences between ECT and IC for the adult and young animals on tissue weights and enzymatic measures. The overall greater statistical significance of results with the younger animals is due in part to the larger numbers of cases of young animals tested. In weight of cortex, the older rats show a greater gain of ECT over IC values than do the younger animals. In weight of the rest of the brain, the adult ECT Groups showed a slight gain, while the younger ECT groups showed a slight loss relative to their IC littermates. With enriched experience, the older rats therefore gain more in total brain weight than do the younger, while in the ratio of weight of cortex to the rest of the brain the younger animals gain slightly more than the older. In gain in total AChE as a consequence of enriched experience, the adult animals show somewhat larger ECT-IC effects throughout the brain than do the younger animals. In AChE activity per unit of weight, both adult and young show ECT-IC differences of about −2% in the cortex, and differences of about +2% in the rest of the brain. Total ChE activity is up in the cortex of both adult and younger ECT rats, as compared with their IC littermates, while the rest of the brain shows no change in total ChE. In ChE per unit of weight, the younger animals show larger and more significant differences than do the adults. Finally, in the ratio of ChE to AChE, the younger rats show slightly (but not strikingly) larger ECT-IC differences than do the adults. The possibility that older and younger brains differ somewhat in their patterns of changes with experiences needs to be investigated further. Nevertheless, it is apparent from these results that the adult rat brain retains considerable plasticity even after the stage of normal growth has ended.

Opposed Effects of Maturation and of Experience

Perhaps the clearest evidence distinguishing effects of maturation from those of enriched experience is that they go in opposite directions on some measures. One example is found in AChE activity per unit of weight in the subcortex. This normally rises swiftly to about 80 days of age, after which it declines. Yet there is a positive ECT-IC difference on this measure for adult as well as for young rats, so normal development and ECT lead to opposed effects (Rosenzweig, Krech, Bennett, & Diamond, 1968, p. 289). Another example is that the occipital cortex of the rat decreases in thickness after the age of about 60 days. But enriched experience, contrary to this developmental effect, leads to increased cortical thickness (Bennett, Rosenzweig, & Diamond, 1969).

Effects of Formal Training

The third line of research is to attempt to differentiate two groups by giving formal training to one and not to the other, while holding all other aspects of their treatment the same. For this purpose some animals have been housed singly and given an hour or two of operant conditioning per day, while their littermates have been in a yoked-control situation. That is, one member of each littermate pair solved a variety of problems, principally to visual stimuli, while the other member was in a yoked Skinner box and received "free" a pellet whenever its littermate earned one. Three replications of this experiment have been conducted, with a total of 32 littermate pairs of S_1 rats.

On most of our cerebral measures the experimental animals showed somewhat higher values than their controls. In ChE activity per unit of weight in the occipital sample of the cortex, the experimental animals had significantly higher activity ($p < .05$). In total cortex, the experimental animals showed significantly greater values than the controls for total AChE activity ($p < .05$), ChE activity per unit of weight ($p < .05$), and total ChE activity ($p < .01$). Thus it appears that formal training alone may be able to produce changes in the brain, although the pattern of changes is somewhat different than that which we have found in the ECT-IC experiments and although the changes induced by the operant training do not seem to be large. Experiments with further control groups are necessary in order to determine whether the observed differences are due to training or may be due to differential stimulation.

SUMMARY

This paper demonstrates that measurable anatomical and chemical changes occur in the brain during exposure to a complex environment and suggests that these changes may be due to learning. Searching for such changes has been called hopeless because of past failures and because investigators have been preoccupied with typical adult learning which involves rapid recombination of already well-learned units. In such adult learning, the cerebral changes may be rapid physiological alterations at a few scattered points in existing neural networks and locating them would indeed be a formidable task. On the other hand, prolonged learning is required for the original formation of complex perceptual and motor organizations in the brain. Although such primary learning is often completed during infancy, it may also occur during adulthood if essentially new experiences are provided. Our work appears to show cerebral effects of varied and prolonged learning, although further controls must be run before this conclusion can be accepted.

To investigate this problem, we gave littermate rats various degrees of experience, the extremes being (a) an enriched physical and social environment coupled with formal training, and (b) social isolation in an impoverished environment. We have found the cerebral cortices of enriched-experience animals to exceed those of impoverished-experience littermates in weight and thickness, total activity of acetylcholinesterase and of cholinesterase, and number of glia. Control experiments have not supported alternative explanations in terms of differential handling or locomotion, isolation stress, adrenal involvement, or differences in body weights. Adult rats show as great cerebral plasticity as do young rats in these experiments.

REFERENCES

Altman, J., & Das, G. D. Autoradiographic examination of the effects of enriched environments on the rate of glial multiplication in the adult rat brain. *Nature*, 1964, **204**, 1161-1163.

Bennett, E. L., Diamond, M. C., Krech, D., & Rosenzweig, M. R. Chemical and anatomical plasticity of brain. *Science*, 1964, **146**, 610-619.

Bennett, E. L., Rosenzweig, M. R., & Diamond, M. C. Time courses of effects of differential experience on brain measures and behavior of rats. In W. L. Byrne (Ed.), *Molecular approaches to learning and memory*. New York: Academic Press, 1969. Pp. 155-89.

Diamond, M. C., with technical assistance by B. Lindner & A. Raymond. Extensive cortical depth measurements and neuron size increases in the cortex of environmentally enriched rats. *Journal of Comparative Neurology*, 1967, **131**, 357-364.

Diamond, M. C., Law, F., Rhodes, H., Lindner, B., Rosenzweig, M. R., Krech, D., & Bennett, E. L. Increases in cortical depth and glia numbers in rats subjected to enriched environment. *Journal of Comparative Neurology*, 1966, **128**, 117-125.

Hebb, D. O. *The organization of behavior*. New York: Wiley, 1949.

Kimble, D. (Ed.) *The anatomy of memory*. Palo Alto, Calif.: Science & Behavior Books, 1965.

Krech, D., Rosenzweig, M. R., & Bennett, E. L. Effects of environmental complexity and training on brain chemistry. *Journal of Comparative and Physiological Psychology*, 1960, **53**, 509-519.

Krech, D., Rosenzweig, M. R., & Bennett, E. L. Environmental impoverishment, social isolation, and changes in brain chemistry and anatomy. *Physiology and Behavior*, 1966, **1**, 99-104.

Opitz, E. Increased vascularization of the tissue due to acclimatization to higher altitudes and its significance for oxygen transport. *Experimental Medicine and Surgery*, 1951, **9**, 389-403.

Riesen, A. H. Effects of stimulus deprivation on the development and atrophy of the visual sensory system. *American Journal of Orthopsychiatry,* 1960, **30**, 23-36.

Rosenzweig, M. R. Effects of experience on brain chemistry and brain anatomy. *Atti della Accademia Nazionale dei Lincei,* 1968, **109**, 43-63.

Rosenzweig, M. R., Krech, D., & Bennett, E. L. Heredity, environment, brain biochemistry, and learning. In *Current trends in psychological theory.* Pittsburgh: University of Pittsburgh Press, 1951. Pp. 87-100.

Rosenzweig, M. R., Krech, D., Bennett, E. L., & Diamond, M. C. Effects of environmental complexity and training on brain chemistry and anatomy: A replication and extension. *Journal of Comparative and Physiological Psychology,* 1962, **55**, 429-437.

Rosenzweig, M. R., Krech, D., Bennett, E. L., & Diamond, M. C. Modifying brain chemistry and anatomy by enrichment or impoverishment of experience. In G. Newton & S. Levine (Eds.), *Early experience and behavior.* Springfield, Illinois: C. C. Thomas, 1968. Pp. 258-298.

Rosenzweig, M. R., Love, W., & Bennett, E. L. Effects of a few hours a day of enriched experience on brain chemistry and brain weights. *Physiology and Behavior,* 1968, **3**, 819-825.

Zolman, J. F., & Morimoto, H. Cerebral changes related to duration of environmental complexity and localized activity. *Journal of Comparative and Physiological Psychology,* 1965, **60**, 382-387.

NEUROPSYCHOLOGICAL CONSEQUENCES
OF ALTERED SENSORY INPUTS[1]

A. H. RIESEN

University of California
Riverside, California

We are seeing significant advances during the 1960's in neuropsychological research. Several areas stand out dramatically. We *used* to hear that although one-third of our lives is spent in sleep, nobody can say why. Now we know that there is a physiological need for sleep, and that sleep *must* meet certain neuropsychological criteria to fulfill this need. True, much remains to be done before behavioral and biochemical benefits of rapid-eye-movement (REM) sleep can be stipulated in detail.

Nonsleep occupies *two*-thirds of our lives. Among other biological gains that accrue during non-sleep, of particular significance are those that derive from sensory stimulation. Here, also, much work remains before behavioral and biochemical benefits are known in detail. This has come to be a particularly lively area of research. Neurophysiologists and neurochemists are entering the field along with physiological psychologists, many of them including behavior in their studies. In point of fact, we had better be on the alert, lest the physiologists and neuropharmacologists take over. They are finding extra excitement when their research has behavioral correlates.

In the very young mammalian organism sleep occupies proportionately a larger share of the total day. Rapid growth is going on. Cellular units of the nervous system are still incorporating protein precursors at a remarkably high rate. Most of the induction mechanism for such growth appears still to originate in endogenous or genetic forces. DNA may still even be guiding some nerve cell proliferation. Although the spinal cord has reached its full complement of cells prenatally, the cortex has not. Why does cell proliferation in the cortex also

[1] Based on address presented at 75th annual convention of the American Psychological Association, September 1–5, 1967, Washington, D.C. Research supported by PHS Grant No. NB-04717.

soon come to a standstill while other organ systems of the developing young mammal are still growing in cell numbers as well as cell size? This is still one of the basic mysteries of life processes.

Eventually most organs reach asymptote. But cells retain properties of change, with shrinkage as well as growth not only possible, but actually going on constantly. The constituents of cells are in flux. Functional demands may determine in part whether their chemical constituents and their size will increase or decrease (Goss, 1966, 1967), even on an hour to hour basis. Some of us are trying to sort out the rapid from the more "chronic" effects of functional demands. This effort is of long standing among biologists studying liver, kidney, and endocrine systems. Only in recent years has the nervous system given up some of its remarkable secrets of structural change.

The effects of functional demands on liver or on muscle are dramatic and well studied. Muscle responds by change in the sizes of its units, the muscle fibers. Liver or kidney may proliferate the units themselves. But even here some substructures change only in size and not by mitosis. And in either case, the changes clearly carry functional consequences that bring about a kind of self-regulation of the growth changes.

What of neural growth and function? On the behavioral side, psychologists are engaged intensively in the study of habituation and arousal, with electrophysiological correlates of these receiving a major emphasis. Subcortex and paleocortex are implicated in these and in that other major consequence of functional demand—*Learning*. Whether we are willing to label the biochemical and the microanatomical alterations that relate to these as "growth" or "decay" phenomena is not important, perhaps, but I feel strongly by now that evidence of common biochemical mechanisms justifies such classification.

Activation (without any intended play on the popular phrase) *is* going on in a diffuse system. As in Lashley's mass action, this property of diffuseness makes neuroanatomical study more difficult. We have needed a more localized function to permit the study of neural correlates, and I believe the discrete sensory projection system is the answer to this need. Sensory restriction gives us a tool, and I would be the last to assert that because we are finding changes worthy of study here, this means that *all* of the important changes are in discrete sensory systems. But I do not go along with those who may wish to put all of the emphasis on the reticular formation or the limbic system or both.

EVIDENCE FOR SENSORY NEURAL CHANGES

I will make no attempt here to review the breakthrough that came in the 1940's and early 1950's from Holger Hydén's laboratory in Sweden. The demonstrations for the vestibular and the visual systems that RNA concentrations could be chronically altered by some few weeks of increased or decreased functional demands were followed by evidence that acute effects could result even from as little as 15 min. of change in stimulation level. Total protein or cell mass does not respond quite this rapidly, but using comparable techniques (X-ray microradiography), Gomirato & Baggio (1962) working in Italy reported that 3 hrs. of altered stimulation level produced significant changes in total dry weights of retinal ganglion cells and in stellate cells in visual cortex. Their base line was normal daylight. The level of stimulation was reduced by using darkness, with and without the added variable of narcosis, or the levels were increased by their use of so-called "dazzling" light.

In the Gomirato and Baggio data we find confirmation of several earlier reports that overstimulation, like understimulation, significantly reduces cell protein from levels that accompany an intermediate physiological optimum. However, this type of decrement in cell mass from overstimulation has been found only in sensory nuclei (including retinal ganglion cells) and *not* in the cortex. Direct electrical stimulation will do this to cortical cells, as shown a dozen years ago by Geiger and independently at about that time by several Russian studies.

Growth Depends upon Nutrition

The blood-brain barrier raises theoretical obstacles for rapid incorporation of protein precursors into neuronal structure. Two solutions to this problem are each supported by some data. Shabadash (1964) found evidence for nucleoprotein interchange within neurons between mitochondria, endoplasmic reticulum, and nucleolus. Hydén (1962) favored a mechanism of interchange between glia and nerve cells.

GROWTH RATES IN BRAIN

That most common measure of growth, gross weight, provides a comparison between postnatal development of brain and other organs. Goss (1964) has compiled results of several studies which show that in the rat many organs continue to grow into adulthood. The brain does so proportionately less than do liver, kidney, or heart.

When body weight reaches approximately 100 gm., the thymus gland stops growing rather abruptly. Biologists have suggested that cessation of growth depends upon feedback from one of the biochemical products of an organ itself, a growth inhibitor. Such a mechanism is undoubtedly involved in controlling neuronal proliferation in the period around the completion of gestation.

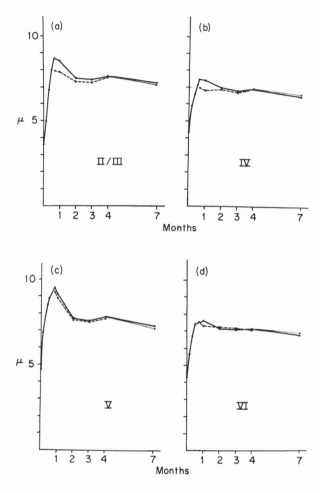

FIG. 1. Mean nuclear diameters in different layers of the visual cortex of dark-reared
(- - - -) and control (————) mice from birth to 4 months (after Gyllensten *et al.,* 1965).

Another set of measures of brain development is in terms of size or complexity of the neuron and its arborizations. In the cells of the cortex in mammalian
species, diameters of cell nuclei are at birth roughly half of their adult size. Most
of this growth differential is accounted for by rapid growth during a few weeks
after birth. Data from Gyllensten, Malmfors, & Norrlin (1965), on nuclear diameters in the mouse visual cortex, show a kind of hysteresis effect, especially
pronounced in layer II/III, the external granular and pyramidal cell layer, and in

the internal pyramidal cell layer. Nuclear diameters reach a maximum at 4 weeks after birth, after which there is some recession (Fig. 1).

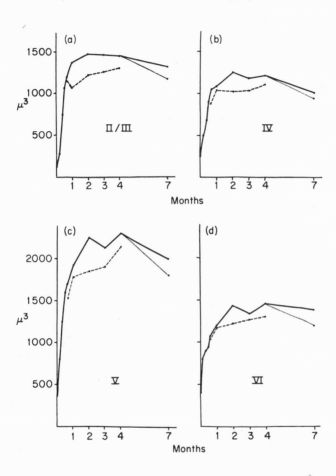

FIG. 2. Mean volume of internuclear material per nucleus in layers of the visual cortex of dark-reared and control mice (after Gyllensten *et al.*, 1965).

There is a small but highly significant lesser degree of growth in cells of mice reared in darkness. Here the rebound is less and by 3 to 4 months from birth there is no longer the difference between mice living in darkness or daylight. Another measure of change in visual cortex was that of mean internuclear volume per nucleus. This change was more general to all layers of the cortex, and somewhat more persistent (Fig. 2). Light-rearing pushes and keeps the cells farther apart.

ABSENCE OF LONG-TERM DARK-REARING EFFECT
IN THE CORTEX OF RODENTS

A key point in these data from Sweden (Gyllensten *et al.,* 1965) is that with *continued* differential visual environments, light versus total darkness, the *cortical* differences produced during early postnatal growth gradually disappear, if not entirely, at least considerably. Robert Ramsey and I have just completed the analysis of similar measures taken from hooded rats after dark-rearing to 200 days of age and beyond. Our results on cell diameters, cell density, and thickness of cortical layers were conspicuously lacking in any differences that were significant. We must bear in mind that these are data for cortex, not sensory relay nuclei, and perhaps we should also not extrapolate beyond rodents. These are data taken after prolonged steady-state conditions (Boas, Ramsey, Riesen, & Walker, 1969).

At these meetings yesterday, or in reading the Proceedings, you learned from Rosenzweig that his continuing work with Bennett, Diamond, and Krech has also resulted in findings that cortex responds initially to their condition of environmental complexity by increases in tissue weights, reaching a peak value in 30 days, and subsiding again while the animals remain in the enriched (but by this time familiar) environment (Rosenzweig, Bennett, & Diamond, 1967).

A recent preliminary report by DeBold, Firsheim, Carrier, & Leaf (1967) at Wesleyan University shows a maximum occipital cortex heavy molecular weight RNA in hooded rats that were reared first in darkness to 80 days and then given light to 105 days of age. Rose (1967) studied tritiated lycine incorporation in visual cortex of dark-reared mice during the initial period of light exposure at 3 weeks of age. He found increased incorporation in brain samples of animals that received 3 hrs. or more of light. The 3-hr. group showed such an increase only if allowed to live an additional 48 hrs. before brain samples were taken.

We thus see in five independent recent studies that it is the introduction of novel and increased stimulation that makes brain grow and show increased protein and lipid metabolism. Could these transitory metabolic growth indices underlie some more permanent neural modification? We should obviously look at what must be the "business" ends of neurons.

CHANGES IN CORTICAL DENDRITES

What can be said today about the development of nerve fibers, dendritic spines, or synapses as these may be dependent upon functional demand? Arthur Hess (1958) has demonstrated a dramatic failure in the proliferation of fibers in visual cortex when an eye is removed during late fetal development in guinea pigs. Excluding light from birth does not have such obvious consequences. Today there is not time to go into studies of surgically produced transneuronal degeneration which I have elsewhere considered as a possible extension of sensory deprivation (Riesen, 1966).

In three littermate pairs of kittens, Coleman and I have looked at dendritic branchings in stellate cells of the dark-reared and light-reared members of each pair at 6 months of age (Coleman & Riesen, 1968). Fibers from cells in the lateral geniculate bodies terminate (as Hubel reminded us yesterday) in the region of the stellate cells in Layer IV of visual cortex. The first-order dendrites are the ones that are attached directly to the cell body and are not changed in number. Second-order dendrites are those that form the first branchings away from cell bodies.

For dendrites of all orders taken together, the light-reared sample gives a larger count. This difference is significant beyond the 1% level of confidence determined by an analysis of variance for repeated measures on the same subjects. This statement is based on the F test applied to the interaction: environment times trial (1 and 4 df, respectively).

As a check on the method of counting branches we also counted, again by a double blind procedure, the numbers of intersections by dendrites of a given cell across a series of circles around the cell body. These circles were drawn concentrically with the radius of each one extended by 18 μ beyond the next smaller circle.

The data for stellate cells of striate cortex and perhaps even more significant comparisons for posterior cingulate, layer III, pyramidal cells will appear in a forthcoming issue of the *Journal of Anatomy*. Whereas for striate cortex one of our pairs of animals did not separate well for the rearing conditions, the separation was consistent for all three pairs in the posterior cingulate, a region found by electrophysiological recording (MacLean, 1966) to respond to light stimulation.

In the data for individual animals, two of three cats are consistently below normals, following dark-rearing, in counts of dendrite crossing for stellate cells. All three pairs separate well in counts made for basal dendrites of pyramidal cells of posterior cingulate gyrus. These cells are 400 to 500 μ below the pia. In layer V of the striate cortex, where we counted to find out whether the effect of dark-rearing was general to cells of the cerebral cortex, there were no differences in either numbers of branches or in counts of intersections.

CHANGES IN DENDRITIC SPINES AND SYNAPSES

Moving on to a still finer structural feature of the cortical dendrites, I can report some fascinating work by Globus and Scheibel of UCLA, and by Dr. F.

Valverde, Chief of the Section of Comparative Neuroanatomy of the Cajal Institute in Madrid, Spain. Their work moves us still closer to the synapse as the
locus of functional alteration.

First, on the basis of monocular eye removal in newborn rabbits, Globus &
Scheibel (1967a) were able to standardize a method of counting dendritic spines
on pyramidal and stellate cells of various regions of the cortex. Their stain was a
variant of the rapid Golgi method. Of major interest to us here is their comparison of cells of the striate and peristriate cortex on the two sides, since in rabbit
most fibers cross over at the chiasm. Monocular enucleation thus provides an
experimental and a control cortex within each individual animal.

In pyramidal cells whose apical dendrites course upward from the cell body in
layer IV and layer III toward the surface of the visual cortex, spines are particularly numerous along the middle portion of the apical shaft. There are no spines
near the base of this shaft, but they are also quite numerous on basal dendrites
and oblique branchings of the apical dendrites.

Counts of spines were made for each quarter of the length of the shaft
separately. Differences were particularly pronounced between shafts from the
denervated side and control shafts for the middle two quartiles of these vertical
distances. The differences averaged 30% and, for some experimental and control
pairs, were as high as 65% in maximally involved areas. Basal dendrites and
dendrites extending obliquely from the main shaft did not show differences in
spine populations, nor was there a difference, to quote the authors, "on the very
limited complement of stellate and short axon neurons characteristic of rabbit
visual cortex."

Globus and Scheibel (1967b) also report effects of dark-rearing. Here the
differences are somewhat less obvious, but clearly in the direction of reduced
fullness in the spines of the dark-reared animal.

In the meantime Dr. Valverde (1967) has published in a recent issue of
Experimental Brain Research a report on dark-reared versus light-reared mice. He
reports so far studies of mice reared to the age of 25 days, but in personal
communication says that he is following additional groups for 50 days and for 6
months of visual deprivation. Valverde counted spines in 50 μ segments of apical
dendrites as these were traversing layer IV from cell bodies in layer V of the
cortex. Mean values showed that sensory deprivation was accompanied by a 22%
reduction in the number of spines. Control counts were done in temporal cortex
and there in layer IV there were no differences in spine count, which can lead
the author of the study (and us) to conclude that the effect is specific to the
system that is normally responsive to visual input. We may say now: What do
spines have to do with the transmission and organization of visual information?
In addition to the implications of these data, we can point to the fact that work
by Gray (1959) and by Hamlyn (1963), through the use of the electron microscope, implicated the so-called "spine apparatus" in providing the anatomical
support for synaptic structures. The foregoing data on dendrites and dendritic

spines, taken in conjunction with a recent preliminary report (Holloway, 1966) provide a reasonably solid base of information to support a conclusion that the increasing environmental demands for sensory transmission augment the anatomical growth of these fine structures of mammalian sensory cortex.

Cragg (1967) has found a change in synaptic density and a shift in the distribution of sizes of synapses (diameters) as a function of light-rearing or dark-rearing for several days starting at the time of weaning. Varying with layers, synapses were enlarged by stimulation or new ones were formed.

White & Westrum (1964) and Ward (1966), at the University of Washington, are finding in the context of research on epilepsy a dearth of dentritic spines in isolated slabs of cortex. Deafferentation, they are contending, results in spine loss following inactivity of cells. The inactivity is in turn responsible for a metabolic buildup that leads to seizure discharges in the region of denuded cells.

SUPPORT OF BEHAVIOR FROM THE DEVELOPED STRUCTURES

We may next ask the question: Is there evidence that the more developed structures will in turn support more advanced forms of behavior? There are at least two ways in which to seek an answer to this question. One is obviously to see whether organisms discriminate more adequately after the structures have been developed under complex stimulation. Another way is to attempt to develop the structures by the use of hormonal growth factors. There is a history of progress in pursuit of both of these procedures.

We have seen the findings of the Berkeley group demonstrating significant changes in cortical layer thicknesses and in brain weight associated with environmental complexity. Animals that have received the benefits of such changes in brain have also shown improved rates of learning where the tasks involved visual discrimination reversals and maze learning (Rosenzweig, 1966). The growth changes in brain were found to recede after their production, without the loss of the behavioral advantages. Let me here point out again that the measures of growth and recession in these longitudinal studies were the gross volumetric or weight changes that I discussed earlier in this talk. They did not include measures of dendritic branching or spine counts nor has there been any information regarding synaptic structures studied with the ultramicroscopic techniques. The crucial gains for behavioral advantage are likely to prove not to involve changes in cortical depth, but rather changes in organelles such as dendritic spines and synapses. This approach to our problem seems to be imminent if not actually already underway.

We have information on complex form discrimination and discrimination of visual movement in kittens that indicates the need for pursuing the study at the organelle and macromolecular levels. Under conditions in which RNA would have advanced and again receded, and in which cortical volumes would have grown and again shriveled, our animals have retained the advantages of the stimulation history (Riesen, 1965). Following 5 months from birth of normal visual exposures and then a second 5 months' period of rearing in total darkness, our kittens equaled or exceeded the performance of animals that were reared under normal conditions during the full period of 10 months. Their entire period of training was under conditions that permitted them to utilize only the visual environment that was visible to them during approximately 10 min. per day of training and testing.

This result was probably obtained in spite of some modest deficiencies in visual acuity, i.e., we do have evidence that late light deprivation can in a matter of 48 hrs. impair somewhat the visual acuity of the squirrel monkey. Unfortunately, we do not have this kind of information for the cat and we are therefore on shaky ground generalizing the result across species. However, the amount of loss of acuity in the squirrel monkeys, while significant, was no more than the acuity deficit suffered by many of us when we have to remove our glasses.

THE USE OF GROWTH HORMONE

Some interesting results have involved the augmentation of neural growth and subsequent tests of possible behavioral advantages. Zamenhof (1942) and more recently Clendennin & Eayrs (1961) succeeded in advancing the development of cortical neurons by injecting bovine extracts of pituitary growth hormone into the mothers of rats during the last two weeks of pregnancy. These workers are not yet in agreement as to whether the effect was to increase the number of neurons, *or* the cell size and the extent of dendrite proliferation, or both (Zamenhof *et al.*, 1966). Although Warden, Ross, & Zamenhof (1942) failed to find differences in the learning by treated and untreated white rats of the Warden and Warren maze problem, the more recent study from England showed significant advantages for hormone treated offspring on Hebb-Williams spatial learning problems. In a recent study from our laboratory, Jaffee attempted to test the assumption that hormone administration could overcome effects of dark-rearing on the Hebb-Williams problem solving tasks. The actual outcome showed that dark-reared rats were helped proportionately less than light-reared animals by the hormone treatment (5½% error reduction versus 16% error reduction). We can at this point state only that no evidence exists to support the notion that internal growth regulation can directly substitute for environmentally induced changes to promote the capacity of mammalian sensory nervous system for mediating complex discriminations.

In our present state of knowledge, we must continue to assume that many essential forms of neural integration are provided for by innate neural growth mechanisms. For vision it seems clear at this point that edge detection is mediated by innately organized mechanisms at least as far along transmission pathways as units in the sensory cortex. Support of structures that are innately provided seems to require early use of these structures. The elaboration of even more complex form detectors must require behavioral elicitation. This statement rests not upon electrophysiological evidence, but upon evidence from behavioral development. So what can we conclude regarding the need for a mutual environmental and neurophysiological interaction if the organism is to establish the means for directing behavior in complex discriminative adaptations?

SUMMARY AND CONCLUSIONS

1. Keeping the environmental input to a minimum results in reduced neurometabolism as shown by measures of RNA concentration in neuronal nuclei and cytoplasm.

2. The addition of more complex stimulation whether in early growth or in adult stages of the life cycle produces an immediate response in the incorporation of RNA into cells of sensory nuclei and sensory cortex. Correlated with this altered metabolism is a growth of fine structures: dendrites and their spines.

3. When the heightened environmental demands are maintained in a steady-state condition, there is a gradual recession in metabolic response. Ongoing research should soon tell us whether the fine structures are retained.

4. Returning the environment to a reduced demand level produces some measurable effects on metabolism, without returning the adaptive capacity of the organism to its former lowest level.

5. Manipulation of neural metabolism by means that are strictly chemical, while it may facilitate the efficacy of environmental pattern repetitions, in no sense substitutes for them. The highest levels of discriminative capacity, I believe, will one day be shown to depend upon neural structures that are established only following optimum programs of environmental support. We are getting closer to identifying such structures, so let us intensify the search.

REFERENCES

Boas, J. A. R., Ramsey, R. L., Riesen, A. H., & Walker, J. P. Absence of change in some measures of cortical morphology in dark-reared adult rats. *Psychonomic Science,* 1969, **15**, 251-252.

Clendennin, B. G., & Eayrs, J. T. The anatomical and physiological effects of prenatally administered somotatrophin on cerebral development in rats. *Journal of Endocrinology,* 1961, **22**, 183-193.

Coleman, P. D., & Riesen, A. H. Environmental effects on cortical dendritic fields. I. Rearing in the dark. *Journal of Anatomy,* 1968, **102,** 363-374.

Cragg, B. G. Changes in visual cortex on first exposure of rats to light. Effect on synaptic dimensions. *Nature,* 1967, **215,** 251-253.

DeBold, R. C., Firsheim, W., Carrier, S. C., III, & Leaf, R. C. Changes in RNA in the occipital cortex of rats as a function of light and dark during rearing. *Psychonomic Science,* 1967, **7 (11),** 379-380.

Globus, A., & Scheibel. A. B. Synaptic loci on visual cortical neurons of the rabbit: The specific afferent radiation. *Experimental Neurology,* 1967, **18,** 116-131. (a)

Globus, A., & Scheibel, A. B. The effect of visual deprivation on cortical neurons: A Golgi study. *Experimental Neurology,* 1967, **19,** 331-345. (b)

Gomirato, G., & Baggio, G. Metabolic relations between the neurons of the optic pathway in various functional conditions. *Journal of Neuropathology and Experimental Neurology,* 1962, **21,** 634-644.

Goss, R. J. *Adaptive growth.* New York: Academic Press (Logos Press), 1964.

Goss, R. J. Hypertrophy versus hyperplasia. *Science,* 1966, **153,** 1615-1620.

Goss, R. J. The strategy of growth. In H. Teir & T. Rytomaa (Eds.), *Control of the cellular growth in the adult organisms.* New York: Academic Press, 1967.

Gyllensten, L., Malmfors, T., & Norrlin, M. -L. Effect of visual deprivation on the optic centers of growing and adult mice. *Journal of Comparative Neurology,* 1965, **124,** 149-160.

Hamlyn, L. H. An electron microscope study of pyramidal neurons in the ammon's horn of the rabbit. *Journal of Anatomy,* 1963, **97,** 189-201.

Hess, A. Optic centers and pathways after eye removal in fetal guinea pigs. *Journal of Comparative Neurology,* 1958, **109,** 91-115.

Holloway, R. G., Jr. Dendritic branching: Some preliminary results of training and complexity in rat visual cortex. *Brain Research,* 1966, **2,** 393-396.

Hydén, A. A molecular basis of neuron-glia interaction. In F. O. Schmitt (Ed.), *Macromolecular specificity and biological memory.* Cambridge, Mass.: M.I.T. Press, 1962.

MacLean, P. D. The limbic and visual cortex in phylogeny: Further insights from anatomic and microelectrode studies. In R. Hasler & H. Stephan (Eds.), *Evolution of the Forebrain.* New York: Plenum Press, 1967.

Riesen, A. H. Effects of visual deprivation on perceptual function and the neural substrate. In J. deAjuriaguerra (Ed.), *Desafferentation experimentale et clinique.* Geneva: Georg; Paris: Masson, 1965. Pp. 47-66.

Riesen, A. H. Sensory deprivation. In E. Stellar & J. M. Sprague (Eds.), *Progress in physiological psychology,* Vol. 1. New York: Academic Press, 1966.

Rose, S. P. R. Changes in visual cortex on first exposure of rats to light. Effect on incorporation of tritiated lysine into protein. *Nature,* 1967, **215,** 253-255.

Rosenzweig, M. R. Environmental complexity, cerebral change, and behavior. *American Psychologist,* 1966, **21,** 321-332.

Rosenzweig, M. R., Bennett, E. L., & Diamond, M. C. Transitory components of cerebral changes induced by experience. *Proceedings of the American Psychological Association,* 1967, **2,** 105-106.

Shabadash, A. L. The histochemistry of the nucleoproteins of the neurons in relation to their functional activity. In A. V. Palladin (Ed.), *Problems of the biochemistry of the nervous system.* New York: Macmillan, 1964. Pp. 196-204.

Valverde, F. Apical dendrites spines of the visual cortex and light deprivation in the mouse. *Experimental Brain Research,* 1967, **3,** 337-352.

Ward, A. A., Jr. The hyperexcitable neuron-epilepsy. In K. Rodahl & B. Issekutz (Eds.), *Nerve as a tissue.* New York: Harper & Row (Hoeber), 1966.

Warden, C. J., Ross, R., & Zamenhof, S. The effect of artificial changes in the brain on maze learning in the white rat. *Science,* 1942, 95, 414.

White, L. E., Jr., & Westrum, L. E. Dendritic spine changes in prepryiform cortex following olfactory bulb lesions–rat, Golgi method. *Anatomical Record,* 1964, 148, 410-411.

Zamenhof, S. Stimulation of cortical-cell proliferation by the growth hormone. III. Experiments on albino rats. *Physiological Zoology,* 1942, 15, 281-292.

Zamenhof, S., Mosley, J., & Schuller, E. Stimulation of the proliferation of cortical neurons by prenatal treatment with growth hormone. *Science,* 1966, 152, 1396-1397.

THE QUESTION OF A MOLECULAR BASIS
FOR THE MEMORY TRACE

HOLGER HYDÉN

Institute of Neurobiology, Faculty of Medicine
University of Göteborg
Göteborg, Sweden

How are memories stored in the brain and how are they recalled? Is a memory trace, engram, formed in the child's brain, throughout the unbelievably complicated structures which make up the central nervous system? These are questions which have captured man's interest and challenged his intellectual capacity through the ages of western civilization. Plato was of the opinion that in learning, we remember what has been laid down and has been residing in our minds for centuries. At the end of the seventeenth century, John Locke advanced the other extreme view that man's mind at birth is a *tabula rasa* on which experience chisels its engraving during the life cycle.

Nobody tries to defend either of these extreme points of view nowadays. With increasing knowledge of the structure, electrical and chemical properties of the brain, and the growing knowledge of instinctive behavior in animals, the problems can be phrased in another way, although the main questions are the same. We can listen to one of the pioneers within the modern field of learning, Karl Lashley. He came to the conclusion that there are no special nerve cells within the brain for special memories. Certain parts of the brain are more essential than others for learning of a particular activity, but within such regions the parts are functionally equivalent. That is to say, the engram, the memory trace if this exists, is present throughout the region. Present man exists in a most complicated society. To encompass the implication of present research in learning and memory, these problems have also to be considered in the context of social questions, education, aging, and the individual's possibility of realizing his brain potentialities during the life cycle.

At present, progress in molecular biology, especially in genetics, strongly influences attitudes and approaches in biological sciences. Some scientists are of the view that the progress which will influence us most during the next twenty years is to be expected in the field of differentiation, immunology, and in neurosciences.

For the past ten years, there has been growing body of knowledge of bio-chemical properties and molecular processes in brain cells. Some main questions can be discerned: Do macromolecular changes occur in brain cells at learning which are specific for learning and which do not occur at simply increased neural function? Can a molecular model be envisaged for learning and remembering, and what may be the relation between macromolecular and electrical pheno-mena in brain cells?

An old theory says that when something is learned and stored, there occurs in millions of nerve cells a facilitation of the messages at the synapses. This is an attractive view, because the activity flow can be made very specific and one big neuron may have 10,000 synaptic knobs on its surface. Figure 1 is a photograph of a surviving nerve cell, isolated by microdissection and stained to show the

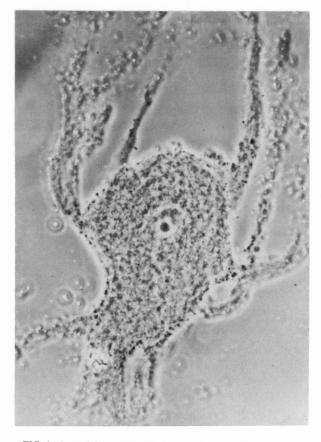

FIG. 1. A surviving nerve cell showing the synaptic knobs.

synaptic knobs, where in focus, they appear on the cell surface as small dots. The theory only scrapes the surface of the problem, however.

Learning means the capacity of a system to react in a new or modified way as a result of experience. Memory is the capacity to store information which can later be retrieved with high distinction to guide the function which is correlated with the new information.

In learning, a short-term memory is first established. This lasts for seconds to hours and is labile and susceptible to interference of various kinds. Short-term memory differs in nature from long-term memory. This storage or fixation process takes place during the learning process immediately after. Long-term memory may last for the better part of a lifecycle. It is remarkably resistant to poisoning and shocks and can be retrieved in a fraction of a second.

It is important to consider that there are three principal components of the brain. Neurons, which differ biochemically, e.g., with respect to transmitter substances and RNA composition. They do not divide and only a small part of their genome is active, about 5%. Glia, the second type of brain cells, also seldom divide and are electrically inexcitable. They are rich in lipoproteins and in rapidly turning over RNA. Figure 2a depicts schematically the relationship between neurons and the surrounding glia. To the right is seen a capillary, at top and to the left, parts of two neurons. In between are various types of glial cells which cover the surface of the neurons except at the sites of the synapses and whose delicate membranous processes interlace. Figure 2b is a microphotograph of such nerve cells, isolated from glia and swimming in a salt solution.

The third compartment of the brain tissue consists of an extra cellular space which seems to amount to around 20%. It presumably contains mucopolysaccharides and mucoproteins.

1. THE GENETIC ROOTS OF LEARNING MECHANISMS

If the outer part of the neuron is the site for the pulse-coded nerve impulse, the inner part handles the energy demands, but also the synthesis of specific substances, and regulates the expression of the gene activities. Synaptic facilitation, therefore, can be expected to be regulated by genetically controlled mechanisms.

Any substance which can serve a memory mechanism for both innate behavior and experiential learning for a lifetime, can be assumed to have a strong relationship with the genes. It may be argued that learning involves an additional activation of the genome of the neuron which, therefore, becomes more richly patterned biochemically and structurally and can respond within a wider range with more selectivity. Such reasoning could obviously lead to a pessimistic view; therefore, many people would find such an idea hard to accept. The limitation

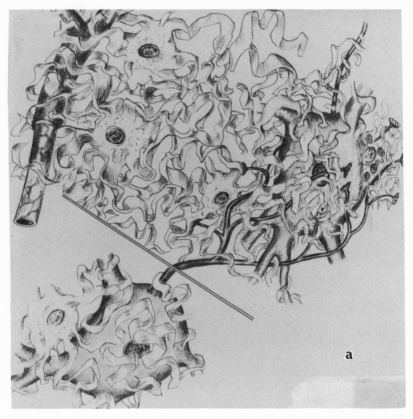

FIG. 2a.

FIG. 2. The relationship between neurons and surrounding glia shown schematically (a) and photographed (b).

of the capacity of the brain would be set. It would mean that only the genetically preprogrammed among our brain cells could be selected for a certain purpose and utilized.

It is true that some neurons are clearly preprogrammed genetically to handle certain types of stimuli. Examples are neurons in the visual cortex. Experience can act as a modifier; e.g., when a tone and a light flash are given *in pair* to an animal, gradually the visual and hearing centers both learn to respond on only one stimulus.

We may now ask if a brain mechanism really can exist in which the genes and the code of the bases in DNA not only permit learning, but also direct the expression of memory. Is it the same mechanism for experiential learning, innate learning, and instinctive behavior? At birth, many types of innate behavior are ready, if not in overt activity. Support a newborn baby in an erect position, let

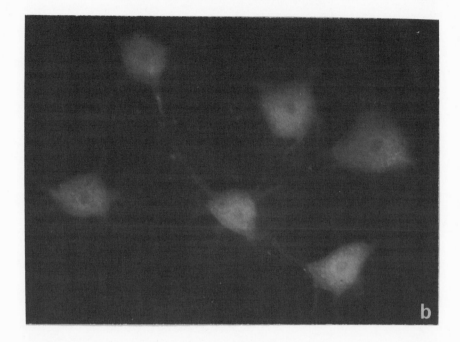

FIG. 2b.

the feet press against the floor, and drag the baby forward. He will make walking and even stepping movements. Many patterns of behavior in animals are clearly inherited and need only a key factor in the environment to be triggered. Then the conclusion cannot be escaped that they are programmed in some way in the sequence of bases in DNA. But if so, the mechanism of expression is much more complicated than the synthesis of a protein.

Interest is now focused on molecular events that form the main operative mechanism underlying learning and remembering. The macromolecules, RNA, and proteins are the most likely candidates to mediate storage of information in the brain, because they have recognition sites. The neurons are rich in RNA and proteins. No other somatic cell can compete with the neuron as an RNA producer.

Table I demonstrates how the amount of RNA per nerve cell varies with species and localization. The data given also show that various types of physiological stimulation leads to an increased amount of RNA per cell. The response varied from a 10 to more than a 100% increase. This reflects an increased synthesis of RNA which has been induced by the stimulation. So far, no base ratio changes have been found in this newly synthesized RNA in mammalian brain cells and the RNA formed has had the base ratio characteristics of ribosomal RNA.

TABLE I
RNA Response of Neurons to Increased Sensory Stimulation

Stimulus	Cell type	RNA increase per cell ($\mu\mu$g)	%	P
Intermittent[a] horizontal rotation 25 min./day, 7 days	Deiters' neurons– rabbit	1550 → 1750	10	.01
Intermittent[b] horizontal rotation 25 min./day, 7 days	Deiters' neurons– rat	680 → 750	10	.02
Intermittent[b] vertical rotation– 30 min.	Deiters' neurons– rat	680 → 850	25	.001
Sodium chloride[c] 1.5% 30 days	Neurons of N. supraopticus– rat	68 → 121	80	.01
Thirst[d] for 7 days	Neurons of N. supraopticus– rat	52 → 129		.001

[a]Hydén-Pigon, 1960.   [c]Edstrom-Eichner, 1958.
[b]Hydén-Egyhazi, 1963.   [d]Edstrom-Eichner-Schor, 1961.

At this point, I would like to stress that no data support the view that brain cells contain mechanistically taping "memory molecules" that store information in a linear way. This is biological nonsense. In current literature, such views are seen, but they do little more than add to the anatomy of confusion. As will be seen, RNA and proteins in brain cells do respond at the establishment of new behavior, but elucidation of the mechanism and its regulation remain for the future.

2. MACROMOLECULAR SYNTHESIS IN BRAIN CELLS AT THE ESTABLISHMENT OF A NEW BEHAVIOR

As was pointed out above, a main question has been: Do macromolecular changes occur in brain cells which characterize the learning process but which do not occur at only increased neural activity? This has been tested by establishing a new behavior in animals and analyzing the brain cells. Another line of research has been to interfere with synthesis of macromolecules in the brain and to observe the effect on behavior. When a new behavior is established, brain cells respond with a synthesis of RNA of a highly specific base composition and a synthesis of several types of acidic proteins.

From our laboratory, I would like to present two types of experiments performed on rats. In the first, neurons were sampled randomly from layers V and VI in a small area of the sensory motor cortex which has been shown to constitute a control area for the transfer of handedness.

Rats are right-handed, left-handed, or − in a small number − ambidextrous. When they execute movements which are complicated for them with their paws, they prefer the paw of one side. They can be induced to switch over to the nonpreferred paw. The performance curve, the number of correct performances per training period and day, is characteristic for this type of learning. It shows a linearly increasing part and, in this case, an asymptotic part after 5 to 6 days with 25 min. training periods twice a day.

The advantage with this experiment is that a paired test can be performed on the analytical values, since control cell material is present contralaterally in the cortex of the same rat.

In the first experiment, right-handed rats were induced to use the left forelimb in retrieving food from far down a narrow glass tube. Multitraining periods of 2 × 25 min. per day were given. The neurons of both sides of the cortex were analyzed, and also those from areas whose destruction prohibits transfer of handedness. These control centers are situated bilaterally in the sensory motor cortex and comprise around 1 mm^3 of the cortex. Layers V-VI are the most important. These neurons have a large nucleus in comparison with the cytoplasm. Therefore, the analytical result will mainly reflect nuclear RNA. Eighty-eight rats were used for the analysis of 14,000 cortical neurons. As was stated above, the advantage of this learning experiment is that the controls are present in the same brain.

A significant increase of the amount of RNA per cell on the learning side of the cortex occurred. In an extension of the work published, the amount of RNA was found to have increased from 220 $\mu\mu$g of RNA per ten nerve cells to 310 $\mu\mu$g.

When the base ratios of the neuronal RNA of the control side were compared with that of the learning side, it was found that the ratio $(G + C)/(A + U)$ had decreased significantly from 1.72 to 1.51 (Table II).

In Table III, the data are divided in two groups. The cell material from the cortex of animals 1 and 2 was taken on the rising part of the learning curve on the third to the fifth day, i.e., during an early part of the learning period. The material from the other two rats was taken on the asymptotic part of the curve on the ninth to the tenth day. In this case, the animals had already reached the maximal number of successful performances per training period on the sixth to seventh day. The increase of the RNA content per neuron of the third to fifth days' animals lies at 25 to 30%. Qualitatively, the RNA formed in the neurons is

TABLE   II

Changes in the RNA Base Composition of Cortical Neurons from the Control (Left) Side
and from the Learning (Right) Side

	Controls Mean	Learning Mean	Change in percent	P
Adenine	18.4 ± .48	20.1 ± .11	+9.2	.02
Guanine	26.5 ± .64	28.7 ± .90	+8.3	.01
Cytosine	36.8 ± .97	31.5 ± .75	−14.4	.01
Uracil	18.3 ± .48	19.6 ± .56	+7.1	.05
$\dfrac{A+G}{C+U}$	0.81 ± .27	.95 ± .35	+17.3	.01
$\dfrac{G+C}{A+U}$	1.72 ± .054	1.51 ± .026	−12.2	.02

TABLE   III

Characteristics of the RNA Formed per Neuron during Transfer of Handedness Correlated
to Training Periods and Performance of the Animals

Animal	Training periods 2 × 25 min/day	Number of successful reaches	Relative increase of total RNA per neuron (percent)	Δ RNA composition
1	3	107	33	A 25.5 G 36.1 C 9.7 U 28.7
2	5	163	23	A 24.5 G 35.7 C 11.7 U 28.1
3	8	625	63	A 26.2 G 34.9 C 16.1 U 22.8
4	9	1041	105	A 21.0 G 35.2 C 24.0 U 19.8

characterized by a DNA-like base ratio composition with adenine and uracil values around 26. (Rat DNA has the following base composition: A 28.6, G 21.4, C 21.5, T 28.4.) The cytosine values were remarkably low. The results were statistically significant. This result was no longer obtained from the animals which had been trained for 8 to 9 days and performed with a maximal number of reaches, i.e., 70 to 80 reaches per period of 25 min. The RNA result deviated both quantitatively and qualitatively from those of group one. The relative RNA increase per neuron in the learning cortex was 60 to 100%. The base ratio composition of the RNA formed was similar to that of ribosomal RNA.

It should be added that when the nerve cells within the learning part of the cortex were taken during the early and acute part of the learning process, the relative RNA increase per neuron was small. The nuclear RNA formed, however, had a DNA-like base ratio composition. Thus, a stimulation of the genome seems to occur early in a learning situation which the animals have not encountered before. A differentiated formation of RNA occurs during a learning period in the neurons engaged, and the beginning seems to be characterized by a genic stimulation, judging by the character of the RNA formed.

In another type of rat learning experiment, an increased production of nuclear RNA was found in neurons and glia clearly engaged in the process. By analogy with results of analysis of other cell material, this brain cell RNA was concluded to be a chromosomal RNA.

A preliminary study of the duration of the RNA in the neurons with the high A/U value gave the following result. Twenty-four hours after stopping the experiment and returning the animals to their home cages, no such RNA fraction could be found. When the training was resumed for 45 min. and the nuclei were analyzed, the RNA fraction with high A/U ratio was found again. The disappearance of the RNA fraction did not mean that the fraction had ceased to be synthesized. It probably means that it is present in such small amounts as to be inaccessible with the present methods of analysis.

A long series of studies has revealed that increase in sensory and motor stimulation and certain drugs easily give rise to an increased synthesis of RNA in engaged nerve cells. But there occurred no change of the proportions of the adenine and uracil components of the newly synthesized RNA as did at the establishment of new behavior. Neither did such changes occur in brain cells during stress experiments.

The observation was obtained by means of the microchemical procedure outlined in Table IV. The protein of nerve cells was separated on polyacrylamide gels in glass capillaries, 300 μ in diameter. Figure 3 shows a photograph of such a microgel. The protein pattern has been stained by amido-black. Fractions 4 and 5 are clearly visible in the middle part of the pattern.

As material, we used the pyramidal nerve cell layer in part of the hippocampus. This area belongs to the phylogenetically old part of the brain. It is a well-known fact that an intact hippocampus is a prerequisite for the formation

TABLE IV

Volume of Sample Prop to Weight of Total Protein in Sample

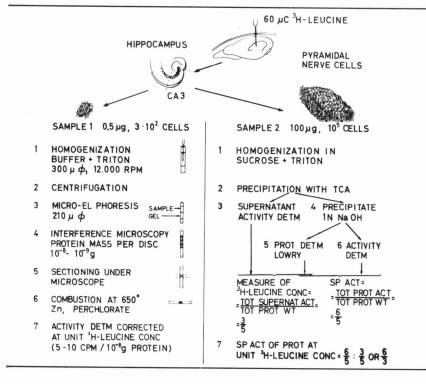

of a long-term memory. In the hippocampal nerve cells, the synthesis of two acidic protein fractions increased by 100% during a learning test in rats.

These proteins are interesting because some of them are produced only in the brain and in no other organ. They have a molecular weight of 30,000 and a composition characterized by a high percentage of glutamic acid and also aspartic acid, but are almost devoid of tryptophane. A protein of such a small size could constitute an electrogenic protein which could respond to electrical fields in 10^{-4} sec. and undergo conformational changes, activate transmitters, and be incorporated in membranes in a more stable configuration.

A question for the future is whether such acidic proteins are the specific executive molecules which operate at the biochemical differentiation of the brain and are also used in mechanisms for storage and retrieval of information.

Another type of learning experiment which involves motor and sensory functions has been performed on goldfish by Shashoua. A piece of plastic foam fastened below the jaw turns the fish around and lifts the head out of the water.

In a while, the fish has learned to swim correctly. During this learning, new RNA was synthesized in the brain; it was of the same type as we had found during learning in rats, with similar ratios of the uracil/cytosine values. No such RNA was produced when the fish performed the same amount of swimming but did not learn, and, most important, stress did not produce these RNA changes. If protein synthesis in the goldfish brain was inhibited by puromycin, no learning occurred.

At this point, I would like to return to the question of the relationship between macromolecules and establishment of behavior and to conclude: At learning, small amounts of nuclear RNA with a highly specific base composition are synthesized in brain cells. Similar RNA responses have not been found up to now as a result of other types of physiological stimulation in brain cells in mammals. The synthesis of certain acidic proteins at learning looks like a specific response.

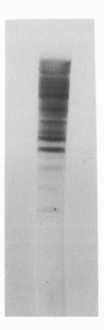

FIG. 3. Polyacrylamidic gel.

The RNA response can be interpreted to reflect an activation of hitherto silent gene areas in brain cells when the animals were faced with a situation they had not encountered before, and which required learning. The task in both of the quoted examples was obviously within the capacity of the species. As learning involving problem solving, the tasks were not difficult to judge by performance and time course.

3. THE NEURON AND ITS CELLULAR ENVIRONMENT
IN LEARNING

Can the glia take part jointly with the neuron in the learning process? For ten years we have analyzed the neuron and its glia in mammals and have come to the conclusion that they together constitute a metabolic and functional unit. When the demand on energy is increased in the neuron, the capacity of the electron transferring system in its respiratory chain increases. In the glia surrounding the neuron, there occurs a switchover to the less-efficient anaerobic glycolysis to cover the glial energy demand. In a pathological process, there occurs first an alteration of the polynucleotide pattern of the glia. Later on, a similar change can be seen in the neurons. Only then do the nervous symptoms become overt. Furthermore, acidic proteins are localized in nuclei of neurons and in cell bodies of glia. There is what we consider good evidence that governing molecules are transferred between the glia and its neuron. RNA seems to flow between these cells. During learning, the glia responded in a way similar to the neurons with respect to synthesis of specific nuclear RNA. Therefore, the glia may be as potent in their function as are the synapses.

The neuron and its glia seem to represent a two-cell metabolic and functional collaboration, a stable system from a cybernetic point of view. The glia may stabilize, influence, and program synthesis in the neurons by transfer of molecules and may modulate electrical properties of the neurons.

4. INTERFERENCE WITH MACROMOLECULAR
SYNTHESIS IN BRAIN CELLS AT THE
ESTABLISHMENT OF NEW BEHAVIOR

In another line of research, the effect of certain antibiotics has been studied on behavior. They have all aimed at blocking the production of protein or nucleic acids of brain in a selective way.

The conclusion of these experiments has been that brain protein synthesis during training is necessary for the formation of long-term memory, as is intact nuclear DNA- and RNA-mediated protein synthesis in the brain cell bodies. Short-term memory, on the other hand, is not dependent on protein synthesis. It can persist concomitantly with the long-term memory and for as long as 6 hrs.

5. THE GAP BETWEEN ELECTRICAL AND BIOCHEMICAL PHENOMENA IN BRAIN CELLS

How can the gap in knowledge between the electrophysiological and biochemical data on brain cells be bridged? This is a question of fundamental importance. There is no straight way to be seen, but we move in the best circles!

Some recent data seem to open up a new lead. Adey and his colleagues have studied intra- and extra-cellular electrical phenomena as well as the EEG during learning experiments. They have advanced the view that there exist current pathways outside the neurons in the extra-cellular spaces which may modulate the neurons. They have suggested that information can be processed in a parallel fashion by a primary system of waves generated in the neurons (50 to 100 μV). These waves are supposed not to be dependent on synaptic connections. The EEG reflects partly such nonlinearly, graded waves. The pulse-coded nerve impulses represent for Adey a secondary system for information processing. It is interesting that clear changes of the EEG pattern have been found to accompany the establishment of a new behavior. There was a decreasing scatter of phase relations in the wave trains of the hippocampus at a higher level of performance.

6. A MOLECULAR MODEL FOR LEARNING AND REMEMBERING

At birth, brain cells have undergone the main differentiation which made them nerve cells. This reflects selected properties collected in the genome of the individual which have been incorporated during evolution.

There are three observations in genetics which are particularly interesting for a neurobiologist. The first is that only part of the genome is active, 5 to 10%. The rest of the gene areas seem to be silent. Secondly, such gene areas can be made active by external factors which have the capacity to penetrate to the genome. Examples are the cells of the reproductive tracts which are induced to synthesize their specific protein products by hormones. Thirdly, large populations of similar nucleotide sequences exist in DNA complements of higher organisms. Furthermore, the repetition RNA does not seem to belong to the ribosomal RNA. This is interesting in view of the fact that brain cells at stimulation produce smaller RNA species in great amounts. One million similar nucleotide sequences seem to constitute 10% of the repeated sequences in the mouse and

15% consisted of 1000 to 100,000 similar nucleotide copies. It was suggested that a sudden appearance of, e.g., 10,000 slightly different nucleotide sequences may lead to an evolutionary event. The products of a set of genes formed from a family of repeated sequences may provide the rich variation of surface proteins upon which relies the intercellular relationships.

I would like to suggest that the redundancy of the gene products provides a basis for the necessary richness of proteins serving as a mechanism for storage of memories. Experience leads to a further differentiation of brain cells.

Additional gene areas become active under the impact of environmental factors. This leads to a synthesis of a great number of RNA species and proteins slightly differing from each other. The detailed mechanism which leads to these events may be the following (see scheme in Fig. 3). The external factors give rise to modulated frequencies in sensory ganglia and brain stem areas, including the limbic area. The modulated frequencies have one quadrature component. I suggest that the 90° vector has a phase shift relative to the quadrature component. The two variables, the frequency and the phase shift, give a high information content of such an electric pattern which may be decisive for the specificity of its effect. In principle, this effect consists of a production of a change in ionic equilibrium through field changes. In the nuclear compartment, these field changes give rise to conformational changes of enzyme protein and induce synthesis of RNA from new gene areas. Even instructional changes could occur. RNA undergoes quite easily hysteresis phenomena by a local change in pH, which are time independent but dependent on the history of the system.

The RNA synthesis will result in a synthesis of specific proteins which will soon be present in the whole neuron, in cell body as well as in synapses. The specific proteins could be incorporated in a more permanent way in the membrane.

With time and experience, the protein pattern of the neuron will become modulated. A differentiation has occurred. RNA and protein species are constantly synthesized to replace and reconstitute this pattern. Each group of neurons will have its own unique protein composition. The uniqueness of the protein pattern decides whether the neuron will respond at retrieval or not. A neuron can therefore respond as a member of a great number of nets or only in a certain area. Each neuron may be a member in a changing Gestalt-combination.

In this reaction the glia do play an active role. The glia are not only support and energy suppliers to their neurons. At learning, the RNA response of the glia is similar to that of the neuron, and RNA response is very rapid.

There occur a transfer of acid protein and a flow of RNA from glia to neuron. These acidic proteins plus RNA may block histones in the nucleus of neurons and maintain gene activation. The induction of synthesis of RNA in glia at learning may occur in the same was as in neurons.

Whatever the flow of RNA from glia to neurons means, it is clear that uptake by neurons of specific macromolecules with recognition sites means program-

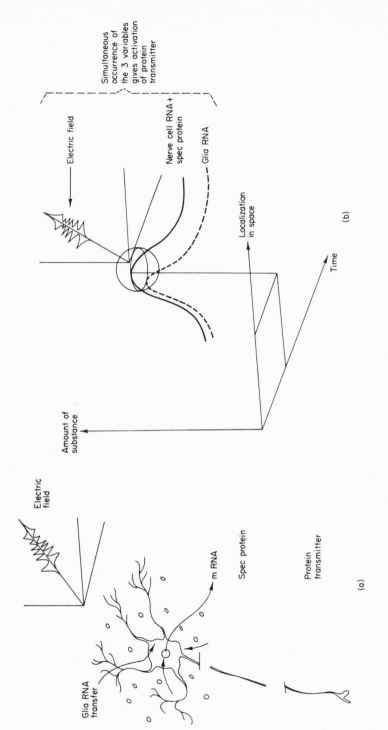

FIG. 4. (a) Differentiation of neuron at learning, (b) retrieval.

ming. It may be a very important mechanism, because to the already complicated structure of the nervous tissue and the thousands of synapses, a third
informational flow between brain cells, a lock-in mechanism between two inter-
dependent units, will be added.

The molecular specificity according to this veiw is placed one step before the
transmitters. This means that only a few types of transmitters are needed.

At learning, a sequence of events leads to a fixation of memory: Informa-
tion-rich modulated frequencies, field changes, transcription into messenger
RNA in both neuron and glia, synthesis of proteins in the neuron, gives a
biochemical differentiation of the neuron-glia unit in millions, a readiness to
respond on a common type of stimulus.

At retrieval, it is the simultaneous occurrence of the three variables: Electrical
pattern, the transfer of RNA from glia to neurons, and the presence of the
unique proteins in the neuron, decide whether the individual neuron will respond or not. (See Fig. 4.)

If the three conditions are fulfilled, the neuron with the specific protein
pattern—or a sufficiently large part of the pattern—will respond on the stimulus
within the Gestalt.

Whether the protein is in a membrane or free, it will respond with an activation of the transmitter since it reacts as in an antigen-antibody-like reaction on
the incoming electrical pattern. In such a model, it is irrelevant if the electrical
instructional changes consist of pulse-coded nerve impulses, or of nonlinear,
graded waves which are generated by dendrites of the neurons and processed in a
parallel fashion.

Whether the next neuron will respond depends entirely on the range of the
protein pattern. The specific protein is activated by the same stimuli which once
induced its synthesis and will rapidly activate the transmitter. Molecular specificity is placed one step before the transmitter.

Such a mechanism does not require only continuous nets of neurons. Millions
of neurons plus their glia in different parts of the brain and in a hierarchical
system can respond to stimuli of the same type. This, by the way, agrees quite
well with observations by Roy John. He found simultaneous electrical response
in cortical neurons at conditioning which could not be accounted for if synaptic
transmission was supposed to occur.

If the whole Gestalt consisting of millions of neurons – and not necessarily in
continuous nets – give a response, then a retrieval of the stored information will
become part of the conscious perception. A graded change of all of the parameters may occur when the functional expression of the phylogenetically older
parts of the brain and the neocortex are considered. Some of the neuron-glia
units may have only part of the protein pattern in common with the rest of the
Gestalt-units. They nevertheless will constitute part of the response. With time,
part of the original protein pattern will probably become changed. I would like

to suggest that this explains the well-known phenomenon that the past is constantly remade by the present.

Experiential learning by additional gene activation and by an instructional mechanism based on recognition sites of macromolecules and hysteresis would both require redundancy of molecular species in the delicate interplay between the various parts of the brain in order to integrate the functional processes.

7. NEURONS, ORDERLINESS AND AGE

Finally, I would like to take up some experiments which deal with orderliness and age of brain cells. The nerve cells share a rare characteristic with a few other cells of the organism. They do not divide. Over a lifecycle, therefore, no order is added to the cells by means of cell division. There will be an increasing danger of errors at synthesis in the cells which means errors in function. Evidence has been presented that neurons may renew their DNA without preparing for division. Future studies have to elucidate what happens in aging neurons, since hybridization analyses have suggested that DNA from an old animal may not be identical with DNA from a young animal.

Old animals do not learn and consolidate the memory with the same alacrity and efficiency as do young animals.

At old age, some organs or systems may be in good shape, including circulation, although the brain function reflected as memory and higher intellectual function may falter. In such cases, can we increase orderliness in the brain cells in order to harmonize the functional output of the various organs? If learning and the expression of memory ultimately reflect potentialities of the genome, then, addition of extraneous gene material with high intrinsic orderliness to such aging brain cells would be a logical attempt. We have, therefore, as a first step, prepared brain DNA of varying degrees of purity. This DNA was injected in the ventricles of the brain in other animals. In 1 hr., protein synthesis was found to increase by more than 100%. Biochemical analyses showed that the DNA had been incorporated in the recipient's brain cells in a polymerized state. It is not surprising *per se* that brain cells can take up macromolecules like DNA, since it is by now a well-known fact that many other somatic cells have this capacity. It was made highly probable by a series of control tests that the incorporation of polymerized DNA had caused the stimulation of protein synthesis in the brain cells, and RNA seemed to mediate the effect. More hard facts are needed. What is the nature of the protein formed? It is functionally valuable or a nonsense protein? How long does the effect last, for hours, days, or years?

How could the observation be utilized in future brain research? I would like to suggest that a way may eventually be found to add orderliness to brain cells of one individual by incorporation of gene material from another. The question is how this would be accomplished. There are several possibilities. The most direct would be to infect the brain with genes attached to a harmless virus entering the brain. Viruses have the capacity of penetrating into host cells and should thus act as transporting agents. A successful counteracting of entropy increase in brain cells could change the whole structure of our society.

REFERENCES

Adey, W. R. In G. C. Quarton, T. Melnechuk, & F. O. Schmitt (Eds.), *The neurosciences.* New York: The Rockefeller Univ. Press, 1967, Pp. 615.

Agranoff, B. W. In G. C. Quarton, T. Melnechuk, & F. O. Schmitt (Eds.), *The neurosciences.* New York: The Rockefeller Univ. Press, 1967, Pp.756.

Bolton, E. T., Britten, R. J., Cowie, D. B., Kohne, D. E., Roberts, R. B., & Szafranski, P. *Carnegie Institution of Washington, Yearbook,* 1965-1966, **65**.

Brattgard, S. O. *Acta Radiologica, Supplementum,* 1952, **96**.

Brawerman, G. *Biochimica et Biophysica Acta,* 1963, **76**, 322.

Dahlstrom, A., & Fuxe, K. *Acta Physiologica Scandinavica Supplementum,* 1964, **232**.

Diamond, M. C., Law, F., Rhodes, H., Lindner, B., Rosenzweig, M. R., Krech, D., & Bennett, E. L. *Journal of Comparative Neurology,* 1966, **128**, 117.

Edstrom, J. E., & Beermann, W. *Journal of Cell Biology,* 1962, **14**, 371.

Edstrom, J. E., & Eichner, D. *Nature,* 1958, **181**, 619.

Edstrom, J. E., Eichner, D., & Schor, N. In S. S. Kety & J. Elkes (Eds.), *Regional neurochemistry.* London, & New York: Oxford University Press, 1961.

Egyhazi, E., & Hydén, H., *Life Sciences,* 1966, **5**, 1215.

Egyhazi, E., & Hydén, H. *Proceedings of the Symposium on Nucleic Acids and Proteins in the Neuron, Prague, May 1967.*

Elul, R., & Adey, W. R. *Nature,* 1966, **212**, 1424.

Flexner, L. B. *Proceedings of the American Philosophical Society,* 1967, **111**, 343.

Galambos, R. In G. C. Quarton, T. Melnechuk, & F. O. Schmitt (Eds.), *The neurosciences.* New York: The Rockefeller Univ. Press, 1967.

Gomirato, G., & Hydén, H. *Brain,* 1963, **86**, 773.

Hamberger, G., & Hydén, H. *Journal of Cell Biology,* 1963, **16**, 521.

Hydén, H. The neuron. In J. Brachet & A. E. Mirsky (Eds.), *The cell,* Vol. 4, Pt. 1. New York: Academic Press, 1960.

Hydén, H. In F. O. Schmitt (Ed.), *Macromolecular specificity and biological memory.* Cambridge, Mass.: The M. I. T. Press, 1962, Pp. 55.

Hydén, H. In J. Wortis (Ed.), *Recent advances in biological psychiatry.* New York: Plenum Press, 1964, Pp.31.

Hydén, H. In G. C. Quarton, T. Melnechuk, & F. O. Schmitt (Eds.), *The neurosciences,* New York: The Rockefeller Univ. Press, 1967, Pp.248.

Hydén, H., & Egyhazi, E. *Proceedings of the National Academy of Sciences, U.S.,* 1962, **48**, 1366.

Hydén, H., & Egyhazi, E. *Proceedings of the National Academy of Sciences, U.S.,* 1963, **49**, 618.

Hydén, H., & Egyhazi, E. *Proceedings of the National Academy of Sciences, U.S.,* 1964, **52**, 1030.

Hydén, H., & Egyhazi, E. *Neurology*, 1968, **18**, 732.
Hydén, H., & Lange, P. W. *Journal of Cell Biology*, 1962, **13**, 233.
Hydén, H., & Lange, P. *Proceedings of the National Academy of Sciences, U.S.*, 1965, **53**, 946.
Hydén, H., & Lange, P. W. *Naturwissenschaften*, 1966, **3**, 64.
Hydén, H., & Lange, P. W. *Science*, 1968, **159**, 1370.
Hydén, H., & Pigon, A. *Journal Neurochemistry*, 1960, **6**, 57.
John, E. R. In G. C. Quarton, T. Melnechuk, & F. O. Schmitt (Eds.), *The neurosciences*. New York: The Rockefeller Univ. Press, 1967, Pp.690.
Kidson, C., & Kirby, K. S. *Nature*, 1964, **203**, 599.
Lashley, K. S. *Symposia of the Society for Experimental Biology*, 1950, **4**, 454.
Locke, J. *Essay concerning the understanding, knowledge, opinion and assent*. B. Rand (Ed.). London & New York: Oxford University Press, 1931.
McEwen, B. S., & Hydén, H. *Journal of Neurochemistry*, 1966, **13**, 823.
Moore, B. W. *Biochemical and Biophysical Research Communications*, 1965, **19**, 739.
Moore, B. W., & McGregor, D. J. *Journal of Biological Chemistry*, 1965, **240**, 1647.
Morrell, F. In G. C. Quarton, T. Melnechuk, & F. O. Schmitt (Eds.), *The neurosciences*. New York: The Rockefeller Univ. Press, 1967. Pp.452.
Oliverio, A., & Bovet, D. *Life Sciences*, 1966, **5**, 1317.
Pelc, S. R. *Journal of Cell Biology*, 1964, **22**, 21.
Plato. *Meno*. R. S. Buck (Ed.). London & New York: Cambridge University Press, 1961.
Riesen, A. H. *Science*, 1947, **106**, 107.
Robins, A. B., & Taylor, D. M. *Nature*, 1968, **217**, 1228.
Schmitt, F. O., & Davison, P. F. *Neuroscience Research Progress Bulletin*, 1966, **3**, 55.
Shashoua, V. E. *Nature*, 1968, **217**, 238.
Skeels, H. *Monographs of the Society for Research in Child Development*, 1966, **31**, No. 3.
Teitelbaum, P. In G. C. Quarton, T. Melnechuk, & F. O. Schmitt (Eds.), *The neurosciences*. New York: The Rockefeller Univ. Press, 1967, Pp. 557.
van Harreveld, A., Crowell, J., & Malhorta, S. K. *Journal of Cell Biology*, 1965, **25**, 117.
von Hahn, H. P. *Gerontologia*, 1966, **12**, 18.

Part III
CHEMICAL TRANSFER

CHEMICAL TRANSFER OF TRAINING: THREE YEARS LATER

ALLAN L. JACOBSON[1] *AND JAY M. SCHLECTER*

University of California
Los Angeles, California

Several years ago, Frank Babich, then a student in my course in physiological psychology, announced to me that he and his cousin, Suzanne Bubash, had successfully transferred a learned habit from one rat to another by injection of a brain extract. Although I had in that very class been discussing experiments on cannibalistic transfer in planarians, I was skeptical that similar effects could be obtained in more complex organisms. Nevertheless, imbued with a scientific daring that several years of association with the intrepid James McConnell had given me, I joined Babich and Bubash in further investigations of their rat transfer phenomenon. After some modifications in their original procedure, we succeeded in replicating, somewhat less dramatically, their pilot results, and we then performed several additional experiments which confirmed and extended the basic finding.

Briefly, the task we employed was magazine- or food-training for rats in a Skinner box. A pellet of food was periodically delivered to a food cup by a dispenser, and the hungry rat soon learned that the click of the dispenser signaled the presentation of food. The response learned was thus a simple instrumental approach, under the control of a discrete exteroceptive stimulus. A rat well-trained in this task seldom approaches the food-cup in the absence of the click, thus demonstrating good stimulus control. The task has the advantages of permitting rapid learning and of ease of reproducibility; it has the disadvantage (for certain purposes) of requiring too much intervention on the part of the experimenter. These topics will be mentioned again later.

From the brains of animals so trained, we extracted material which we described as "ribonucleic acid," but which clearly contained quantities of at least certain other substances. The label "RNA" was, it would seem, more applicable to the extraction procedure than to the extract. We were careful to point this

[1] Present address: Department of Psychology, San Francisco State College, San Francisco, California.

out in our first published paper (Babich, Jacobson, Bubash, & Jacobson, 1965), but some critics have felt that these qualifiers were not emphatic enough. In any case, we injected the extract into the peritoneum of untrained rats and after several hours, tested, at periodic intervals, the responsiveness to click of these recipient rats in the Skinner box. While the details of these experiments need not be presented here, it should be further noted that no food was given during testing, that tests were conducted in blind fashion, and that the data we reported were not a biased sample of the experiments we actually performed (one previous experiment had been discarded because of difficulties with the injection procedure, which were subsequently remedied).

In brief, our finding was that experimental recipients, injected with extracts from trained rats, showed a significantly greater tendency to approach the food-cup upon click presentation than did control rats, which were injected with extract from untrained rats. A possible source of bias was that the experimenter activated the click, but our use of a blind procedure would help to deal with this problem. Nonetheless, in a subsequent experiment (Babich, Jacobson, & Bubash, 1965), we tightened our control further by recoding recipient Ss after every five trials of testing and still obtained positive results. In this experiment, we also gave control donors handling and apparatus-exposure equated to that received by experimental donors, thus obviating another criticism of our first study. A final, and important, innovation of this later study was our use of two different species, hamsters as donors and rats as recipients. In spite of the additional treatment given to controls, the more elaborate blind procedures, and the change of donor species, we obtained very clearcut transfer effects in this experiment. In this case, then, a systematic replication (Sidman, 1960) proved most fruitful — we were able to replicate our basic effect while also gaining additional information. Of course, by incorporating several changes in procedure at once, we ran the risk of obscuring our results, but perhaps gambling, in science as elsewhere, is to some degree a matter of temperament. On this occasion it was most worthwhile.

Another experiment (Jacobson, Babich, Bubash, & Jacobson, 1965) in this series provided related and confirmatory evidence regarding the necessary conditions for transfer. Two groups of rats were trained according to the general procedure of our first study, except that for one group a blinking light rather than a click served as the cue for cup-approach. A given recipient was injected with extract from only one of these trained donor groups, but all recipients were subsequently tested (blind) with both stimuli. The two groups proved to be differentially responsive to the stimuli to a significant degree, but the clarity of this conclusion was not ideal: Recipients of extract from click-trained donors responded significantly more to click than to light; recipients of extract from light-trained donors responded more, but not significantly more, to light than to click. The indication of specificity was thus strong but not complete. Still, the significant difference between the two groups bore out the idea that the transfer effect we had obtained depended on the conditions of training of donors and could not be produced simply by nondifferential stimulation. (For further discussion of the specificity question in transfer work, see Jacobson, 1967a.)

Despite several positive replications in other labs, the bulk of investigators who undertook to repeat our work were unsuccessful (Byrne *et al.*, 1966). I see no point in dwelling on these efforts here, since other approaches to the transfer problem have been developed and our original paradigm is no longer in use. In our laboratory, we too have been attempting to work out improved methods of studying transfer effects, but with only erratic results at best. In a moment, we shall characterize these efforts and offer some observations about the present status of transfer work. First, however, I would like to discuss some experiments on planarians which were designed to clarify several questions arising from earlier transfer studies on that organism.

McConnell's (1962) and John's (1964) data indicated rather clearly that a transfer effect could be obtained in planarians when cannibal worms ate victim worms which had been classically conditioned with light and shock. It was not apparent, though, whether the effect was dependent on conditioning of victims, as opposed to sheer stimulation, since control victims in both studies had received no treatment at all. The experiment I shall now discuss (Jacobson, Fried, & Horowitz, 1966a) assessed these alternative interpretations. One group of planarians was classically conditioned with paired light and shock. A second group received the same number of lights and shocks, hence the same total stimulation, but the stimuli were unpaired. A third group received no stimulation. A phenol extraction procedure, designed to secure RNA, was then performed on each of these three groups, the extract obtained was injected into three groups of untrained planarians, and these recipient planarians were tested in the experimental situation some 24 hrs. later. Two methodological points deserve comment here: (*a*) extraction, injection, and testing were all conducted blind; (*b*) no shock was used during testing of recipients – their tendency to respond to light was assessed in the absence of explicit conditioning. (For a discussion of reinforced versus nonreinforced testing, see Jacobson, 1967a.)

The results showed quite clearly that only the experimental group manifested more than a base-line level of responding to light. The scores of recipients of extract from stimulated donors were indistinguishable from the scores of recipients of extract from unstimulated donors, whereas the score of recipients of extract from conditioned donors did not even overlap with those of the two prior groups. It was clear that the transfer effect in planarians satisfies at least one of the major criteria of specificity (Jacobson, 1967a). Several follow-up studies substantiated this finding when a more purified RNA extract was employed. A final experiment (Jacobson, Fried, & Horowitz, 1966b) in this series found that extinction of the conditioned response in donor worms did not impair the transfer effect – an intriguing lead for theorists in this area.

Let us return now to the rodent studies. Somewhat sporadically during the past two years, the present two authors, along with several assistants, have attempted to establish a procedure for obtaining a robust, convincing, and easily interpretable transfer effect. Our guiding principle has been that of employing as simple chemical and behavioral procedures as we could. Thus in some of our work we have used whole brain homogenates (Dyal, Golub, & Marrone, 1967; Reinis, 1966), and, in other work, we have used the supernatant of centrifuged homogenates (Byrne & Samuel, 1966; Ungar, 1967). These procedures, besides yielding successful results in other laboratories, seemed to involve a minimal number of steps. Behaviorally, we have employed several responses, including barpressing for food and conditioned fear of a compartment associated with shock. Again, these tasks were selected because they are rapidly learned and amount of training can thus be controlled nicely. To be very concise, our search for a reliable transfer paradigm, like Lashley's search for the engram, met with failure. Perhaps more unfortunately, our failures did not yield the types of accessory information which made Lashley's efforts such an important contribution. At times, we achieved positive, even significant results, but in contrast to the earlier work, our attempts at replication were unsuccessful. In some cases, these failures of replication were due to extraneous causes, and in the perspective of time, it now appears that we may not have been persistent enough at certain points in tracking down promising leads. Nonetheless, the fact remains that by any strict criterion, our quest of the past two years has failed. It would be possible to discuss our procedures in detail, but since we have not isolated any variables which are critical for obtaining good results, such a description would provide no more advantage than any other unreconciled negative report. We would emphasize, on the basis of our efforts, the difficulty of replicating all the features, both behavioral and chemical, of any given transfer experiment. Some labs which early reported positive effects have continued to be successful (e.g., Rosenblatt & Miller, 1966; Ungar, 1967). At least one laboratory which originally obtained negative results subsequently obtained, and has continued to obtain, positive results (Byrne & Samuel, 1966). To our knowledge, ours is the first laboratory to obtain first positive and then negative results. Of course, the numerous changes in personnel and procedure have undoubtedly been important in this process, but we simply do not know the key features.

We may conclude with some observations on the present status of the transfer work, and a tentative hypothesis about the source of variability in results from one laboratory to another. Several of the investigators who originally reported transfer effects are still obtaining positive results (to our knowledge, this includes at least Fjerdingstad, McConnell, Reinis, and Ungar). In addition, of course, a number of other laboratories have reported success. The recent (December 1967) AAAS symposium on this topic revealed that some fourteen laboratories have now obtained positive results. In the face of this wide-spread activity, and despite the numerous failures, the emphasis has shifted from a vitriolic verbal battle concerning the validity of the phenomena to a more considered discussion of the causes of confusion and inconsistency. Initially, the transfer work, departing as it does in some ways from conventional views, evoked strong emotional reactions from some scientists. In this respect, at least, the work follows in the grand tradition of innovation in science (as well as in other human endeavors). Early research on new topics has often been muddled, and there will always be scientists around who, because of vested interests or sheer "conservatism," will make confident and even dogmatic assertions about the ultimate outcome of new ventures into the unknown. As in these earlier cases, the emotional reactions to the transfer work have proved premature and irrelevant in light of clarifying research efforts (see Jacobson, 1967b). In the transfer case, as in some others, the "impossible" seems once again to have proved itself.

In any event, the report of the AAAS symposium, which is being prepared by William Byrne, represents the most authoritative summary of transfer research to date and will be an invaluable source for those interested in pursuing this work.

As the Byrne compilation will show, several variables have been empirically related to the degree of transfer obtained in a given task. Two examples are amount of training of donors and dosage of extract injected (Ungar, 1967). While such findings are extremely important, they very likely do not shed light on the causes of failure of those replication attempts in which no transfer effects at all are found. The present authors have followed a certain line of thinking in this regard, and even though we have been unable to substantiate it experimentally, the argument might be worth presenting here. It is simply this: Each of several laboratories, including those of Drs. Rosenblatt, McConnell, and Ungar, has obtained transfer effects in several or many different learning tasks. Dr. Ungar, for example, has studied at least habituation, spatial discrimination, and passive avoidance, all with considerable success. Within each of these laboratories, while the behavioral procedures have varied grossly, the chemical procedures have varied only slightly. In general, a standard extraction procedure, once developed and adopted, has yielded transfer effects in each of several, often widely disparate learning tasks. This line of reasoning suggests the conclusion that, in situations where no obvious anomalies in the training of donors or preinjection testing of recipients have occurred, variations in chemical rather than in behavioral procedures are primarily responsible for failures of replication. We know of one case in which two skilled chemists, working side by side, obtained quite different results in "identical" transfer experiments. Obviously a phenomenon this difficult to replicate will cause disagreement; fortunately, replication attempts in other laboratories have been more successful. But discrepancies of this sort offer opportunities to isolate critical and often subtle variables. Clearly there is ample reason to pay attention to details of technique in transfer work, and we believe that details of chemical procedure will prove most important in the development of robust transfer paradigms.

REFERENCES

Babich, F. R., Jacobson, A. L., & Bubash, S. Cross-species transfer of learning: Effect of ribonucleic acid from hamsters on rat behavior. *Proceedings of the National Academy of Sciences, U.S.,* 1965, **54**, 1299-1302.

Babich, F. R., Jacobson, A. L., Bubash, S., & Jacobson, A. Transfer of a response to naive rats by injection of ribonucleic acid extracted from trained rats. *Science,* 1965, **149**, 656-657.

Byrne, W. L., *et al.* Memory transfer. *Science,* 1966, **153**, 658-659.

Byrne, W. L., & Samuel, D. Behavioral modification by injection of brain extract prepared from trained donors. *Science,* 1966, **154**, 418.

Dyal, J. A., Golub, A. M., & Marrone, R. L. Transfer effects of intraperitoneal injection of brain homogenates. *Nature,* 1967, **214**, 720-721.

Jacobson, A. L. Inter-organism transfer of response tendencies by injection of material from trained animals. *Excerpta Medica International Congress Series* 1967, **129**, 161-168. (a)

Jacobson, A. L. Reply to a Russian scientist. *Journal of Biological Psychology,* 1967, **9**, 38-39. (b)

Jacobson, A. L., Babich, F. R., Bubash, S., & Jacobson, A. Differential approach tendencies produced by injection of ribonucleic acid from trained rats. *Science,* 1965, **150**, 636-637.

Jacobson, A. L., Fried, C., & Horowitz, S. D. Planarians and memory: I. Transfer of learning by injection of ribonucleic acid. *Nature,* 1966, **209**, 599-601. (a)

Jacobson, A. L., Fried, C., & Horowitz, S. D. Planarians and memory: II. The influence of prior extinction on the RNA transfer effect. *Nature,* 1966, **209**, 601. (b)

John, E. R. Studies on learning and retention in planaria. In M. A. Brazier (Ed.), *Brain Function,* Vol. 2. Berkeley: University of California Press, 1964. Pp. 161-182.

McConnell, J. V. Memory transfer through cannibalism in planarians. *Journal of Neuropsychiatry, Supplement,* 1962, **3**, 542-548.

Reinis, S. Influence of brain homogenate injection on the speed of the formation of alimentary conditional reflex in rats. *Worm Runner's Digest,* 1966, **8**, 7-24.

Rosenblatt, F., & Miller, R. G. Behavioral assay procedures for transfer of learned behavior by brain extracts, Parts I and II. *Proceedings of the National Academy of Sciences, U.S.,* 1966, **56**, 1423-1430, 1683-1688.

Sidman, M. *Tactics of scientific research.* New York: Basic Books, 1960.

Ungar, G. Transfer of acquired brain information by brain extracts. *Journal of Biological Psychology,* 1967, **9**, 12-27.

ATTEMPTS TO TRANSFER APPROACH AND AVOIDANCE RESPONSES BY RNA INJECTIONS IN RATS[1]

JAMES V. McCONNELL, TSUYOSHI SHIGEHISA, AND HAROLD SALIVE

Mental Health Research Institute
University of Michigan
Ann Arbor, Michigan

Three different experimental paradigms were used to study the so-called "memory transfer" phenomenon. In the first set of studies, donor rats were trained to approach a cup to get a pellet of food when a buzzer sounded. RNA from the brains of these animals was injected intraperitoneally into untrained animals that were subsequently given unreinforced test trials in the same chamber. Recipients that received RNA from trained donors approached the food cup significantly more often than did recipients that received RNA from untrained control donors or that received hydrolyzed RNA fron trained donors. In the second paradigm, food deprived rats were trained to approach a milk dipper in an operant conditioning chamber in response to a distinct "click" made by the dipper when it was elevated into the chamber. An RNA extract was prepared from the brains of these animals, as well as from the brains of control animals that had received no such training. The RNA was injected into the brains (subarachnoid space) of naive recipients, who were then required to learn to press either of the two bars in the chamber in order to elevate the dipper and get milk. Recipients injected with RNA from trained donors typically learned the problem within 5 days. Recipients that received RNA from untrained donors or hydrolyzed RNA from trained donors typically did not learn the problem until after 5 days, if at all. In the third paradigm, donor animals were trained to avoid drinking a saccharin solution by pairing consumption of the saccharin solutions

[1] The following is a revised version of a paper read by the senior author at the annual meeting of the American Association for the Advancement of Science in New York City on the 30th of December, 1967. The research reported in this paper was supported by contract AT(11-1)-825 from the U.S. Atomic Energy Commission, by grants NIH K3 MH-16697 and MH-13151, by a grant from the Michigan Memorial Phoenix Project, and by the Mental Health Research Institute at The University of Michigan, Ann Arbor.

with injections of apomorphine hydrochloride. An RNA extract was obtained from the brains of some of the donors and injected into the brains (subarachnoid space) of naive recipients; the homogenized brains of other trained donor animals were put through dialysis, and either the dialysate or the nondialysable fraction was injected into the peritoneum of naive recipients. Following injection, the consumption of saccharin solution by the recipients was measured. While some statistically significant results were obtained, the magnitude of the "transfer" effect was considerably smaller than in the first or second paradigm.

INTRODUCTION

The first studies suggesting that an interanimal "transfer of acquired behavioral tendencies" was possible was conducted in this laboratory in 1960 (Humphries & Jacobson, 1961; McConnell, Jacobson, & Humphries, 1961; McConnell, 1962). Planarians given classical conditioning training in which light was the conditioning stimulus (CS) and electric shock the unconditional stimulus (UCS) were, following training, chopped in pieces and fed to untrained, cannibalistic flatworms. The latter were then given conditioning trials. The response rates to light (CS) of these experimental animals were, from the first set of training trials, significantly greater than the response rates of control cannibals fed the bodies of untrained victims. In 1962, we were the first to show that a crude RNA mix extracted from the bodies of conditioned planarians and injected into the bodies of untrained flatworms apparently caused an elevation in response rates in the experimental animals, as compared with the behavior of several groups of control animals injected with a crude RNA mixture extracted from the bodies of various groups of untrained planarians (Zelman, Kabat, Jacobson, & McConnell, 1963). In recent years, these early experiments have been replicated in several other laboratories under more controlled conditions than obtained in the original research (Fried, & Horowitz, 1964; Fuchs, Harrington, Lariviere, & Robinson, 1966; Jacobson, Babich, Bubash, & Goren, 1966a; Jacobson, Fried, & Horowitz, 1966b; John, 1964; Kabat, 1964; McConnell, 1966, 1967a; Pickett, Jennings, & Wells, 1964, 1965; Ragland & Ragland, 1965; Rieke & Shannon, 1964; Westerman, 1963a). While there remains some argument as to what it is (behaviorally) that transfers in the case of planarians, it seems relatively clear that the "transfer effect" itself is a valid one, at least in flatworms.

The first experiments suggesting that a similar "transfer effect" could be obtained in higher organisms, such as rats and hamsters, were performed in Czechhoslovakia by Reinis (1965, 1966), in Copenhagen by Fjerdingstad, Nissen, & Roigaard-Petersen (1965), in Houston by Ungar and his associates (Ungar & Oceguera-Navarro, 1965), and in Los Angeles by Jacobson and his colleagues (Babich, Jacobson, & Bubash, 1965a; Babich, Jacobson, Bubash, & Jacobson,

1965b; Jacobson, Babich, Bubash, & Jacobson, 1965; Jacobson, Fried, & Horowitz, 1966c). Our own work with rats began in 1965 when we attempted to repeat the experiments reported by Jacobson and his collegues showing that if one extracted an RNA mixture from the brains of rats trained to approach a food cup when a click sounded, and then injected this mix intraperitoneally into untrained animals, the recipients tended to approach the food cup more than did control animals when presented with the click. Our work yielded statistically significant results, and the use of additional control groups indicated that the "transfer molecule" was probably RNA.

In our first experiments, we used a training apparatus built as closely as possible to the specifications for the one employed by Jacobson and his associates (Babich et al., 1965a), a masonite box (26 cm^3) with a grid floor. In one corner of the box was a metal food cup into which food pellets could be dropped from a tube outside the box. A buzzer was mounted in the exact center of the bottom of the box, beneath the grid floor. The walls of the box were painted gray; however, an area of 63 cm^2 around the foodcup was white and constituted the "food cup area." The subjects were 64 male hooded rats (Long-Evans) from Maxfield Farms in Cincinnati. The animals were approximately 60 days old, and weighed approximately 250 gm., when used. Both donor and recipient animals were put on a food deprivation schedule and maintained at approximately 80% body weight. The recipients were 48 hrs. deprived when tested. Twenty-four of the donors were trained 5 days by hand-shaping to approach the food cup to get a pellet of food whenever the buzzer sounded. By the end of training, all the animals were responding appropriately at least 95% of the time. The 8 untrained donors were handled and deprived in the same fashion as were the trained donors but were not put in the training box. Immediately after their last training session, the donors were dropped into liquid nitrogen and frozen. The whole cerebrum (i.e., the portion of the brain posterior to the olfactory lobes and anterior to the cerebellum) was used for extraction purposes. The brains were individually placed in a cold homogenizer and ground with 10 vol. of phosphate buffer for approximately 2 min. An equal volume of 88% phenol was added to the homogenate and the mix stirred for 1 hr. at $2°C$. The mixture was then centrifuged at $20,000 \times g$ for 5 min. at $2°C$. The phenol layer was carefully removed and discarded, and an additional half-volume of phenol was added and the mix was stirred for 30 min. The aqueous phase was carefully drawn off and centrifuged at 3500 rpm for 15 min. The RNA was precipitated by addition of .1 vol. of 20% potassium acetate and 2.5 vol. of 95% ethanol. The RNA was separated by centrifuging at 3000 rpm for 15 min., washed with ethanol-water (3:1) twice, and then was dissolved in 1 ml. of isotonic saline after the remaining ethanol was evaporated off. This preparation constituted the "unpurified" or "crude" RNA mixture.

Some of the "crude" RNA was then hydrolyzed with ribonuclease. This RNA was dissolved in a solution of (1 mg/ml) ribonuclease (bovine pancreatic, phos-

phate free and lyophylized) instead of the isotonic saline and was incubated at
$37°C$ for 5 hrs. To the incubated solution, 10 μg/ml bentonite were added and
the clear supernatant was drawn off after the mixture had been centrifuged at
10,000 X g for 1 hr. This preparation constituted the hydrolyzed "crude" RNA
mixture.

For the preparation of "purified" RNA from both trained and untrained
donors, the "crude" precipitated RNA was dissolved in 3 ml. of distilled water.
To this solution, 1 vol. of 2.5 M K_2HPO_4, .05 vol. of 33.3% H_3PO_4, and 1 vol.
of 2-methoxyethanol were added, in that order. The mixture was shaken vigorously and allowed to stand at room temperature for 15 min.; it was then centrifuged at 3000 rpm for 15 min. The top layer (containing most of the RNA) was
then carefully drawn off. A small amount of the top layer was poured back into
the lower layer and this mixture was shaken vigorously and then allowed to
stand for 5 to 10 min. so that separation into two layers again occurred. This
procedure was repeated 3 times. Then the combined top layers were centrifuged
at 10,000 X g for 1 hr. to remove any remaining 2-methoxyethanol. The RNA
was precipitated from the clear supernatant obtained by this centrifugation.
RNA yields were determined from the optical density at 250 mμ with 10 mm.
cell length. For the "crude" RNA preparation, the average yield was .96 mg/gm
of brain tissue; the yield was .62 mg/gm for the "purified" RNA from both
trained and untrained donors.

Four groups of recipients were used. The 9 animals in Group I were injected
with the "purified" trained RNA, the 8 animals in Group II received "crude"
trained RNA, the 7 animals in Group III received hydrolyzed "crude" trained
RNA, while the 8 animals in Group IV received "purified" untrained RNA. Each
recipient was injected intraperitoneally (without anesthetic) with an amount of
the appropriate preparation that represented the RNA from one donor brain.
The animals were assigned code numbers, and injection and testing were performed "blind."

Six test sessions of five trials each were given. The first such session occurred
6 hrs. after injection; additional test sessions were given once each 24 hrs.
thereafter for 5 days. Each animal thus received a total of 30 test trials. A test
trial was not begun unless (a) the animal was at least one body length distant
from the food cup, (b) unless the animal was turned at least $90°$ away from the
cup, and (c) unless the animal was not making any gross locomotor movements.
At the start of a test trial, the buzzer was sounded and if any part of the animal's
body crossed into the white "food cup area" within 5 sec., the response was
scored as an "approach." No food or other reward was given to any of the
recipients while they were in the test chamber. Two observers recorded all
responses independently.

One week after the recipients had been given the 30 unreinforced test trials,
each animal was given 100 reinforced trials during which a pellet of food was
dropped into the food cup immediately after the buzzer sounded. If the animal

reached the food cup in 5 sec. after the buzzer sounded, the response was considered "correct."

The results of this first set of experiments are shown in Tables I, II, and III. As the data in Table I indicate, the animals that received either "crude" or "purified" RNA from the brains of trained donors were significantly superior to the animals in both control groups in terms of the number of approaches they made to the food cup during the 30 unreinforced test trials. The data in Table II

TABLE I

Number of Approaches to the Food Cup for Four Groups of Rats Injected with Various Substances [a]

	Purified trained RNA I	Crude trained RNA II	Hydrolyzed crude trained RNA III	Purified untrained RNA IV
Ss				
	1	1	0	1
	3	2	0	1
	3	3	2	2
	5	3	2	3
	5	4	3	3
	5	5	3	4
	6	5	3	4
	6	7		4
	7			
Mean	4.6	3.8	1.9	2.8

[a]By the Mann-Whitney U Test, Group I is significantly superior to Groups III and IV, and Group II is significantly superior to Group III.

show that the animals receiving the "purified" untrained RNA made significantly fewer errors during the subsequent 100 reinforced trials than did the animals in any other group, while the animals receiving the hydrolyzed "crude" trained RNA were significantly the poorest group. If we look at the last trial on which each animal failed to respond correctly during these 100 reinforced trials (Table III), we find much the same picture.

These data suggest to us that one must measure several different "transfer" effects: There seems to be a "nonspecific," excitatory, perhaps pharmacological effect on performance from injecting any kind of an RNA mixture into untrained animals. This nonspecific effect shows up during reinforced training trials but is not apparent during unreinforced test trials. In addition, it would seem

TABLE II

Number of Incorrect Responses out of 100 Reinforced Trails for
Four Groups of Rats Injected with Various Substances [a]

	Purified trained RNA	Crude trained RNA	Hydrolyzed crude trained RNA	Purified untrained RNA
	I	II	III	IV
Mean	4.0	3.6	5.1	2.0

[a]By the Mann-Whitney U Test, Group IV is significantly different from all three other groups. Group II approaches significant difference from Group III (p = .076).

TABLE III

The Last Trial on Which Each Animal Failed to Respond Correctly during 100
Reinforced Trials for Four Groups of Rats Injected with Various Substances[a]

	Purified trained RNA	Crude trained RNA	Hydrolyzed crude trained RNA	Purified untrained RNA
	I	II	III	IV
Mean	36	27.9	46	7.7
Median	31	27.5	44	6

[a]By the Mann-Whitney U test, Group IV differs significantly from all other Groups. Group II differs from Group III at the p = .168 level of confidence.

that one can obtain both facilitatory and inhibitory "transfer" effects from injecting material from trained brains into recipients. The facilitory effect shows up most clearly during unreinforced trials, but to some extent also during subsequent reinforced trials, while the inhibitory effect shows up most clearly during the reinforced trials.

In point of fact, these findings should not be too surprising. For decades now, learning theorists have emphasized that in any learning situation, the animal surely acquires both approach and avoidance tendencies whether the reinforcement used to control the animal's behavior in positive or negative. Thus the animal's behavior is seen as reflecting some kind of "algebraic sum" of several different excitatory and inhibitory processes. In our opinion, the outcome of any "transfer" experiment hinges on the balance obtained among several different "transfer" factors, at least one of which is inhibitory. We believe it likely that one reason that several laboratories have been unable to replicate the many successful "transfer" experiments now in print stems from their use of procedures that maximize the "transfer" of inhibitory factor(s) rather than excitatory or faciliatory factors.

OPERANT CONDITIONING STUDIES

Although we were successful in replicating the work of Jacobson and his colleagues in our first experiments, several considerations prompted us to switch to a different experimental paradigm. To begin with, the Jacobson procedure involved the use of observers who watched the animal and merely recorded whether or not it moved to the food cup within 5 sec. after the buzzer had sounded. While we obtained high interjudge reliability in these studies (96%), we believed that use of a procedure in which the recipient's responses were automatically recorded might free us from any lingering suspicion that "experimenter bias" was somehow affecting the results of our experiment. Then too we wished to find a paradigm that would let us determine what experimental conditions would maximize the facility factors and minimize the inhibitory factors described above. The use of an operant conditioning chamber (Skinner box) and a specific experimental technique called "magazine training" seemed to fulfill our requirements best. The next eight studies were then begun using this technique.

In the standard operant conditioning apparatus, the lever or bar that the rat must depress is always located near the food cup that delivers the positive reinforcement the animal gets when it presses the bar. In general, the further away the food cup is from the lever, the more difficult it is for the animal to associate pressing the bar with the appearance of the food. If the cup is directly opposite the lever in a fairly large chamber, most rats learn the problem fairly slowly. One may make the task even more difficult by substituting a dipper arrangement of some kind for the food cup. Usually, when the animal presses the bar, a pellet of food drops into the cup and remains there until the animal finds it; the experimenter has no way of removing the pellet once it has been dropped into the cup. The dipper, which typically contains a liquid reinforcer such as sweetened milk, can be elevated into the chamber automatically, but if the animal does not find and drink the milk within a period of a few seconds (the exact time being specified by the experimenter), the dipper is automatically withdrawn until the animal presses the bar again. The solenoid operating the dipper typically makes a loud and rather distinct "click" noise as it elevates the dipper, a fact that makes most rats avoid the vicinity of the dipper at least at the beginning of training. Under these conditions, a great many rats fail to learn to bar press since they must somehow learn to rush from one side of the chamber to the other in order to claim the reward.

If one wishes to teach a rat to bar-press under these conditions, one typically must break the training up in two parts. At the beginning of the experiment, the rat is put in the chamber and the machinery set so that the lever is nonfunctional and the dipper is automatically elevated into the chamber at irregular intervals. The rat soon learns to sit by the dipper and wait for its daily ration of "manna from heaven" to appear. This first part of the procedure is called "magazine training," because what the animal learns to do is to approach the food magazine on signal. Once the animal knows the significance of the dipper, and associates the loud "click" with the presence of a reward, the second stage of training begins. In the second part of training, the dipper is set to operate only when the animal presses the bar. A rat beginning this part of training typically sits quietly by the dipper for a while, waiting for it to operate automatically. When, after a few minutes, no food appears, the rat often begins wandering about the chamber and, presumably by accident, presses on the lever. The dipper elevates into the chamber, and the loud "click" made by the apparatus reminds the rat that food is now present. The second stage of training usually proceeds very rapidly, and the animal learns to press the bar to get the milk without further difficulty. However, if the "magazine training" sessions are omitted, the rat learns the task slowly if at all.

In the present series of experiments, the donor animals were always trained to go to a dipper to obtain milk when a click sounded; the recipients were forced to learn to press a bar in order to activate the dipper, but the recipients were never given the all-important first-stage "magazine training." It was our belief that if the tendency to approach the milk dipper when the click sounded could be transferred chemically, the recipients that were injected with "trained" brain materials would learn the bar-press task rapidly, while the control recipients injected with "untrained" brain materials would learn slowly, if at all.

It was our opinion also that injecting the RNA directly into the brains of the recipient animals was more likely to yield success than the intraperitoneal injections used in earlier experiments. We chose the technique of injecting into the subarachnoid space of the forebrain described by Lindberg & Ernster (1950) since these authors present evidence that materials injected by their method diffuse rapidly to different parts of the brain and because the RNA thus injected is presumably "inside" the "blood-brain barrier."

An extraction procedure similar to the one that yielded the "crude" RNA in the first experiments was used throughout this second set of studies. Some modifications were introduced, however: During homogenization of the brains, isotonic saline was used rather than phosphate buffer, the homogenate was stirred with phenol but once, for 30 min., then centrifuged at 20,000 $\times$ g for 60

min.; .1 vol. $MgCl_2$ (1 M) and ethanol were added and the RNA was precipitated overnight in a freezer. The RNA was collected after centrifugation at 2500
rpm for 30 min. and was washed with 75% ethanol three times or more. Yields
of RNA were approximately 1.5 mg/gm of brain tissue, but measurable amounts
of DNA, protein, and polysaccharides were present in the mix. Rather than
freezing the whole animal in liquid nitrogen and removing the brain afterwards,
as we did in the first studies, we decapitated the animals and removed the brain
and froze it by placing it in powdered dry ice. Decapitation took place 8 hrs.
after final training of the donors. All experiments save the first one reported
below were performed "blind"; in all experiments, however, the data were recorded automatically.

The subjects were male hooded rats of the Long-Evans strain (obtained from
Maxfield Animal Supply Co., Cincinnati, Ohio, and from Blue Spruce Farm Inc.,
Altamont, New York), having an average body weight of 250 gm and were 50-60
days old at the beginning of the handling and deprivation schedules. The animals
were maintained in group cages and received food (Rockland Diet) and water *ad
lib.* for 5 days. On the sixth day after arrival, each animal was moved to a metal
individual cage and handling and deprivation begun. Except as noted below, all
animals were brought down to 80% of their body weight and maintained there
for the balance of the experiment; the handling schedule was maintained for
more than 10 days in the donors before their training began and for more than
20 days in the recipients before pre-injection testing (except for Experiment
MT-2a, described below).

Apparatus for Training and Testing

All training (donors) and testing (recipients) was conducted in two identical
wooden two-bar operant conditioning chambers (Fig. 1) with a 16 X 14 in. mesh
floor and with 7 in. high walls one of which, a sliding door, consisted of a
one-way glass. The chambers were housed in separate sound-insulated enclosures
covered with fiber glass. The interior walls and floors of the chambers were
painted flat black. The ceilings were glass through which the inside of the chambers were illuminated by 14-W cool white bulbs (fluorescent).

The manipulanda, two square bars (1 X 1 X .25 in.), protruded, 8 in. apart,
into the chambers through vertical slits in one of the walls 2 in. above the floor.
A vertical force on each bar of approximately 24 gm. triggered a solenoid that
raised a metal dipper which delivered .08 ml. of milk through the hole in the
bottom of the dipper area. A cavity was made 2 in. above the floor so as to form
the dipper area (2.5 in. in diameter, 1.25 in. deep) in the wall opposite to the
one in which the bars were set. A solenoid, placed behind the dipper, generated a
distinct click (which was much louder than the usual clicks in conventional
Skinner boxes) and lifted up the dipper through the hole. A milk dish which was

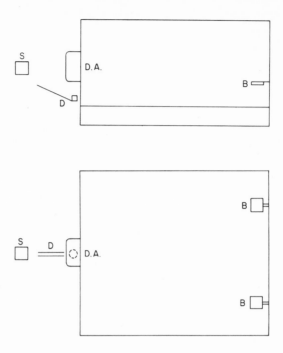

FIG. 1. Apparatus used in the magazine training and the pre- and postinjection tests (S = solenoid; D = dipper; D. A. = dipper area; B = bar).

placed directly under the dipper area was sufficiently large to contain enough milk for 180 continuous reinforcements and deep enough to prevent the recipients from stealing the milk by stretching their forelegs through the hole.

In our later experiments, a photocell device was attached to the dipper area so as to record the number of times the animal stuck any part of its body inside the dipper area.

A jet of air was introduced into the sound-insulated enclosure through a small hole (.5 in. in diameter) made in an upper part of a wall. Another small hole was connected with a vacuum device. These two attachments provided cool fresh air, constant white noise, and removed warm stale air from the inside of the chamber throughout the experiment. The temperature inside the chambers was kept at approximately 70-75°F.

The milk dish, dipper, and the dipper area (inside and outside of the chamber), bars, and bar area were cleaned and fresh sawdust was placed in the tray under the mesh floor of the chamber whenever necessary (usually every 4 hrs.). Condensed milk to which was added 10% sucrose was used as a reinforcer.

During the donor training, both bars were disconnected from the dipper mechanism so that a bar-press did not activate the click noise of dipper. During the recipient testing, the bars were connected to the dipper mechanism so that each bar-press activated the dipper (which made a "click" as it elevated into place).

Training and testing of both donors and recipients proceeded automatically throughout all experiments. The animals were put into the chamber when it was dark. Immediately after the door was closed, the house light was turned on and the first dipper presentation occurred (in donor training).

Training of Donors

Each donor animal was trained to approach the dipper under a variable interval (VI-45 sec.) schedule. The animal was given 60 trials per session for 5 days (plus one extra session at the start for hand-shaping). During the first 2 days, the dipper was elevated for 20 sec. during each training trial. On Day 3, the time was cut to 10 sec. for each presentation, to 7.5 sec. on Day 4, and to 5 sec. on the final day of training. The donors were maintained at 80% body weight and were trained when 23 hrs. deprived. After each training session, the animal was weighed and given enough Rockland Diet to bring it back up to 80% of body weight.

During the preliminary shaping session, the dipper (with milk in it) was held up by E's hand from the beginning of the session until the animal found it and consumed the milk, The animal was given the milk 10 times in this manner whenever it approached the dipper. No click was sounded at this stage of shaping. Next, the click was sounded while the animal was sticking its nose inside the dipper area deep enough so that it could very easily find the dipper with milk immediately after the click in spite of any emotional response the animal might evince to the onset of the click. This click-dipper presentation was repeated successively more than 10 times until the rat consumed the milk within 20 sec. 10 times in succession. Then, the click-dipper presentation was withheld until the animal moved away from the dipper area an inch or two. After the click-dipper presentation was repeated for 50 to 10 times under this condition, the intertrial interval was gradually increased up to 60 sec., and then it was gradually shifted to the VI-45 sec. dipper-presentation schedule. Total number of dipper presentations per day during this and subsequent days was approximately 60. Almost all animals established a dipper-approach response during this shaping session.

Untrained donor animals were treated similarly to the trained donors outside of the chamber situation. These animals had been handled, deprived, and maintained at 80% body weight throughout. During the last 6 days prior to sacrifice, untrained donors were given extra handling equivalent in time to the trained donors and weighed, fed, and maintained at 80% body weight. The untrained donors did not experience the chamber situation, however, and were not fed milk. Trained and untrained donors were sacrificed in pairs.

Injection Procedure

Fourteen hours prior to its first postinjection test session, the recipient animal was injected with RNA from a trained or untrained donor. The injection was made into the space between the olfactory bulbs so as to facilitate rapid diffusion of the injected materials into the subarachnoid space of the brain.

Prior to injection of the RNA, each animal was anesthetized with an intraperitoneal injection of sodium-pentobarbital in a manner that minimized emotional disturbance. A cut was made along the line of suture sagittalis between the animal's eye balls with a sharp knife, the remaining muscles were pushed aside, and the skull was exposed. The incision area was thoroughly sterilized (with zephiran-chloride: ca. .2%). A dental drill with a 1 mm.-wide tip was used to make a hole in the suture sagittalis directly between the eye balls (i.e., above the space between the olfactory bulbs). The drill tip was placed on the suture sagittalis so as to form an angle of 45° with the frontal plane (Lindberg & Ernster, 1950).

The hole was drilled gently only about 2/3 of the way through the skull, to prevent mechanical leakage of the RNA solution after injection. A 27-gauge needle was placed in the hole and was rotated several times under moderate pressure for 10 to 15 sec. to pierce slightly the remaining bone. This needle was then removed, and a $250\,\mu$l. tuberculin syringe with a 30-gauge ¼-in.-long needle was used to inject the RNA. This syringe had been kept in a refrigerator and was loaded with $200\,\mu$l. of cool RNA solution immediately before the injection. The tip of the needle was introduced by rotation under minimum pressure. The needle was kept at a 45° angle with the frontal plane, 2 mm. deep from the outside surface of the skull. Two hundred μl. of the cool RNA solution were injected into each recipient over a 5 min. period.

The needle was withdrawn slowly after the injection was made so that leakage of the injected solution was minimized. After complete withdrawal of the needle, the incision was sterilized and the epidermal tissues were dried slightly with cotton for 30 sec. The incisions was closed without suturing by pressing the skin edges together with moderate pressure from a pair of forceps.

Testing Procedure

(A) Preinjection Test

Each recipient animal was tested 10 hrs. before injection (i.e., 14 hrs. before the first session of the postinjection test) under the same experimental conditions as obtained during the postinjection test. Animals were then assigned to experimental or control groups according to baseline response tendencies during the preinjection test.

The preinjection test lasted for 60 min., during which time a bar-press elevated the dipper for 20 sec. It was typically the case that few if any animals actually obtained the milk during the pre-injection test, however.

In several of our early experiments in this series, we found a significant correlation between the number of bar-presses the rat made during preinjection testing (regardless of whether or not it obtained reinforcement) and the probability that it would eventually learn to press the bar to obtain the milk. In general, it appears that animals with a high preinjection response rate (more than 10 bar-presses during the hour's test) will learn the task no matter what one injects them with, while animals with a very low response rate (0-2 bar-presses) fail to learn no matter what one injects them with. The reasons for this fact are obvious and have nothing to do with "memory transfer" *per se*. Rats with a very high initial response rate are highly active animals, hence much more likely to explore the box immediately after a bar press, hence more likely to discover the connection between the milk and pressing the bar. Rats that are (for some reason) low responders tend to be frightened animals that cower in the corner of the box and do not explore; this high emotionality appears to overwhelm the effects of injection of trained material.

It is important to note, then, that the "transfer effect" can best be demonstrated in this paradigm when one uses animals with a "medium" preinjection response rate (2-10 bar-presses) and when one makes sure that experimental and control groups are balanced in terms of this factor.

It has been our experience that the average preinjection response rate varies widely in animals obtained from the same supplier at different times. We found it expedient to order at least twice as many recipient animals as we planned to use so that we could discard the very high and low responders prior to injection.

(B) Postinjection Test

Following the preinjection test, each animal was weighed but was not fed; thus when it was given its first postinjection test 14 hrs. after the injection, the animal had been food-deprived for 48 hrs. The postinjection testing procedure was the same as was used for the preinjection test. The dipper was elevated for 20 sec. after each bar-press, the intersession interval was 24 hrs., the animals were food-deprived for 23 hrs. (after the first session) and were maintained at 80% of body weight across sessions.

Criterion for learning was specified as being 60 "correct" bar-press responses within 30 min. "Correct" bar-press responses were defined as those responses that actually actuated the dipper. Any responses the animal made during the 20 sec. dipper-holding period (after a "correct" response) were thus not counted. The animals were tested for 10 sessions, or until they met the criterion.

Results

Experiment MT-1

The results of this experiment are shown in Table IV. Although the data were recorded automatically, the experiment was not run "blind." All of the rats injected with "trained" RNA learned within 9 days; none of the rats injected

TABLE IV

Number of Bar-Press Responses during Each 1-hr. Daily Test Session for Naive Rats Injected with RNA from Trained and Untrained Donors (Experiment MT-1)

	Injected with RNA from brains of trained donors				
	Rat number				
Day	1	2	5	7	10
1	11	6	26	9	2
2	55	13	55	2	46
3	60	60	60	5	60
4	60 ^{a}	34	60	3	60
5		60 ^{a}	60 ^{a}	5	60 ^{a}
6				28	
7				60	
8				60	
9				60 ^{a}	
10					

	Injected with RNA from brains of untrained donors				
	Rat number				
Day	3	4	6	8	9
1	2	2	4	2	0
2	0	3	0	0	1
3	3	3	2	1	4
4	1	1	0	1	6
5	1	4	2	2	4
6	1	4	2	2	4
7	1	4	1	0	0
8	1	4	2	0	0
9	0	4	2	0	0
10	0	1	8	0	2
	0	3	6	1	4

^{a}Criterion is 60 responses in less than 30 min.

with RNA from untrained donors learned within 10 days. Rat No. 7 in the Experimental Group was in poor health during the first 5 days following injection. The two groups differ significantly ($p < .01$).

Experiment MT-2

Because Experiment MT-1 was not performed "blind," we attempted an immediate replication using "blind" techniques. In our rush to get the experiment underway, however, we gave the recipients but 3 days' handling prior to injection and did not bring them down to 80% body weight. They were not 48 hrs. deprived when given their first test, but were maintained on a 24 hr. deprivation schedule thereafter. The experiment (MT-2a) was halted after four days' training for obvious reasons, and all the animals were given a week of handling and were brought down to 80% body weight. They were then reinjected with additional "trained" and "untrained" RNA. Since one of the control animals had reached criterion and two others died, two of the animals that were injected with "trained" RNA the first time were injected with "untrained" RNA the second time. After the second injection, the animals were again assigned code numbers and the data gathered "blind" (MT-2b).

The results of Experiment MT-2, shown in table V, strongly suggest that the recipients must be well-gentled and deprived if the "transfer" phenomenon is to be demonstrated in a food-approach situation, a fact first pointed out by Reiniš (1966). The fact that animals No. 14 and No. 18, which received "trained" RNA on the first injection and "untrained" RNA the second, did not reach criterion rapidly suggests that there were few if any "lingering" effects of the first injection still present by the time the second injection was made. During the second part of Experiment MT-2, the experimental animals were significantly superior to the controls ($p < .01$).

Experiment MT-3

The first two experiments suggested strongly that some kind of "transfer" effect could be obtained under the conditions we had employed, but the results of these two studies could easily be attributed to some kind of nonspecific, pharmacological agent in the RNA mix. For example, one possible explanation would be that the "trained" RNA contained some kind of "general activator" substance, and that the experimental recipients were therefore more active than the control animals, hence more likely to learn the bar-press task. Also, we had no assurance that, even if we had discovered a genuine "transfer" of acquired behavioral tendencies, RNA was the molecule that mediated the "transfer." Experiment MT-3 was designed to test both these possibilities.

Donor animals were trained as before. Prior to injection, however, the recipients were given 2 hrs. of testing. During the first ½ hr., each recipient was put in a specially designed activity chamber that had the same internal dimensions as the operant test chamber. Rather than having two bars at one side and a milk

TABLE V

Number of Bar-Press Responses during Each 1-hr. Daily Test Session for Naive Rats Injected and Then Reinjected with RNA from Trained and Untrained Donors (Experiment MT-2a and 2b)

	Injected with RNA from brains of trained Donors								Injected with RNA from brains of untrained donors					
	Rat number								Rat number					
Day	3	6	11	13	14[a]	18[a]	19	20	2	4	10	15	16	17
1	7	4	7	10	3	3	5	3	3	3	6	5	6	41
2	2	3	1	5	0	1	6	0	7	2	3	4	3	60
3	2	0	0	2	2	1	2	1	1	0	1	9	3	60[b]
4	3	2	12	1	1	3	6	3	2	2	0		5	60[b]

	Reinjected with RNA from brains of trained donors					Reinjected with RNA from brains of untrained donors				
	Rat number					Rat number				
Day	1	3	11	13	19	4	10	14[a]	16	18[a]
1	1	60[b]	60[b]	60[b]	60	7	3	1	2	4
2	9	60[b]			60[b]	13	0	2	1	3
3	60[b]					20	0	1	2	1
4	60[b]					5	0	1	5	7
5						8	0	1	3	4
6						15	0	0	2	2
7						60[b]				
8						60[b]				

[a] Note that rats numbered 14 and 18 were injected with mix from trained donors the first time but with mix from untrained donors the second.

[b] Criterion is 60 responses in less than 30 min.

dipper at the other, however, the activity chamber had built into its wooden floor two metallic plates measuring 3.5 X 5 cm. The plates were on opposite sides of the chamber. During all tests in the activity chamber, we measured the total number of times that the animal pressed on either plate, as well as the number of times that it pressed both plates within 20 sec. Our belief was that these two measures would tell us something about the gross activity levels of the recipients, as well as whether any of them showed a tendency to move rapidly from one side of the chamber to the other (as would be the case if the animals learned during the postinjection tests in the operant chamber).

Following the first 30 min. in the activity chamber, each recipient was put for 1 hr. into the operant conditioning apparatus for its preinjection test. Then the animal was given a second 30-min. period in the activity chamber. The animals were then divided into four groups that scored roughly the same number of bar-presses during the preinjection test. Some 14 hrs. after the conclusion of the preinjection tests, the animals were injected with one of four different solutions: Group A received RNA from trained donors, Group B was injected with hydrolyzed RNA from the brains of trained donors, Group C received RNA from the brains of untrained donors, while Group D received hydrolyzed RNA from the brains of untrained donors. Hydrolysis of the RNA was accomplished as it had been during our first series of experiments, described above.

About 14 hrs. after injection, the entire preinjection series of tests was given again to each animal; about 23 hrs. later, this procedure was repeated. Thereafter, the activity measures were dropped and only the daily training session was given. At the end of the fifth day, all of the animals in Group A, but none of the animals in any other group, had reached criterion, so the training was terminated.

The bar-press data for experiment MT-3 are shown in Table VI. Only the animals in Group A, which received "trained" but unhydrolyzed RNA, reached criterion in 5 days. Since the animals in Group B, which received hydrolyzed "trained" RNA, were if anything somewhat inferior to all other groups, we have tentative evidence that the "transfer factor" in this situation is indeed RNA.

There were no significant differences between the four groups in terms of activity levels before or after injection. The highly significant differences between Group A and the other three groups in bar-press activity following injection do not seem to be the result of any nonspecific, pharmacological activator.

Experiment MT-4

An inspection of the data from Experiment MT-3 suggested to us that, within any one of the four groups, there was a correlation between the animals' preinjection response rates and the speed with which they reached or approached criterion after injection. In Experiment MT-4 we hoped to maximize the differences between experimental and control recipients by selecting only the very lowest responders on the preinjection response test.

TABLE VI

Number of Bar-Press Responses before Injection and during Each 1-hr. Daily Test Session for Naive Rats Injected with Hydrolyzed or Unhydrolyzed RNA from Trained and Untrained Donors (Experiment MT-3)

	Group A Injected with RNA from brains of trained donors				Group B Injected with hydrolyzed RNA from brains of trained donors				Group C Injected with RNA from brains of untrained donors				Group D Injected with hydrolyzed RNA from brains of untrained donors			
Rat number	14	9	6	2	13	10	17	16	15	11	3	12	1	7	4	5
Preinjection responses	2	2	4	7	1	2	4	8	1	2	6	6	0	3	4	9
Day																
1	5	8	5	4	0	1	0	4	0	2	3	1	0	1	1	0
2	8	7	3	22	1	2	0	5	0	3	0	3	1	0	1	2
3	60	15	3	60	0	0	0	4	0	1	1	6	1	1	3	16
4	60[a]	60	60	60[a]	0	0	0	8	1	2	2	47	0	2	3	19
5		60[a]	60[a]		0	1	0	24	0	2	1	60	1	44	4	51

[a] Criterion is 60 responses in less than 30 min.

In order to decrease emotionality in the recipients, they were all given 5 days of preinjection (but reinforced) testing in the chamber. Seven animals were injected with "trained" RNA, six animals with "untrained" RNA. The two groups were balanced in terms of their responses to the lever on the final preinjection day of testing. The average preinjection response rate on the fifth day was less than 2 responses in both groups.

The subjects were all Long-Evans hooded rats from Blue Spruce Farm, Inc., Altamont, New York; the recipients were younger and smaller than usual since the supplier could not provide us with animals of the weight and age we had used in previous experiments.

The yield of RNA was 1.0 mg/gm of brain tissue, somewhat smaller than usual.

No measurable "transfer" effect was recorded in Experiment MT-4. Only one animal (one that received "trained" RNA) reached criterion within 5 days. By the end of 10 days' training, 3 experimental animals and 3 control animals reached criterion, and a fourth experimental animal was close to criterion. Five of these seven animals were the highest responders during the 5 days of preinjection testing.

The data from Experiment MT-4 suggest that the "transfer" effect is difficult to demonstrate in animals with very low preinjection response rates since almost none of the animals reach criterion within 5 days without regard to the substance with which they are injected.

Experiment MT-5

Since Experiment MT-4 failed to yield a "transfer" effect, we believed we should attempt to repeat our original three experiments using the magazine training paradigm.

The animals were from Blue Spruce Farm, Inc., but were of the same size and age as were the animals in the first three studies. Only those animals with preinjection response rates of 4 to 14 bar-presses were used. We had hoped to use animals with response rates of 2 to 10 bar-presses, but there were not enough animals with these response rates.

The results of this experiment, which are shown in Table VII, are encouraging but must be taken with a grain of salt since the two groups were not adequately balanced for preinjection response rates. However, it is pertinent to note that the fastest learners among the experimental animals were not those with the very highest response rates, and that control rats with response rates greater than many experimental rats failed to learn at all.

Experiment MT-6

Donor training and recipient testing in this experiment were the same as in previous experiments, but the recipients received two injections 24 hrs. apart. Each injection was the equivalent of the RNA extracted from one-half a cere-

TABLE VII

Number of Bar-Press Responses during Each 1-hr. Daily Test Session for Naive Rats Injected with RNA from Trained and Untrained Donors (Experiment MT-5)

	Rat Number										
	Experimental rats						Control rats				
	1	4	5	6	8	11	2	3	7	9	10
Preinjection session	5	8	14	14	5	11	4	9	6	5	5
Postinjection session											
1	0	32	2	4	33	42	3	6	2	1	1
2	1	60	5	3	60	60	1	2	1	1	0
2	1	60^a	60	53	60^a	60	4	1	0	2	3
4	0		60^a	55		60	5	0	2	1	2
5	2			60^a		60^a	7	1	1	0	2
6	1						2	1	1	0	2
7	0						4	3	1	2	2
8	0						5	1	1	15	5
9	0						1	1	1	60	60
10	0						1	1	2	60	60^a

^{a}Criterion is 60 responses in less than 30 min.

brum; hence these animals all received about twice as much RNA as did the animals in the earlier experiments. The animals came from Maxfield Animal Supply Co. and were of the same age and weight as those used in the first experiments. The two groups were well-balanced in terms of their preinjection test scores (2-11 bar-presses).

The results of Experiment MT-6 appear in Table VIII. The two groups differed significantly on the first day of postinjection training ($p < .05$) and in when they reached criterion. Four of the five animals in the experimental group reached criterion before any of the 5 animals in the control group did. Since the "transfer" effect was not significantly stronger than that found in prior studies, we conclude that a double injection of "trained" RNA does not necessarily yield a greater effect than does a single injection as administered in this situation.

TABLE VIII

Number of Bar-Press Responses during Each 1-hr. Daily Test Session for Naive Rats Injected with RNA from Trained and Untrained Donors (Experiment MT-6)

	Rat number									
	Injected with RNA from brains of trained donors					Injected with RNA from brains of untrained donors				
	2	5	7	8	9	1	3	4	6	10
Preinjection session	7	10	4	8	4	11	7	6	7	2
Postinjection session										
1	23	30	11	22	8	5	7	1	10	6
2	60	60	60	11	2	3	7	3	60	5
3	60[a]	60[a]	60[a]	60	2	13	4	1	60	1
4				60[a]	2	41	3	6	60	0
5					0	60	4	21	60[a]	2

[a]Criterion is 60 responses in less than 30 min.

Experiment MT-7

One of the variables Ungar (1967) reported as influencing the strength of the "transfer" effect was the amount of training given donor animals. In this experiment, we tested the potency of this variable by giving donor animals varying degrees of training prior to sacrifice. One group of donors was given 10 days of magazine training; a second group was given but the usual 5 days we have employed in all previous experiments. Deprivation, handling, extraction, injection, and training were all as before. Five animals that were given 10 days' training and 10 animals that were given 5 days' training were used as donors. Six recipients were injected (subarachnoid space) with RNA from the 10-day-trained donors, while 12 animals were injected with RNA from the 5-day-trained donors. The groups were balanced in terms of their preinjection response scores. Both injection and training of recipients were performed "blind."

The curves showing the average number of bar-press responses per session for the recipients are shown in Fig. 2. As can be seen, the animals receiving RNA from the 10-day-trained donors had a significantly higher response rate than did the animals receiving RNA from the 5-day-trained donors.

Experiment MT-8

In an attempt to extend the findings of Experiment MT-7, we gave 5 groups of donor animals different experiences. Group 1D donors received 5 days' magazine training, Group 2D received 10 days' magazine training, Group 3D received

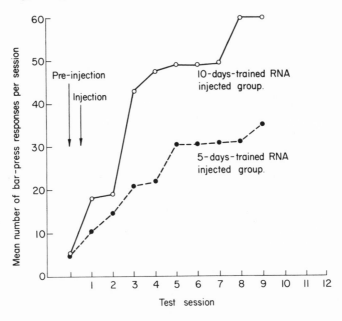

FIG. 2. Number of bar-press responses during each 1-hr. daily test session for naive rats injected with nucleic acid mix (RNA) from 10-days-trained and 5-days-trained donors (mean of each group).

20 days' magazine training, Group 4D donors were not given any training but were housed under normal laboratory conditions, while Group 5D donors were kept under conditions of moderate sensory deprivation for a period of 30 days from age 60-90 days, being housed in a light-proof box that had constant white noise present to mask external sounds. Deprivation, handling, extraction, injection, and training were all as above. We did make one additional change in procedure, however: A photocell device was added to the cup containing the milk dipper. Each time an animal put its nose (or any other part of its body) into the cup, a relay was broken, and a "magazine entry" was recorded automatically. There were 6 animals in Group 1R (that received subarachnoid space injections of RNA extracted from the Group 1D donors), 5 recipients in Group 2R, 5 in Group 3R, 6 in Group 4R, and 6 in Group 5R. The groups were balanced in terms of their preinjection response levels. Injection and testing were performed "blind."

The mean number of bar-press responses per session for each of the 5 groups is shown in Fig. 3. The Group 2R animals were significantly superior to all other groups for the first 2 days following injection and from Groups 3R, 4R, and 5R for the final 3 days. The Group 1R animals were no different from Groups 3R, 4R, and 5R on the first 2 days, but were significantly superior to these groups on Days 3-5.

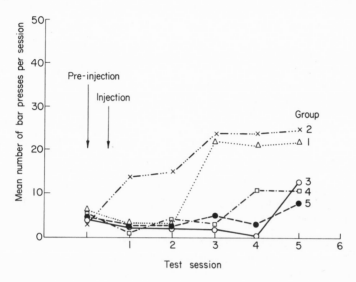

FIG. 3. Number of bar-press responses during each 1-hr. daily session for naive rats injected with nucleic acid mix (RNA) from 20-, 10-, and 5-days trained, untrained, and sensory deprived donors.

It would appear that, as in one case described by Ungar (1967), the relationship between amount of donor training and the strength of the "transfer" effect is U shaped, with a peak near 10 days' training, a result consistent with our findings in Experiment MT-7. The fact that there were no significant bar-press differences between the animals in Groups 4R and 5R suggests that RNA extracted from the brains of untrained donors does not affect speed of learning a bar-press response in recipients whether or not the donor animals had undergone moderate sensory deprivation prior to sacrifice.

The average number of "magazine entries" recorded by the photocell device on the cup containing the milk dipper are shown in Fig. 4. As will be seen, the Group 1 and Group 3 animals showed more magazine entries during the preinjection test than did the animals in the other three groups (it is difficult, if not impossible, to balance 5 groups of recipients in terms *both* of their bar-press responses *and* of their magazine entries prior to injection). Since the Group 2 animals were inferior to Groups 1 and 3 on this measure prior to injection, yet

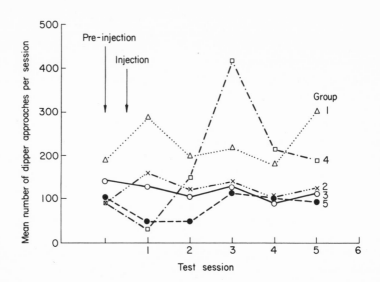

FIG. 4. Number of dipper approach responses during each 1-hr. daily test session for naive rats injected with nucleic acid mix (RNA) from 20-, 10-, 5-days trained, untrained, and sensory deprived donors.

were significantly superior to Groups 1 and 3 immediately after injection (in terms of the actual number of bar-press responses made), we may conclude that "magazine entries" are not as meaningful a measure of the "transfer effect" in this situation as are "bar-press responses" following injection. This conclusion is supported by an inspection of the data yielded by individual animals. Almost all rats that eventually learn to press the bar to get milk show a peak number of magazine entries 2 to 3 days prior to reaching criterion. As they approach criterion, however, the number of magazine entries drops significantly. Animals that maintain a very high number of magazine entries for several days often do not learn to press the bar at all, but rather spend all their time exploring the food cup area and trying with paw or nose to reach the milk in the reservoir below. The rat that actually learns the problem spends a large proportion of its time shuttling back and forth from the bar to the dipper and in pressing the bar; its magazine entries tend to come only during the period immediately after it has pressed the bar.

Discussion

The "magazine transfer" paradigm has yielded highly significant "transfer" results in our laboratory for some two years now, and we have performed enough parameter studies that we begin to appreciate what the critical factors are that influence the success of these experiments. The factors we believe to be critical include the following: (*a*) The amount of RNA injected should be at least the equivalent of that taken from half a donor brain; (*b*) the recipients should be well-gentled and well habituated prior to injection; (*c*) the recipients should be well-deprived prior to injection; (*d*) the donors should be given an optimal amount of training prior to sacrifice, and this optimal amount of training must (at the moment at least) be determined empirically in any given training situation; (*e*) and perhaps most important of all, the preinjection response tendencies of the recipients must be measured carefully and taken into account if the transfer effect is to be maximized. Additionally, we recommend that the donor animals be sacrificed within minutes after their last training session in a situation such as the one that we have employed, and that the injections be intracranial if RNA is used as the transfer material (McConnell, 1967a).

We have had little success in attempting to use dialyzed materials in the magazine-approach experiments; indeed, we have some tentative evidence that use of dialysate from the brains of animals trained in an operant conditioning chamber causes what appears to be a "negative" transfer effect. In one piece of pilot work (not reported above), we trained donor animals to press the lever in order to activate the dipper (on a fixed ratio schedule of 1 reinforcement for each 50 bar-presses); recipients injected with dialysate from the brains of these trained donors learned significantly more *slowly* than usual, while animals injected with "untrained" dialysate were not retarded in their speed of learning. Such results are consonant with our findings (in our early attempts to replicate the procedure used by Jacobson and his colleagues described above) that intraperitoneal injections of materials from trained brains could significantly retard learning when food reinforcement was given the animals during training, even though a positive "transfer" effect could be demonstrated in the same recipients during unreinforced trials. It is fascinating to speculate that "approach" tendencies may be mediated by large molecules, such as RNA, while "avoidance" tendencies may be mediated by small molecules, such as would be found in a dialysate. The fact that most successful "transfer" studies in which dialysate was used were, in fact, "avoidance" learning paradigms, lends some further credence to this kind of speculation. The "saccharin avoidance" studies to be described below are, in part, an attempt to test this hypothesis.

The "magazine training" paradigm we have employed in these experiments does seem to yield striking results, although somewhat more sophisticated equipment is required than has been used in most other laboratories working in this field. We do not as yet know whether or not the "transfer" achieved is stimulus-specific, nor can we guarantee that it is "learning" or "memory" (as opposed to some motivational component) that is being "transferred," but we are relatively sure that the effect is not one that involves a mere change in the recipients' activity level. All in all, the "magazine training" paradigm seems worthy of considerable further study.

ATTEMPTS TO TRANSFER AN AVOIDANCE RESPONSE

In the past three years (1964-1967), there have been reports from several laboratories of successful attempts to transfer acquired behavioral tendencies from one rat or mouse to another, by extracting substances from the brains of trained animals and injecting these extracts into untrained recipients. In almost all cases, the training given to the donor animals in these experiments has been the sort that lasts over many trials and usually over several days; to the best of our knowledge, no one has yet been able to transfer anything like "one trial" learning, although several investigators have made the attempt. Indeed, in both our laboratory and in Georges Ungar's, evidence has been obtained that suggests that the more training one gives the donor animals, at least up to a certain maximum (as we showed above), the stronger the resulting transfer (Ungar, 1967). In some ways, such a finding is rather surprising, for many of the "one trial" learning situations employed by experimental psychologists yield rather strong and long-lasting effects and the "one trial" situation has proved an effective tool in studies of memory consolidation. One might intuitively think that the stronger the learning, and the more easily it comes about, the more likely it is that it could be transferred chemically from one animal to another. (Another charm of a one-trial learning situation, of course, is that it leads to considerable savings of the experimenter's time.) This section of our paper, then, is a progress report of a new series of experiments we have recently begun in which we attempt to transfer an easily established conditioned aversion to a novel-tasting food in rats.

In the spring of 1967, Samuel H. Revusky visited the Mental Health Research Institute at the University of Michigan and described some research that he and Frank DeVenuto had performed at the U.S. Army Medical Research Laboratory at Fort Knox, Kentucky. Briefly stated, they trained rats to avoid a saccharin solution by giving X irradiation to the animals shortly after the animals were given the saccharin solution. After the saccharin aversion had been established, they extracted RNA from the brains of the donor animals using a cold phenol technique, then injected the material subcutaneously into 40 recipient animals. Another 40 rats received RNA injections from control donors. Both groups of recipients were then tested under 24 hr. liquid deprivation to see if any part of the saccharin aversion had transferred chemically. The results of the study by Revusky and DeVenuto were equivocal, but they did find some statistically significant results in the predicted direction (Revusky & DeVenuto, 1967).

As Revusky and DeVenuto point out, the experimental paradigm they employed is interesting in a great many ways. In the first place, it is a simple matter to train large numbers of donors. Only two or three pairings of the saccharin solution with X irradiation, or with an injection of a nauseating agent such as apomorphine, are necessary for a very strong and long-lasting aversion to take place. The control donor animals can be given exactly the same experiences as the experimental donors, but if the X irradiation is paired with tap water rather than with saccharin, the donor animals will actually show an increased consumption of the saccharin solution rather than developing an aversion towards it. We thought that this paradigm had a great deal to commend it, so we set out to replicate the experiment.

The subjects in our first experiment were 18 adult male Sprague-Dawley rats; 6 of these animals were donors, while 12 were recipients. We began by giving the donor animals 10 days of restricted access to water. During these 10 days, they were allowed to drink all they wanted during a 10 min. period each day, but were not given water at any other time. After these 10 days, the saccharin aversion training began. On Days 11, 13, and 15, the donors were given 10 min. access to a solution of saccharin in drinking water. Fifteen minutes after they had drunk the saccharin soultion, the donors were injected intraperitoneally with apomorphine hydrochloride (15 mg/kg) (Garcia, Erwin, & Koelling, 1966). On Days 12 and 14, the donors were given plain tap water and were not injected. As we expected, their response to this training was a dramatic aversion to the saccharin solution. On Day 15, the donors drank about one-third as much of the saccharin solution as they did on Day 11. Their consumption of plain drinking water on Days 12 and 14, however, remained the same as before the injections began—obviously it was the saccharin flavor, and not liquid *per se*, that the rats were avoiding.

Four hours after the apomorphine hydrochloride injection on Day 15, the donors were sacrificed by decapitation and their brains immediately frozen. Three of the brains, chosen at random, were used for RNA extraction; the other three donor brains were put through dialysis. The RNA extraction method we employed was the same as that described above. The brains that underwent dialysis were homogenized with 5 vol. of saline and then dialyzed against 20 vol. of distilled water for 48 hrs. The volume of the dialysate was then reduced to 1 ml. per brain by lyophilization. As many of you will recognize, this is the dialysis procedure used by Ungar and his associates (Ungar, 1967).

Our 12 recipient animals were given 14 days of restricted water intake. During this period of time, they were allowed 10 min. of free access to liquid daily, the 10 min. being divided into two contiguous 5-min. periods. During the first 8 days, the recipients were given ordinary tap water during both of the 5-min. periods. On Day 9, we established a preference baseline for all the recipients. Half of them were given saccharin during the first 5-min. period and water during the second; the other half of the animlas were given water and saccharin solution in reverse order. In all cases, the recipients consumed more liquid during the first 5-min. period than during the second 5-min. period. This is, of course, just the sort of behavior you would expect from a very thirsty rat.

For the next 5 days following the preference test, all recipients were given ordinary water during both 5-min. periods of time. On the Day 14, the 12 recipients were split into three groups of 4 animals each; the groups were balanced for baseline saccharin preference and matched for weight. The 4 animals in Group I received 200 μl. of RNA extract injected into the subarachnoid space of their brains; the animals were injected under pentobarbital anaesthesia. The 4 animals in Group II received 1 ml. of dialysate injected intraperitoneally without anesthesia, while the 4 animals in Group III received 1 ml. of nondialyzable material intraperitoneally, also without anesthesia. About 14 hrs. after injection, each of the animals was given a repeat of its preference baseline test—that is, the rat received water during one 5-min. period and saccharin solution during the other 5-min. period. Half the animals received the water first, while the rest of the animals received the saccharin solution first. For the next 3 testing days, the order of presentation was reversed daily. Thus half the recipients received water first on test days 1 and 3, while the other half received water first on test days 2 and 4, and the experiment was balanced throughout.

Our analysis of variance did show a triple interaction between extracts and solution between days that was significant at the .025 level, and inspection of the behavior of the animals in the various subgroups could lead one to speculate about interesting processes going on here and there, but frankly, if there was a transfer effect, it was not what you might call outstandingly noticeable.

Perhaps these results were only to be expected. For one thing, we made the classic mistake of trying to "improve" on the paradigm used by Revusky and DeVenuto. These experimenters failed to find a strong transfer effect with RNA injections when their recipients were run under 24 hrs. water deprivation. However, when they offered one group of animals continual access to both water and saccharin solution, they found a very significant drop in saccharin solution consumption on Day 2 of testing. It is possible that we would have found significant differences had we also tested our animals under conditions of reduced drive and when they had free access to both water and saccharin solution. We intend to do so immediately.

It is also true that we had fewer donors per recipient than did Revusky and DeVenuto. While this fact might not have mattered as far as the RNA group was concerned, for we injected as much RNA as we have in some two dozen past experiments that yielded positive transfer results, we were certainly using far fewer donors in the dialysate groups than Ungar and his associates find necessary. And I regret to report that we have some evidence that our RNA extract may not have contained very much intact RNA. Analysis of an RNA extract we obtained on a subsequent experiment showed no intact RNA present at all, just breakdown products; we are not entirely sure why there was no intact RNA present. This finding suggests strongly, however, that one should save a portion of the RNA extract from each donor group and analyze it afterwards to make sure how much RNA the extract actually contained.

We are now in the process of repeating the saccharin aversion work with a larger group of animals and making every effort to correct the mistakes that we made in our first experiment. It is our opinion that the evidence obtained so far is sufficiently encouraging to warrant further work on the saccharin avoidance paradigm. At the moment, however, we cannot recommend it as a paradigm in which it is easy to demonstrate the chemical transfer of acquired behavioral tendencies.

SUMMARY AND CONCLUSIONS

During the past thirty months, we have used more than a thousand rats in a dozen or more experiments to test whether or not acquired behavioral tendencies can be transferred chemically from one animal to another by extracting various substances from the brains of trained animals and injecting them into untrained recipients. In general, our results strongly support the hypothesis that some kind of informational "transfer" can indeed be achieved, and we believe we now know what some of the critical factors are that affect the "transfer" phenomenon. We are not as yet sure what types of "information" can thus be passed from one animal to another, nor how "stimulus-specific" the effect is, but it does appear that the storage and "transfer" of different types of information may well be mediated by different kinds (or at least by different sizes) of molecules. Hopefully, further research in our own and other laboratories will help answer some of the knotty problems as yet unsolved.

We would like to close by emphasizing a point too often forgotten in the controversy that the "transfer" idea has engendered, namely, that our primary interest is in how memories are encoded, stored, and decoded in the brains of the *donor animals*. The transfer technique is primarily useful as a kind of "behavioral litmus paper" to tell us more about the processes going on in the brains of the donors during the learning process. We know by now from the large number of successful reports from laboratories all around the world that we can get an effect of some kind by injecting untrained recipients with chemicals taken from the brains of trained animals. Even if subsequent experiments should prove conclusively that the effect is not really that of an implantation of "memories" into the brains of the recipients, it is still quite likely that the "transfer" technique itself will be a useful tool in our attempts to learn what goes on in the brains of the donor animals when they learn whatever task we set them.

ACKNOWLEDGMENTS

We wish to thank the following people for their assistance in various parts of these experiments: Arthur Aaronson, Richard Block, Patricia Fox, Frank Masiarz, Donald Newman, Barbara Salive, Jessie Shelby, Nancy Slater, Jon Sterngold, William Straugh, Paul Yoder, and Kenneth Zuckerman. We also thank Marlys Schutjer for her help in preparing the manuscript.

REFERENCES

Babich, F. R., Jacobson, A. L., & Bubash, S. Cross-species transfer of learning: Effect of ribonucleic acid from hamsters on rat behavior. *Proceedings of the National Academy of Sciences, U.S., 1965,* **54,** 1299-1302. (a)

Babich, F. R., Jacobson, A. L., Bubash, S., & Jacobson, A. Transfer of a response to naive rats by injection of ribonucleic acid extracted from trained rats. *Science,* 1965, **149,** 656-657. (b)

Babich, F. R., Jacobson, A. L., Bubash, S., & Jacobson, A. Behavioral modifications in naive rats produced by injection of ribonuclei acid extracted from trained rats. *Worm Runner's Digest,* 1965, **7,** 11-14. (c)

Fjerdingstad, E. J., Nissen, T., & Roigaard-Petersen, H. H. Effect of ribonucleic acid (RNA) extracted from the brain of trained animals on learning in rats. *Scandinavian Journal of Psychology,* 1965, **6,** 1-5.

Fried, C., & Horowitz, S. Contraction—a leaRNAble response. *Worm Runner's Digest,* 1964, **6,** 3-6.

Fuchs, A., Harrington, R., Lariviere, R., & Robinson, T. Degree of learning and degree of memory transfer in planarians. *Worm Runner's Digest,* 1966, **8,** 28-31.

Garcia, J., Ervin, R. R., & Koelling, R. A. Learning with prolonged delay of reinforcement. *Psychonomic Science,* 1966, **5,** 121-122.

Humphries, B. M., & Jacobson, R. The effect of ingestion of conditioned planaria on the response level of naive planaria: II. *Worm Runner's Digest,* 1961, **3,** 165-170.

Jacobson, A. L., Babich, F. R., Bubash, S., & Goren, C. Maze preferences in naive rats produced by injection of ribonucleic acid from trained rats. *Psychonomic Sciences,* 1966, **4,** 3-4. (a)

Jacobson, A. L., Babich, F. R., Bubash, S., & Jacobson, A. Differential approach tendencies produced by injection of ribonucleic acid from trained rats. *Science,* 1965, **150,** 636-637.

Jacobson, A. L., Fried, C., & Horowitz, S. Planarians and memory: I. Transfer of learning by injection of ribonucleic acid. *Nature,* 1966, **209,** 599-601. (b)

Jacobson, A. L., Fried, C., & Horowitz, S. Planarians and memory: I. Transfer of learning by injection of ribonucleic acid. *Nature,* 1966, **209,** 601. (c)

John, E. R. Studies on learning and retention in planaria. In M. A. Brazier (Ed.), *Brain function* Vol. 2. Berkeley: University of California Press, 1964 Pp. 161-182.

Kabat, L. Transfer of training through ingestion of conditioned planarians by unconditioned planarias. *Worm Runner's Digest,* 1964, **6,** 23-27.

Lindberg, O., & Ernster, L. The turnover of radioactive phosphate injected into the subarachnoid space of the brain of the rat. *Biochemical Journal,* 1950, **46,** 43-47.

McConnell, J. V. The biochemistry of memory. In S. C. Ratner & W. C. Corning (Eds.), *The chemistry of learning* New York: Plenum Press, 1967, Pp. 310-322. (a)

McConnell, J. V. Comparative physiology: Learning in invertebrates. *Annual Review of Physiology,* 1966, **28,** 107-136.

McConnell, J. V. Factors affecting the "transfer of training" effect in rats. *Journal of Biological Psychology,* 1967, 9(1), 40-48. (b)

McConnell, J. V. Memory transfer through cannibalism in planarians. *Journal of Neuropsychiatry, Supplement,* 1962, **3,** S42-S48.

McConnell, J. V., Jacobson, R., & Humphries, B. M. The effects of ingestion of conditioned planaria on the response level of naive planaria. *Worm Runner's Digest,* 1961, **3,** 41-45.

Pickett, J. B., Jennings, L. B., & Wells, P. H. Influence of RNA and victim training on maze learning by cannibal planarians. *American Zoologist,* 1964, **4,** 158.

Pickett, J. B., Jennings, L. B., & Wells, P. H. Influence of RNA and victim training on maze learning by cannibal planarians. *Worm Runner's Digest,* 1965, 7, 30-38.

Ragland, R. S., & Ragland, J. B. Planaria: Interspecific transfer of a conditionability factor through cannibalism. *Psychonomic Science,* 1965, 3, 117-118.

Reiniš, S. The formation of conditioned reflexes in rats after the parenteral administration of brain homogenate. *Activitas Nervosa Superior,* 1965, 7, 167-168.

Reiniš, S. Influence of brain homogenate injection on the speed of the formation of alimentary conditioned reflex in rats. *Worm Runner's Digest,* 1966, 8, 7-24.

Revusky, S. H., and DeVenuto, F. Attempt to transfer aversion to saccharin solution by injection of RNA from trained to naive rats. *Journal of Biological Psychology,* 1967, 9(2), 12-27.

Rieke, J., & Shannon, L. The effects of deoxyribonuclease and ribonuclease on the transfer of learning by cannibalism in planarians. *Worm Runner's Digest,* 1964, 6, 7-9.

Ungar, G. Transfer of learned behavior by brain extracts. *Journal of Biological Psychology,* 1967, 9 (1), 12-21.

Ungar, G., & Oceguera-Navarro, C. Transfer of habituation by material extracted from brain. *Nature* 1965, 207, 301-302.

Westerman, R. A. Somatic inheritance of habituation of responses to light in planarians. *Science* 1963, 140, 676-677. (a)

Westerman, R. A. A study of the habituation of responses to light in the planarian *Dugesia dorotocephala. Worm Runner's Digest,* 1963, 5, 6-11. (b)

Zelman, A., Kabat, L., Jacobson, R., & McConnell, J. V. Transfer of training through injection of "conditioned" RNA into untrained planarians. *Worm runner's Digest,* 1963, 5, 14-21.

Part IV

NEURONAL PLASTICITY

CELLULAR MODELS OF LEARNING AND CELLULAR MECHANISMS OF PLASTICITY IN *APLYSIA*[1]

I. KUPFERMANN AND H. PINSKER

*Department of Physiology and Biophysics
and Department of Psychiatry
New York University Medical School
New York, New York*

This paper reviews a number of different hypotheses about the cellular mechanisms of learning and, for some of the hypotheses, briefly considers relevant electrophysiological data obtained from studies of single units. In recent years, a variety of simple neural preparations from arthropods and mollusks has been used to study behaviorally relevant problems. The data we will consider have all been drawn from one particular preparation, the isolated abdominal ganglion of the marine mollusk, *Aplysia*. This ganglion contains very large nerve cells which can be identified from preparation to preparation (Frazier, Kandel, Kupfermann, Waziri, & Coggeshall, 1967). A particular advantage of this preparation is that long-term intracellular recordings can be obtained from these large cells, permitting detailed analysis of cellular mechanisms.

In order to facilitate our review of hypothetical cellular mechanisms of learning, we would like to present some highly simplified neuronal models of classical and operant conditioning. The function of these models is to illustrate certain principles rather than to explain all of the complexities of actual learning.

A minimal neuronal model of learning must contain two features: (*a*) a feature of plastic change, and (*b*) a feature of specificity. A plastic change refers to an enduring change in some functional property of a neuron. Recent thinking has emphasized two broad classes of plastic changes. One type of plasticity involves changes in synaptic efficacy, that is changes in the size of synaptic potentials. A second type of plasticity involves changes in the frequency of firing of spontaneously active neurons. The present models have been organized

---

[1] This paper is based on a talk given at the 1967 annual meeting of the American Psychological Association. For a more detailed discussion of some of the topics included, the interested reader is referred to Kupfermann & Pinsker (1969).

around these two broad classes of plastic change. Each of these plastic changes can be produced in several ways. The term "cellular reinforcing event" will be used to refer to the necessary and sufficient neural conditions that produce a plastic change. Under the two broad classes of plastic change, several hypothetical cellular reinforcing events will be examined, and the minimal additional assumptions to achieve specificity will be outlined. Specificity has a somewhat different meaning in classical and operant conditioning. In classical conditioning, it refers to the dependence of the conditioning upon the specific pairing of the conditioned stimulus with the unconditioned stimulus. In operant conditioning, specificity refers to the dependence of the conditioning upon the specific pairing of some behavior with a reinforcing stimulus.

We would first like to consider models in which the cellular reinforcing event leads to a persistent increase in the efficacy of an excitatory synapse. Changes in synaptic efficacy can be readily utilized in models of classical conditioning, but we will show that the same models can be modified to handle operant conditioning. In all of these models the synapse at which the plastic change occurs is shown as a large filled triangle and will be referred to as the "plastic synapse" (Fig. 1). The models all contain a response neuron which sends an output either to an effector organ or to some other part of the brain. The response neuron receives afferent inputs, either directly from the periphery or from an interneuron.

One of the oldest notions concerning the plastic change underlying learning postulates that repeated use of a synapse increases synaptic efficacy. Eccles (1953) has been particularly concerned with a mechanism of this type, and he has developed a model that is designed to explain classical conditioning on the basis of synaptic use. A simplified form of this model is represented in part A of Fig. 1. In model A the cellular reinforcing event is activity or use of the plastic synapse. In order to obtain specificity, it must be assumed that "use" has an effect only when above some minimal level. If this condition is not met, repeated unpaired presentation of the conditioned stimulus (CS) will gradually increase the efficacy of the learning synapse, resulting in sensitization. With the above assumption, specificity to pairing can be achieved by having the CS and UCS converge on an interneuron. Neither the CS nor the UCS alone can fire the interneuron at a sufficiently high rate so that its synaptic end terminal shows use-plasticity. Before conditioning, the plastic synapse is so ineffective that the CS does not fire the response neuron even though it fires the interneuron. When the CS and UCS occur close in time, summation of the excitatory synaptic potentials leads to firing of the interneuron at a rate high enough to satisfy the requirements of the cellular reinforcing event, and the plastic synapse becomes more effective. The CS can then fire the response neuron. We will not discuss that data relevant to the use hypothesis other than to mention that a number of studies have shown that under certain conditions short-term intense synaptic use does increase synaptic efficacy for periods up to several hours.

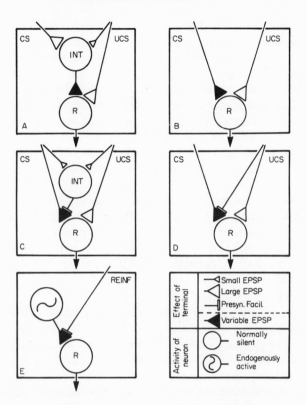

FIG. 1. Simple neuronal models of learning in which the plastic change involves an increase in the efficacy of an excitatory synapse. The locus of the plastic change is indicated by the solid black triangle (plastic synapse). The large empty triangle represents a synaptic terminal that produces an excitatory postsynaptic potential (EPSP) that is capable of firing the postsynaptic cell. The small triangle indicates an EPSP that can fire the postsynaptic cell only when summated with another EPSP. R indicates the response neuron, which is the output of the model. INT indicates an interneuron which is needed to obtain specificity in models where specificity is not part of the cellular reinforcing event. Parts A, B, C, and D. Models of classical conditioning in which the cellular reinforcing event involves: (A) use of the plastic synapse; (B) use of the plastic synapse *and* firing of the postsynaptic cell (successful use); (C) presynaptic activity at the plastic synapse; (D) presynaptic activity *and* activity of the plastic synapse. Part E. Model of operant conditioning. The CS path in model D has been replaced by an endogenously active neuron (from Kupfermann & Pinsker, 1969).

Another important hypothesis is Hebb's (1949) proposal that the fundamental event underlying learning involves use of a synapse in association with the firing of the postsynaptic neuron. This may be termed the successful use hypothesis. Part B of Fig. 1 shows a model of classical conditioning based on such a mechanism. In this model the cellular reinforcing event involves two things: synaptic activity and postsynaptic firing. The UCS serves to insure one of the necessary conditions, i.e., firing of the postsynaptic cell. The CS leads to the other necessary condition, i.e., use of the plastic synapse. In this model, in contrast to the previous "use" model, no additional neural machinery is needed in order to obtain specificity. The specificity is part of the cellular reinforcing event. Although the successful use hypothesis has been influential in a number of theoretical treatments of the learning process, there have been very few experimental studies of this hypothesis. It has been specifically studied in *Aplysia* neurons by Kandel & Tauc (1965b) and later by Wurtz, Castellucci, & Nusrala (1967), but these workers could find no evidence for a mechanism of this sort. Thus this very elegant hypothesis has not yet received any experimental support.

In the two models we just discussed, changes in synaptic efficacy essentially involved use of the plastic synapse. In the models we will now consider, long-lasting increases in the efficacy of the plastic synapse are produced by activity of another synapse that ends directly on the plastic synapse, producing so-called presynaptic facilitation. A mechanism of this type was first suggested by Kandel & Tauc (1965b).

In one type of presynaptic facilitation (nonspecific), facilitation occurs whenever the presynaptic fiber is active, independent of the activity of the plastic synapse. Burke (1966) has presented some models based on this mechanism, and Part C shows one such model of classical conditioning. Specificity to pairing is achieved in a manner that is similar to that used in model A, that is, convergence of the CS and UCS on an interneuron.

Several experimental studies have provided evidence for presynaptic facilitation. It was first described by Kandel and Tauc (1965a) in a study on the giant cell of *Aplysia*. This study utilized intracellular recording while a stimulus sequence derived from the classical conditioning paradigm was presented to the ganglion. Electrical stimulation of two nerves was used to provide analogs of the CS and UCS. One nerve was stimulated weakly with a test stimulus which produced a small excitatory synaptic potential that did not fire the cell (Fig. 2, Part 1). Another nerve was stimulated strongly with a priming stimulus which produced a large EPSP that fired the cell. Pairing of the test and priming stimuli (Part 2) produced an increase in the size of the test EPSP and the facilitation lasted for up to 40 min. (Parts 3, 4). Control experiments showed that the pairing of the two stimuli was *not* necessary for the facilitation to occur, i.e., presentation of the priming stimulus *alone* also facilitated the test EPSP. Further control experiments by Kandel and Tauc and later experiments by Tauc & Epstein (1967) provided strong evidence that the increased EPSP resulted from a presynaptic facilitation of synaptic terminals in the test pathway.

Kandel and Tauc hypothesized another type of presynaptic facilitation (specific) that produces its effects only if the presynaptic activity is associated with activity of the plastic synapse on which the presynaptic fibers impinge. This model is shown in Part D of Fig. 1. As in the "successful use" model, the cellular

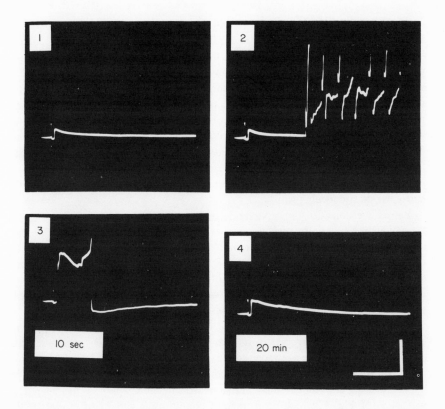

FIG. 2. Presynaptic facilitation of an EPSP in the giant cell (R2) of *Aplysia*. 1. Test EPSP produced by stimulation of the genital nerve before pairing. 2. First of nine pairing trials of test EPSP and response to priming stimulus (6/sec. train of 1 sec. duration to the siphon nerve). 3 and 4. Test EPSP 10 sec. and 20 min. after pairing. The tops of the spikes in frames 2 and 3 have been cut off in photography. Calibration is 10 mV and 500 msec (modified from Kandel & Tauc, 1965a).

reinforcing event involves two conditions. The UCS functions to directly produce one of the conditions, i.e., activity of the presynaptic fiber. The CS functions to produce the other condition, i.e., activity of the plastic synapse.

A number of experiments have been done to test this interesting hypothesis but the results have not been conclusive. Kandel & Tauc (1965a) originally reported in a study of unidentified cells in *Aplysia* that pairing of a weak stimulus to one nerve with a strong stimulus to another nerve facilitated the synaptic potential produced by the weak stimulus. Unpaired presentation of the strong stimulus did not produce facilitation. These results could be explained by the mechanism of specific presynaptic facilitation hypothesized in model D, although alternative explanations are possible. In a later study, Von Baumgarten

& Djahnparwar (1967) failed to find the complete specificity reported by Kandel and Tauc, but they found evidence for incomplete specificity: that is, both the paired and unpaired procedure produced facilitation, but the paired procedure produced larger facilitation than the unpaired procedure. Recent studies by Kupfermann and Kandel (unpublished observations) have also failed to replicate the original findings of Kandel and Tauc. In these studies the paired procedure was occasionally more effective than the unpaired, but the differences were small and inconstant. Even if we could conclude that partial specificity can be reliably demonstrated in *Aplysia* neurons, such specificity need not result from the kind of specific presynaptic facilitation hypothesized in the model we just outlined. Thus there are no direct data that unambiguously support this particular plastic mechanism.

Before we consider the next model, which deals with operant conditioning, we would like to briefly review what we have covered up to this point. We have outlined four models of classical conditioning based on four hypotheses of plasticity of synaptic efficacy. Two of the models, A and C of Fig. 1, postulate a *nonspecific* plastic mechanism and an interneuron is needed to obtain specificity to pairing in these models. The other two models, B and D, postulate a type of *specific* plastic mechanism, and in these models specificity to pairing can be obtained without an interneuron. The experimental data provide support for both of the nonspecific plastic mechanisms. However, neither of the specific plastic mechanisms have yet received conclusive support.

All of these models can be modified to handle operant conditioning simply by substituting an endogenously active neuron in the CS path, as has been done in Part E of Fig. 1, which is an operant conditioning variant of model D. The endogenously active neuron can fire in the absence of synaptic input, and, in addition, has the property of undergoing spontaneous alterations of firing rate. In such models, conditioning would occur whenever the endogenously active unit fired sufficiently fast to fire the response unit. When the response unit fired, the experimenter or the environment would provide a reinforcing stimulus along the equivalent of the UCS pathway, and the plastic synapse would show enduring facilitation, since all of the requirements of the cellular reinforcing event would be met. Therefore, during conditioning, even though the average frequency and pattern of firing of the endogenously active unit would not change, a given amount of firing would produce a larger amplitude synaptic potential at the response neuron and hence the overall frequency of firing or probability of a response would increase. Kandel (1967) has pointed out how such a transformation from the amplitude domain (of the synaptic potential) to the frequency domain (firing of the response unit) opens up the possibility of moving from classical conditioning models to operant conditioning models, and Burke (1966) has applied similar notions to the model of classical conditioning shown in Part C.

We would now like to consider models in which the cellular reinforcing event leads to alterations in the frequency of endogenous spiking activity. Since operant conditioning involves a change in the frequency of spontaneously occurring behavior, such conditioning can be readily modeled by a plastic change in the average firing rate of an endogenously active neuron. We will also show that changes in endogenous activity can be used in models of classical conditioning. Frazier, Waziri, & Kandel (1965) have postulated two types of endogenous plasticity. One form (nonspecific or noncontingent) assumes that the change in activity is dependent only on synaptic input and does not depend upon the firing of the endogenously active unit. A second form of the hypothesis (specific or contingent) assumes that enduring alteration resulting from synaptic input is dependent upon the state of firing of the endogenously active unit at the time of the synaptic input. In both cases, the cellular reinforcing event is mediated synaptically, but the plastic change occurs not in the synaptic terminals but in the postsynaptic cell.

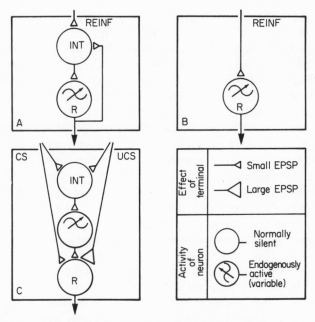

FIG. 3. Simple neuronal models of learning in which the plastic change involves an increase of the average firing frequency of an endogenously active neuron. Parts A and B. Models of operant conditioning in which the cellular reinforcing event involves: (A) synaptic input to the endogenously active neuron (nonspecific effect); (B) synaptic input *and* firing of the endogenously active neuron (specific effect). Part C. Model of classical conditioning utilizing plasticity of an endogenously active neuron and nonspecific cellular reinforcing event (from Kupfermann & Pinsker, 1969).

Part A of Fig. 3 schematizes a model of operant conditioning, in which the cellular reinforcing event involves synaptic input independent of the state of firing of the endogenously active unit. The synaptic input is assumed to produce a plastic change which leads to a persistent increase in the probability of the neuron firing. In this model, specificity could be accomplished by having the R neuron send a recurrent collateral to an interneuron. Synaptic input from this interneuron would constitute the cellular reinforcing event, and this would occur only under the conditions of synaptic summation provided by the combined input from the reinforcing stimulus and the recurrent collateral from the response unit. The experimental evidence for nonspecific alterations in endogenous activity is fairly strong. Studies on endogenously active cells in *Aplysia* have shown that brief strong synaptic input can produce prolonged increases in firing frequency (Frazier *et al.*, 1965). These experiments demonstrated *nonspecific* plasticity since the presence or absence of endogenous spike activity at the time of the synaptic input did not alter the effect of that input.

In the *specific* variant of the models involving changes in endogenous activity, it is postulated that the cellular reinforcing event has two aspects: synaptic activity and activity of the endogenously active unit. For example, synaptic activity could produce a persistent increase of firing of the endogenously active unit, but only when the synaptic activity occurs close in time with the firing of the postsynaptic neuron. Such a cellular reinforcing event could be the basis of a very simple model of operant conditioning which is shown in Part B of Fig. 3. In this model the cellular reinforcing event has specificity built into it, and no additional neural machinery is needed. Several studies in *Aplysia* have demonstrated a type of specific mechanism involving changes in endogenous activity. These studies have been done on cells that are endogenously active and fire in regularly occurring bursts of spikes. Part 2 of Fig. 4 shows a complete burst cycle, consisting of a burst of spikes and a quiet period. The burst onset interval is the duration of the burst cycle. A study by Frazier *et al.* (1965) showed that when weak synaptic input resulting from stimulation of a nerve occurred during the early part of the burst (contingency A), the burst onset interval was shortened. When the same synaptic input occurred later in the burst cycle (contingency B), the burst onset interval was lengthened. In other words, contingency A stimulation led to more bursts per unit time, whereas contingency B led to fewer bursts per unit time. When contingency B nerve stimulation was presented repeatedly, each successive burst onset interval was longer than the previous one. Following the cessation of repeated stimulation, the succeeding burst onset intervals could remain lengthened for up to 20 min.

Nerve stimulation produces a complex synaptic input to the bursting cells, and it is therefore difficult to exactly specify the synaptic input that leads to the specific plastic change just described. However, Pinsker & Kandel (1967) have obtained similar results with pure IPSPs produced by intracellular stimulation of

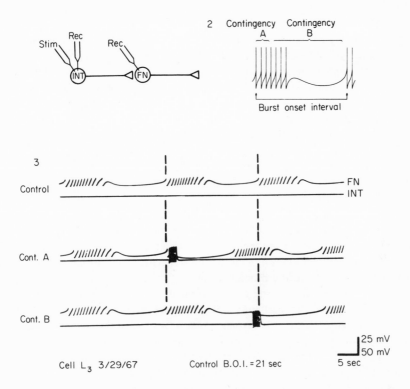

FIG. 4. Part 1. Schematic diagram of experimental arrangement for studying an interneu-ron (INT) and one of its follower neurons (FN). By means of independent intracellular electrodes for stimulating and recording, the firing of the interneuron can be controlled to provide synaptic input contingent upon the activity recorded from the follower neuron. Part 2. Idealized burst cycle of an endogenously active left upper quadrant bursting cell in *Aplysia*. Synaptic input produces opposite effects on the burst onset interval depending upon the phase of the burst cycle in which it is presented. Contingency A stimulation shortens the burst onset interval whereas contingency B stimulation lengthens the burst onset interval. (Unpublished figure from Frazier *et al.*, 1965.) Part 3. Specific effects of inhibitory synaptic input (from cell L10) on an endogenously active bursting cell (L3). In each part, the bursting cell (FN) is shown on the upper trace, and the interneuron (INT) is shown (at reduced gain) on the lower trace. Control. Regular bursting rhythm in the absence of stimulation. Dashed lines indicate the control burst onset interval (B.O.I). Cont. A. Effect of contingency A stimulation. A high frequency train of IPSPs produced by stimulation of the interneuron inhibits spikes when presented at the onset of the burst onset interval. Cont. B. Effect of contingency B stimulation. The same synaptic input presented later in the burst cycle lengthens the burst onset interval. The tops of the spikes have been cut off in photo-graphy. (Unpublished figure from Pinsker & Kandel, 1967.)

an identified interneuron (L10) that synapses with the bursting cells. Figure 4, Part 3 shows simultaneous records from a bursting cell on the upper traces and from the inhibitory interneuron on the lower traces. The control shows the regular bursting pattern in the absence of stimulation from the interneuron. In contingency A, the interneuron was made to fire at the onset of the burst. It inhibits the remaining spikes and shortens the burst onset interval. In contingency B, the interneuron was made to fire during the quiet period. Now it leads to an increase in the burst onset interval. With repeated contingency A stimulation with the pure IPSP, the shortening of the burst onset interval produced by each stimulus tends to gradually increase. When the stimulation was discontinued, the burst onset interval gradually returned to the control level. These experiments with a monosynaptic input from an interneuron provide strong evidence that synaptic input can directly produce specific alteration in the endogenous properties of a cell.

We have outlined two models of operant conditioning based on plasticity of endogenous activity. In parallel with the previous models using plasticity of synaptic efficacy, one of the models, A, postulates a nonspecific plastic mechanism, and an interneuron is needed to obtain specificity in this model. The other model postulates a specific plastic mechanism and it does not need an interneuron to obtain specificity. The experimental data provide support for both the nonspecific and specific mechanisms of plastic change of endogenous activity.

Cellular reinforcing events involving plastic changes in the frequency of firing of endogenously active neurons need not be limited to models of operant conditioning. Part C of Fig. 3 shows a model of classical conditioning based on the nonspecific plastic mechanism utilized in model A. In this model the endogenously active unit fires constantly, providing a tonic level of depolarization of the response unit. The CS and UCS converge on an interneuron whose firing provides a synaptic input to the endogenously active unit and thereby produces a persistent increase in its firing rate. This increased firing, in turn, leads to an increase in the tonic depolarization of the response unit, bringing it closer to the firing level, so that the CS will now produce a response.

We would like to briefly summarize the main points we have tried to make. The plastic properties of single nerve cells can be studied in detail in simple invertebrate preparations. Studies on the isolated abdominal ganglion of *Aplysia* provide support for two types of plastic mechanisms: plasticity of synaptic efficacy and plasticity of endogenous activity. Both of these mechanisms can be utilized in simple neural models of either classical or operant conditioning. It should be emphasized that there is an enormous gap between the understanding of relatively short-term plastic changes demonstrated in simple preparations and the understanding of the cellular basis of mammalian learning. However, it is our feeling than an understanding of the detailed functional properties of single cells and of simple aggregates of cells can provide meaningful hypotheses that can be tested in mammalian brains. Furthermore, recent studies have demonstrated behavioral modifications in *Aplysia* (Kupfermann, 1968; Kupfermann & Pinsker, 1968; Lickey, 1968) and it should be possible to relate the plastic changes that have been described in the isolated nervous system to the behavioral plasticity of the intact animal (Castellucci, Pinsker, Kupfermann, & Kandel, 1970; Kupfermann, Castellucci, Pinsker & Kandel, 1970; Kupfermann & Kandel, 1968, 1969; Pinsker, Kupfermann, Castellucci & Kandel, 1970).

ACKNOWLEDGMENTS

The authors thank Dr. Eric R. Kandel and Dr. William Alden Spencer for their helpful comments on this paper. The figures were prepared by Susan Smith and Kathrin Hilten.

Original research reported in this paper was supported, in part, by NINDB grant R01 NB 07621-02 EPB, and NIH grant NB 05980-02. In addition Dr. Harold Pinsker was supported by the NIMH Research Training Program in Psychiatry and the Biological Sciences at New York University Medical School.

REFERENCES

Burke, W. Neuronal models for conditioned reflexes. *Nature,* 1966, **210**, 269-271.

Castellucci, V., Pinsker, H., Kupfermann, I., & Kandel, E. Neuronal mechanisms of habituation and dishabituation of the Gill withdrawal reflex in *Aplysia*. *Science,* 1970 (in Press).

Eccles, J. C. *The neurophysiological basis of mind.* London & New York: Oxford University Press, 1953.

Frazier, W. T., Kandel, E. R., Kupfermann, I., Waziri, R., & Coggeshall, R. E. Morphological and functional properties of identified neurons in the abdominal ganglion of *Aplysia californica. Journal of Neurophysiology,* 1967, **30**, 1288-1351.

Frazier, W. T., Waziri, R., & Kandel, E. Alterations in the frequency of spontaneous activity in *Aplysia* neurons with contingent and noncontingent nerve stimulation. *Federation Proceedings,* 1965, **24**, 522.

Hebb, D. O. *The organization of behavior.* New York: Wiley, 1949.

Kandel, E. R. Cellular studies of learning. In F. O. Schmidt (Ed.), *The neurosciences.* New York: Rockefeller Univ. Press, 1967. Pp. 666–689.

Kandel, E. R., & Tauc, L. Heterosynaptic facilitation in neurones of the abdominal ganglion of *Aplysia depilans. Journal of Physiology (London),* 1965, **181**, 1-27. (a)

Kandel, E. R., & Tauc, L. Mechanism of heterosynaptic facilitation in the giant cell of the abdominal ganglion of *Aplysia depilans. Journal of Physiology (London),* 1965, **181**, 28-47. (b)

Kupfermann, I. A circadian locomotor rhythm in *Aplysia californica. Physiology and Behavior,* 1968, **3**, 179-181.

Kupfermann, I., Castellucci, V., Pinsker, H., & Kandel, E. Neuronal correlates of habituation and dishabituation of the Gill withdrawal reflex in *Aplysia. Science,* 1970 (in Press).

Kupfermann, I., & Kandel, E. Reflex function of some identified cells in *Aplysia. Federation Proceedings,* 1968, **27**, 348.

Kupfermann, I., & Kandel, E. Neuronal controls of a behavioral response mediated by the abdominal ganglion of *Aplysia. Science,* 1969, **164**, 847-850.

Kupfermann, I., & Pinsker, H. A behavioral modification of the feeding reflex in *Aplysia californica*. *Communications in Behavioral Biology, Part A* 1968, **2**, 13-17. biology,

Kupfermann, I., & Pinsker, H. Plasticity in *Aplysia* neurons and some simple neuronal models of learning. In J. Tapp (Ed.), *Reinforcement*. New York: Academic Press, 1969. Pp. 356-386.

Lickey, M. E. Learned behavior in *Aplysia vaccaria*. *Journal of Comparative and Physiological Psychology,* 1968, **66**, 712-718.

Pinsker, H., & Kandel, E. R. Contingent modification of an endogenous bursting rhythm by monosynaptic inhibition. *Physiologist,* 1967, **10**, 279.

Pinsker, H., Kupfermann, I., Castellucci, V., & Kandel, E. habituation and dishabituation of the Gill withdrawal reflex in *Aplysia*. *Science,* 1970 (in Press).

Tauc, L., & Epstein, R. Heterosynaptic facilitation as a distinct mechanism in *Aplysia*. *Nature,* 1967, **214**, 724-725.

Von Baumgarten, R. J., & Djahnparwar, B. Time course of repetitive heterosynaptic facilitation in *Aplysia californica*. *Brain Research,* 1967, **4**, 295-297.

Wurtz, R. H., Castellucci, V. F., & Nusrala, J. M. Synaptic plasticity: The effect of the action potential in the postsynaptic neuron. *Experimental Neurology,* 1967, **18**, 350-368.

THE AFTEREFFECTS DUE TO AN INTRACELLULAR ELECTRIC STIMULATION OF THE GIANT NEURON "A" IN THE LEFT PARIETAL GANGLION OF THE MOLLUSK *LIMNAEA STAGNALIS*

E. N. SOKOLOV, A. PAKULA, and G. G. ARAKELOV

Department of Neuropsychology
Moscow State University
Moscow, USSR

Increased interest in mechanisms of memory results nowadays in a more accurate attitude to the aftereffects taking place in single neurons due to prolonged or repeated stimulation. Making use of the giant neurons of mollusks enables us to perform long-lasting intracellular recordings and to study such complex forms of aftereffects as hibituation (Holmgren & Frenk, 1961), facilitation (Szabo & Fessard, 1961), and conditioned response (Tauc, 1966).

Sokolov, Arakelov, & Levinson (1967), dealing with the neurons of the abdominal and the cerebral ganglia of *Limnaea stagnalis,* have demonstrated an effect of a stable increase of excitability of neurons after a repeated orthodromic stimulation had been used. After several applications of orthodromic shocks, a neuron which was nonactive started spike generation. The probability of neuron response increases and latency of spike generation decreases in the course of a stimulation. Application of a train of stimuli evokes temporary autogeneration of spikes; i.e., when spikes are generated in the absence of stimuli. In the course of further stimulation, a neuron showed habituation for an orthodromic stimulation. The probability of spike generation decreased and latency of response increased. Both extinction of the neuron's responses as well as its activation exhibited marked aftereffects.

However, it is an extraordinarily difficult task to separate the participation in the aftereffects of the presynaptic structures from that of the postsynaptic ones when orthodromic stimulation is used. In the explication of a mechanism of the aftereffects, the main attention is paid to the mobilization of the transmitter in a presynaptic membrane as described for posttetanic potentiation in the excitatory and inhibitory synapses. The problem concerning the role of internal structures of a postsynaptic neuron still remains unsolved.

Extinction of unitary responses may be explained with the help of the mechanism, including participation of inhibitory interneurons. At the first state of habituation, "parallel inhibition" is believed to increase, while at the second, presynaptic inhibition seems to be present (Sokolov, Arakelov, & Levinson, 1967). However, the possible modification of excitability of the postsynaptic membrane is not discussed.

Direct stimulation of a neuron's soma by means of an imbedded microelectrode presents one of the possible ways for determination of the role of intracellular structures in aftereffects. And here subthreshold stimulation of long duration seems to be very appropriate for influencing directly the excitability of a neuron via intracellular structures without immediate involvement of the membrane's generatory mechanisms electrically. For these goals, the giant neurons of mollusks are very convenient. The large size of nuclei in these cells (about 70% of the cell diameter) enables the researcher to exert influence on the nuclear structures as well as on the cytoplasmic ones and on the cell membrane.

This paper deals with the aftereffects occuring at the intracellular level in the giant neuron A of the left (small) parietal ganglion of the mollusk *Limnaea stagnalis* due to electric stimulation of long duration through the recording microelectrode.

METHOD

The principal obstacle to the investigation of intracellular mechanisms of aftereffects in a single neuron is in the difficulty of making compatible two opposing demands:

(1) maintenance of the normal functional state of the neuron, and, at the same time,

(2) elimination of extracellular stimuli to the maximum extent possible.

Our choice for the intracellular registration of an electric activity of single units in a whole mollusk preparation was made to fulfill maximally the demand for the relatively normal functioning of a neuron. Although in this case the demand for the maximal elimination of extracellular influences was not fulfilled, an intracellular registration made it possible to evaluate the most important synaptic messages coming to the cell. If such influences during a definite time-span exhibit sufficient stability, then using intracellular electric stimulation, makes it possible to discover the contribution of postsynaptic intracellular mechanisms to the aftereffects. Also, if direct electric stimulation does not evoke recurrent influences via interneurons, it means that we have a situation favorable to the study of the extrasynaptic contributions to the aftereffects.

The mollusks used for the experiments were collected in the pool of the University Botanic Garden. The procedure of preparation was as follows. Having separated a mollusk from its shell, two cuts were made: one along a "foot," and another along a "back," starting from the mouth's aperture. Then the sides of a "back"-cut were fixed by pins in the wax chamber, and the thus made visible esophagus was cut in the region of the pharynx and removed from the ring of ganglia through which it passes. Such whole preparation of a mollusk was put into a special chamber. A cone-like plastic pivot projecting from the center of the chamber was fitted to enter the "foot"—cut and then passed through the ring of ganglia to fix the position of the latter. In this position, it was possible to introduce a microelectrode into the neurons of different ganglia. In our experiments, we dealt with the same identified giant neuron ("neuron A," see Yarmizina, Sokolov, & Arakelov, 1968) in the left parietal ganglion of *Limnaea stagnalis,* so some additional operations related to the specific location of this neuron were necessary. Nervus pallialis sinister, the only nerve connecting the left parietal ganglion with the rest of body, was cut at its peripheral end, picked up, and rolled upon the pivot. In this way, all the giant neurons (4-5 in total) of the left parietal ganglion were easily recognized and had a sufficiently stable (from sample to sample) location. The most characteristic location of the neurons in this ganglion is shown in Fig. A. In this position, neuron A (the diameter of which ranges from 170 to 280 μ approximately) was found protuberant in the upper quadrant of the ganglion.

During an experiment, a mollusk preparation was immersed in Ringer's solution for Mollusca (NaCl $-$ 6.5 gm.; KCl $-$ .14 gm.; $NaHCO_3$ $-$ .2 gm.; $CaCl_2$ $-$ .12 gm.; H_2O dist. $-$ up to 1000 cm^3).

An electrophysiological experiment was followed by a histological procedure for marking the position of a microelectrode's tip in a neuron. Using $FeCl_3$ as an electrolyte for micropipettes enabled us to mark not only a neuron whose activity was recorded during an experiment (which already has become more or less common practice in intracellular experiments), but also the position of the tip in the neuron (Sokolov, Arakelov, & Levinson, 1966). The low mobility and the protein-binding properties of the ferric ions resulted in a limited distribution of these ions in a region around the tip of the microelectrode. In the stained sections, this was visible as a blue spot of from 4 to 20 μ diameter. For marking position in this way, it was not necessary to apply currents of high intensity. In most cases an application of positive subthreshold (10^{-9} A) current for 20 min. was sufficient.

Glass micropipettes filled with a solution of 2.75 M $FeCl_3$ were used as microelectrodes. The micropipettes were made from pyrex glass tubing of 1.2 to 1.4 mm. o.d. using the vertical puller of Marinytchev's system, and were filled only if the o.d. of the tips did not exceed 1 μ. A special investigation of the properties of such microelectrodes has demonstrated that their resistance does not change when currents up to 10^{-8} A are applied. Only with further increase in

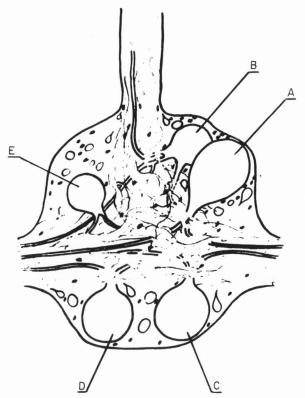

FIG. A. Location of the giant neurons in the left parietal ganglion of *Limnaea stagnalis.* Nervus pallialis sin. is shown going upward.

intensity does a microelectrode start to exhibit the properties of a nonohmic resistance, rising abruptly from the initial 10 - 20 MΩ up to several thousand megohms. The stability of the microelectrode's resistance over such a range of current intensities was sufficient for our experiments. The tip potential of the microelectrodes was from 2 to 15 mV with negligible fluctuations in time.

For registration of the neuron's electric activity, a microelectrode was connected through the agar-agar bridge with the device for the registration of cell activity consisting of a cathode-follower, microelectrode amplifier MZ-3B, and universal dual-beam oscilloscope VC-7A with a continuous-recording camera mounted on it (manufactured by Nihon Kohden Co., Ltd., Tokyo, Japan). Also, simultaneous registration by a recording potentiometer EPP-09 M2 was provided. Electric stimuli to the neuron were applied from the electronic stimulator MSE-3R through the isolating unit MSE-JM (both manufactured by Nihon Kohden Co., Ltd., Tokyo, Japan). The Wheatstone bridge modification (Frank,

1959) was used since the electric stimuli were applied through the recording electrode.

Altogether the activity of 117 A neurons was registered. In this paper, the results of the experiment on A neuron, No. 39, are discussed principally, because at this neuron different kinds of aftereffect were apparent at once that are usually dissipated over the population of single neurons.

The duration of the continuous recording in this case was 7 hrs. The mark of the microelectrode's tip was identified in the nucleus of the neuron.

RESULTS

1. Time-Dependent Modification of the Neuron's Electric Activity after Penetration by the Microelectrode

The neuron discussed, after the penetration of the microelectrode, started spike generation of high firing rate which persisted for a while (Fig. 1A). Gradually the firing rate decreased, accompanied by the development of a hyperpolarizing shift of membrane potential of about 20 mV. After that the membrane potential remained constant for hours. Even this initial shift was apparently determined more by the transient processes taking place at the tip of the microelectrode, as a result of the changes of the tension potential after the introduction of the pipette into the cell, than by the proper reaction of the neuron itself. This was concluded because the amplitude of spikes was almost unchanging during the development of the "hyperpolarization." The drift of the electronic device was negligible.

The decrease of firing rate continued after the termination of the negative shift of transmembrane potential and finally the spike activity reduced to single spikes and almost completely ceased. EPSPs were not present. Generation of spikes was evoked by pacemaker potentials (see Fig. 1A) and the decrease of firing rate was caused by the reduction of frequency and amplitude of the pacemaker potential.

2. Activation of Spike Generation Occurring Spontaneously or Evoked by Adequate Stimuli

After the transmembrane potential became stable and the pacemaker potentials and spikes gradually disappeared, we observed a spontaneous activation of spike generation, when during a period of from 1 to 3 min. the spikes preceded by the pacemaker potentials were generated (Fig. 2A). Then the neuron again ceased generating spikes.

Similar temporary activation of spike generation might be evoked by adequate stimuli, too. A drop of saline solution, falling upon the skin of the mollusk from a height of approximately 5 cm., initiated the trains of spikes as well (Fig. 2B).

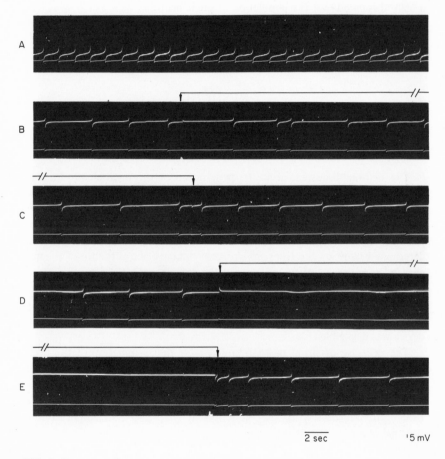

2 sec   '5 mV

FIG. 1. Response of neuron No. 39 to the injection of chlorine ions by a "hyperpolarizing" current. A. A spontaneous activity of the neuron at the fifth minute after the introduction of microelectrode. B and C. Application of a prolonged dc pulse of a next-to-threshold value. The mean rate of spike generation almost coincides with that of background but the "on" and "off" effects are already expressed (see, respectively, B and C). At "on" the interspike intervals are becoming greater, at "off," shorter. D and E. A current of a higher intensity (-1.7×10^{-9} A) produces complete suppression of the spontaneous activity. In E an effect of "rebound" in response to switching off the current is clearly shown. The moments when the current was switched on and off are marked by arrows. Calibration of amplitude is given only for the trace of lower amplification.

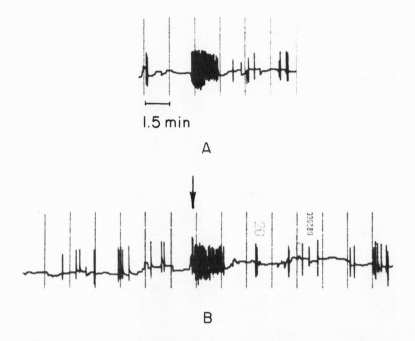

FIG. 2. Reaction of the neuron to the adequate stimuli. Registration was made with the recording potentiometer. Calibration of amplitude is not given in all the records made with this potentiometer because there were great distortions of amplitude of spikes when using this kind of registration. A. Spontaneous activation of the spike generation process. Duration – about 2 min. The background activity consists of occasional spikes. B. Similar activation of the neuron in response to a falling drop of saline solution. Membrane potential – 50 mV. The vertical bars mark time intervals.

3. Activation of Spike Generation Due to an Iontophoresis of Positive Ions

The activation of spike generation due to an application of adequate stimuli as well as spontaneous activation occurred on the background of a stable mean level of the membrane potential. Each spike was evoked by the pacemaker potential. Considering the pacemaker potential of the endogenous event, we may assume the possibility of such an interaction among the neurons, for which the presence of EPSPs is not essential, and all the influences are manifested at the level of the intrinsic mechanisms of the postsynaptic neuron.[1] Therefore, one may expect that similar effects could be obtained by direct electric stimulation of the internal structures of a neuron by the same recording microelectrode.

[1]This paper was in press when evidence of such an interaction in stomatopod heart ganglion was reported by Watanabe et al. (1969).

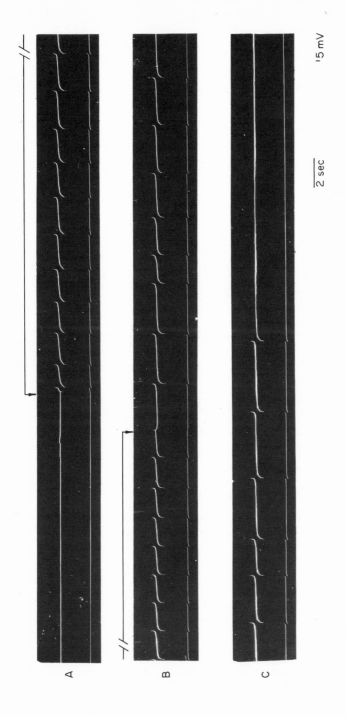

FIG. 3. Response of neuron No. 39 to the injection of ferric ions by a "depolarizing" current of overthreshold intensity (1.5 × 10⁻⁹ A). A background spike activity is not present. After the current is switched on, spikes appear immediately (A), and they persist even after it is switched off (B); only after 2 to 2.5 min. does the initial background activity become reestablished (C). Because the current was applied for a long time, in this case the record of changes in spike activity made by the recording potentiometer (see Fig. 4) is more revealing. The moments when the current was switched on and off are marked by arrows. Calibration of amplitude is given only for the trace of lower amplification.

The application of a prolonged positive dc pulse of 1.5×10^{-9} A (for 23 min.), resulting in an iontophoresis of positive ions (Fe^{+++}) into the neuron, did not influence the mean level of the membrane potential, but did evoke a gradual increase of firing rate. Although the membrane potential remained stable (with accuracy of ± 1 mV), the changes in the neuron's activity were evident and a long-lasting aftereffect testifies to this. The neuron generated spikes during the 2 to 3 min. after the iontophoresis had been terminated (Fig. 3B,C and Fig. 4). Then the firing rate decreased again and the single spikes became more and more random.

1.5 min

FIG. 4. Response of the neuron to a prolonged dc pulse of 1.5×10^{-9} A (see the fragments of continuous film recording in Fig. 2). Registration was made with the recording potentiometer. At the beginning of stimulation the neuron discharged by bursts lasting from 1 to 1.5 min. The rhythmic activity persists for a time after the current has been switched off. "On" and "off" of current are marked by arrows. Membrane potential -47 mV. The vertical bars mark time intervals.

The analysis of the details of the electrogenesis under the conditions of iontophoresis of positive ions into the cell has shown that the activation of the pacemaker potential in this instance was similar to that due to the penetration of a cell by a microelectrode.

4. Suppression of Spike Generation Due to an Iontophoresis of Negative Ions

In order to evaluate the dependence of the activity of the spike generating mechanism on the direction of an iontophoretic current, the microelectrode was made negative and chlorine ions were injected into the neuron. This led to the opposite effect. Although the membrane potential again suffered no changes, this time the neuron's spike activity was suppressed completely (Fig. 1D). This resulted from a low pacemaker potential generation rate and its lower amplitude at the increased critical firing threshold. After the current was switched off, a phenomenon of "rebound" took place, and the frequency of spikes was for a while rather higher than the mean firing rate in the interstimulus intervals (Fig. 1E).

5. Dependence of Spike Activity on Current Intensity during an Iontophoresis of Positive Ions

No Changes in spike activity were noted when using stimuli up to 1.3×10^{-9} A. This stimulus gave only a statistically detectable reaction. The evidently noticeable activation of spike generation started at a current value of 1.4×10^{-9} A. The increase in the current's intensity led to an increase of firing rate (Fig. 5).

1.5 min

FIG. 5. Response of the neuron to a "depolarizing" current of different intensity. Registration was made with the recording potentiometer. A current of 1.3×10^{-9} A does not evoke any appreciable reaction of the neuron, while those of 1.4×10^{-9} A and of 1.5×10^{-9} A yield pronounced reactions. "On" and "off" of current are marked by arrows. Intensity of the current increases to the right. Membrane potential − 47 mV. The vertical bars mark time intervals.

It is necessary to stress once more that an increased activity of pacemaker and spike generating mechanisms, caused by the augmented iontophoresis of positive ions, may not be related to any changes in the membrane potential.

6. Sensitization of Spike Generation Due to Repeated Stimulation

After the series of electric stimuli, the neuron started to exhibit regular spike activity even during the interstimulus intervals. This coincided with the decrease in the threshold of the activation effect. Consequently a stimulus of 1.1×10^{-9} A, which had been subthreshold at the beginning of the experiment, started to evoke an activation of spike generation, while a stimulus of 1.3×10^{-9} A noticeably increased its effectiveness (Fig. 6A).

The sensitization of the spike generation also took place in the case of repeated application of negative dc pulses. This resulted in the suppression of the spike activity at the lower values of the applied current (cf. Fig. 1B,C and Fig. 6B).

Thus, repeated intracellular stimulation by the prolonged dc pulses of both polarities brought about the permanent sensitization of a neuron. This effect was made clear by the decreased activation-inactivation threshold stimuli. This kind of aftereffect persisted for as long as several times 10 min.

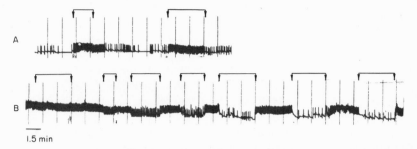

1.5 min

FIG. 6. Sensitization of the neuron due to repeated application of prolonged "depolariz-ing" and "hyperpolarizing" dc pulses. Registration was made with the recording potentio-meter. A. After the series of "depolarizing" stimuli, sensibility of the neuron to the stimula-tion became greater than it was initially (cf. Fig. 5), and the neuron started to respond to currents of 1.2×10^{-9} A and of 1.3×10^{-9} A. "Rebound" effect is not present, but another kind of aftereffect — an after-activation — takes place. B. Sensibility of the neuron to the stimulation changes as well when prolonged "hyperpolarizing" stimuli are used. A threshold of desensitization gradually decreases in a course of repeated stimulation and in consequence the background activity is suppressed by the currents that initially had no apparent influence on the spike activity. Gradual decrease of the background spike genera-tion rate also bears witness to an inactivating influence of the "hyperpolarizing" current on pacemaker potential generation. Intensity of the stimuli (from the left to the right):

(i) 1.2×10^{-9} A;   (iii) 1.5×10^{-9} A;   (v) 2.0×10^{-9} A;   (vii) 1.4×10^{-9} A.
(ii) 1.3×10^{-9} A;   (iv) 1.7×10^{-9} A;   (vi) 2.5×10^{-9} A.

Membrane potential — 46 mV. The vertical bars mark time intervals.

DISCUSSION

The aftereffects noted in this experiment, despite the stability of the mem-brane potential, indicate a crucial role of pacemaker potentials in these phenom-ena. For better understanding of the possible mechanisms of the activation-inac-tivation of the pacemaker, it is necessary to have a more explicit notion of the processes taking place within the neuron during the stimulation. In this sense, important information might be obtained from knowledge of the location of the microelectrode's tip.

Using the method of marking by ferric ions, we found that the tip of the microelectrode in this experiment, as in many other cases, had been in the nucleus of the neuron. The limited volume of the mark shows that, in spite of the local character of the iontophoresis of ferric ions, it may influence the neuron's activity regulating generation of pacemaker potentials. Since the den-sity of current at the membrane was too low to involve the membrane mecha-nisms in the spike activity directly, the first effect of iontophoresis was not a modification of the membrane potential, but an involvement in the evident activ-ity of the intracellular structures responsible for the control of the metabolic processes in the cell. Upon local stimulation, the nucleus of the neuron exhibited a prolonged summation of effects of stimulation, a result not found when only the membrane is involved in the reaction. The prolonged summation of sub-threshold currents corresponded with the long-lasting aftereffects, such as a persistence of the spike activity after switching off the positive current, or a lowering of the activation threshold as a consequence of the stimuli applied previously. Also, these aftereffects were not related to the reactions of the membrane potential.

The iontophoresis of negative ions (chlorine) had an inactivating effect on spike generation and evoked similar aftereffects. However, in this case, it was difficult to state any conclusion about the mechanism of the changes which occurred because no chlorine tracing was done and hence nothing was known about its distribution in the neuron. We may only guess that the analogous alterations in the case of the chlorine iontophoresis indicate mechanisms analogous to those of an activation phenomenon due to the iontophoresis of ferric ions.

All the activating and inactivating influences during the experiment were expressed via a pacemaker potential. This gives reason to presume the importance of the intracellular influences upon the pacemaker potential, especially as the endogenous origin of the latter seems at present doubtless (Alving, 1968). Autonomy of the pacemaker potential in preserving the rhythm of the spike discharge in the pacemaker neurons was demonstrated by T. H. Bullock (1961). Pacemaker neurons in the motor center of *Cicada* are of great interest from this point of view. The pacemaker neuron there may be triggered by an adequate as well as by an orthodromic electric stimulation and continues a certain rhythm for some 20 sec. Moreover, the threshold of the triggering of the pacemaker grew lower after repeated stimulation (Sviderskij & Karlov, 1967). The authors underline an extraordinary autonomy in the activity of the pacemaker neurons. This autonomy does not exclude, however, the possible influences of adequate and nonadequate stimuli which result in triggering or blocking of the generation of the pacemaker potential. Grundfest (1957) has described three types of pacemaker neurons in different species of electric fish. In some species, frequency was completely independent of applied stimuli; in others, it was affected somewhat; and in still others, the applied stimuli caused great changes in pacemaker activity. Also temperature changes are known to modify the frequency of the discharge in the different neurons of electric fish and mollusks (Grundfest, 1965; Carpenter, 1967).

The facts mentioned in the previous paragraph argue in favor of the intracellular origin of pacemaker activity, although this does not mean that the reverberation theory has nothing to do with this kind of nervous activity. The evidence of the intracellular origin of pacemaker rhythm related to the pacemaker neurons was reinforced recently by the excellent work of Dr. B. O. Alving (1968) that was performed on the pacemaker neurons of the sea-hare *Aplysia*.

Isolating by ligatures the somata of neurons from the synaptic regions that are situated in *Mollusca* on the process of the cell at some distance from the soma, showed that the pacemaker locus is located on the soma. Despite the fact that no synaptic messages arrived at the soma, pacemaker activity persisted.

The point of the problem, however, is in the question, to what degree might Adrian's statement about a presumed tendency of the nerve cells to act, if not prevented, in synchronized autorepetitive activity, be expanded in reality. In other words, can every neuron under the appropriate conditions act as a pacemaker? At this point it is necessary to clarify what is meant by the term "pacemaker." This term is often found in the literature but seldom is its concrete meaning explained. As a consequence of this, there are several conceptions of the term "pacemaker" existing at the same time. One is that a neuron is considered "pacemaker" if it exhibits an autorepetitive spike activity. Another definition requires that a neuron, in addition to autorepetitiveness of spike generation, must "drive" other cells.

In our experiments on the different neurons of *Limnaea stagnalis,* we have found neurons which acted autorepetitively, but we could not say how they "drove" other cells. However, we do not regard this as a deficiency because the point of the problem, in this case, is something else. More important seems to be the fact that many neurons, without a permanent autorepetitive activity, might be triggered for a time to produce pacemaker potentials, but not necessarily the spikes "driving" the activity of other cells. Repetitive activity found in our experiments was of two kinds: Some neurons discharged permanently during all the experiment, while others only for some time after the penetration of the neuron by the microelectrode. Afterwards the latter gave trains of pacemaker potentials now and then spontaneously or as a response to the applied stimuli. The efficiency of these pacemaker potentials depended on their amplitude, which as a rule waxed and waned in time. This type of pacemaker activity was characteristic also of the neuron discussed in this paper, although by accepted criteria it does not fall into the group of pacemaker neurons.

In general it seems more reasonable to characterize a capability of neurons for pacemaker activity, not by a criterion of permanent autorepetitive spike activity or by presence of "driven" neurons, but first of all by a capability of the neuron to generate the pacemaker potentials. As became evident from our experiments (see Sokolov, Pakula, & Arakelov, 1969; Sokolov & Pakula, in press) many neurons considered nonpacemakers according to the criterion of permanent autorepetitiveness, often possessed latent pacemaker activity in the sense that they generated pacemaker potentials, which might or might not give rise to spike generation, depending upon whether the threshold was reached. This alludes to the possibility of the existence of an intrinsic mechanism of pacemaker potential generation in all "normal" neurons which may be discovered in certain neurons and not discovered in others, because of different concrete conditions. Such conditions might be the level of the membrane potential, temperature, functional state, and perhaps some others, in so far as they are known to influence the pacemaker activity in "pure" pacemaker neurons (Grundfest, 1961, 1965; Carpenter, 1967). These factors are supposed to influence the permeability of the neuron's membrane for sodium as well as the repolarizing mechanisms, both of them believed to determine the endogenous oscillatory changes of the membrane potential called pacemaker potentials (Grundfest, 1965). If this is really so, then it is evident that the generation of the pacemaker potentials should be in close relation with the metabolic processes occurring in the neuron, and might be triggered, activated, or blocked by induced alterations in these processes. At the same time, it is known that the bulk of the physiological rhythms are related to DNA, which controls the rhythm of different processes by means of the system DNA - m-RNA - protein. Therefore it is plausible that the capability for pacemaker activity, i.e., for generation of the pacemaker potentials, is determined by this system as it is supposed, for example, in another instance of the latent form of the neuron's repetitive response — in so-called "natural response" (Luco, 1964).

From the results obtained in the experiments performed on the A neurons of *Limnaea stagnalis* we have concluded that there exists the possibility of influencing neuron activity not only with electric current of high intensity, but also by involving internal mechanisms of the cell through the subthreshold electrical or mechanical stimulation of the nucleus. This kind of stimulation gives rise to the long-lasting aftereffects related to the activation or suppression of the endogenous pacemaker potential generation. Three types of aftereffects were encountered more frequently than others and all of them were present in A neuron, No. 39. They were:

(1) the cumulative effect, or summation of the subthreshold currents for several minutes, resulting in the appearance of a pacemaker potential (if positive ions were injected into the neuron) or in the disappearance of it (if negative ions were injected);

(2) the maintenance of the evoked repetitive spike generation for several minutes after the termination of the prolonged stimulation; and

(3) the decrease of the threshold for the triggering or blocking of pacemaker potential generation as a consequence of repeated, prolonged electric stimulation applied intracellularly.

No synaptic messages were found to play any role in these cases, while activation or suppression of the pacemaker potential generation was always evident. The possibility of controlling the generation of pacemaker potentials by direct electric stimulation of the cell's nucleus, either by mechanical stimulation of the latter (which is inevitable when a microelectrode is introduced into the cell; see Sokolov, Pakula, & Arakelov, in press), or by adequate stimuli, endow those neurons capable of exhibiting pacemaker activity with the mechanisms necessary to a realization of different kinds of aftereffects.

SUMMARY

1. One-Hundred-seventeen identified giant A neurons in the left parietal ganglion of *Limnaea stagnalis* were studied by intracellular technique.

2. Three kinds of nonsynaptic aftereffects were found as a consequence of a prolonged electric stimulation:

    a. appearance (if positive ions were injected into a neuron) or disappearance (if negative ions were injected) of a spike activity;

    b. maintenance of an evoked repetitive spike generation for a time after termination of stimulation; and

    c. decrease of the threshold for triggering or blocking activity after repeated stimulation.

3. All these aftereffects took place on the background of a stable membrane potential.

4. Aftereffects were determined by changes in a mechanism of pacemaker potential generation.

5. It is likely that the pacemaker mechanism is latently present in many neurons, and that it represents a special form of manifesting trace effects occurring in a cell and particularly in its nucleus.

REFERENCES

Alving, B. O. Spontaneous activity in isolated somata of Aplysia pacemaker neurons. *Journal of General Physiology*, 1968, **51**, No. 1, 29-45.

Bullock, T. H. Initiation of nervous impulses in receptor and central neurons. In G. M. Frank (Ed.), *Current problems in biophysics*. Moscow: Izdatel'stvo Innostr. Literat., 1961. Pp. 248-262. (In Russian)

Carpenter, D. O. Temperature effects on pacemaker generation, membrane potential, and critical firing threshold in *Aplysia* neurons. *Journal of General Physiology*, 1967, **50**, No. 6 (Pt. 1), 1469-1484.

Frank, K. Identification and analysis of single unit activity in the central nervous system. In J. Field & H. W. Magoun (Eds.), *Handbook of physiology, Sect. 1. Neurophysiology*, Vol. 1. Washington, D. C.: American Physiological Society, 1959. Pp. 261-277.

Grundfest, H. The mechanisms of discharge of the electric organs in relation to general and comparative electrophysiology. *Progress in Biophysics and Biophysical Chemistry*, 1957, **7**, 1.

Grundfest, H. Ionic mechanisms in electrogenesis. *Annals of the New York Academy of Sciences*, 1961, **94**, 405.

Grundfest, H. Some determinants of repetitive electrogenesis and their role in the electrical activity of the central nervous system. Proceedings of the International Symposium on Comparative and Cellular Pathophysiology of Epilepsy. *Excerpta Medica International Congress Series*, 1965, **124**, 19-46.

Holmgren, B., & Frenk, S. Inhibiting phenomena and "habituation" at the neuronal level. *Nature*, 1961, **192**, 1294, 1295.

Luco, J. V. Plasticity of neural function in learning and retention. In M. A. B. Brazier (Ed.), *Brain function.* Vol. 2. Berkeley: Univ. of California Press, 1964. 135-159.

Sokolov, E. N., Arakelov, G. G., & Levinson, L. B. Marking of the position of a microelectrode inside a separate neuron. *Tsitologiya,* 1966, 8, No. 4, 567-569. (In Russian)

Sokolov, E. N., Arakelov, G. G., & Levinson, L. B. "Habituation" to repetitive electrical stimuli by neurons showing no spontaneous activity in the gastropod mollusc *Limnaea stagnalis. Zh. Evol. Bioch. i Fiziol.,* 1967, 3, No. 2, 147-153. (In Russian)

Sokolov, E. N., Arakelov, G. G., & Pakula, A. Adaptation of the pacemaker neuron to microelectrodes in the visceral ganglion of the mollusc *Limnaea stagnalis.* In V. V. Parin (Ed.), *System organization of physiological functions.* Moscow: Meditsina, 1969. Pp. 65-75. (In Russian)

Sokolov, E. N., & Pakula, A. Responses of pacemaker neuron in the visceral ganglion of *Limnaea stagnalis* to intracellular electric shocks. In E. N. Sokolov et al. (Eds.), *Neuronal mechanisms of the orienting reflex* (in press).

Sokolov, E. N., Pakula, A., & Arakelov, G. G. Some features of adaptation to mechanical injury in the giant A neuron of *Limnaea stagnalis.* In E. N. Sokolov et al. (Eds.), *Neuronal mechanisms of the orienting reflex* (in press).

Sviderskij, V. L., & Karlov, A. A. Rhythm generator (pacemaker) in the motor center of the cicada *Lyristes plebeius.* In E. M. Kreps (Ed.), Evolutionary neurophysiology and neurochemistry. Leningrad: Nauka, 1967. Pp. 45-53. (In Russian)

Szabo, T., & Fessard, A. La facilitation de post-activation comme facteur de plasticite dans l'établissement des liaisons temporaires. In J. F. Delafresnaye (Ed.), *Brain mechanisms and learning.* Oxford: Blackwell, 1961. Pp. 353-373.

Tauc, L. Physiology of the nervous system. In K. M. Wilbur & C. M. Yonge (Eds.), *Physiology of mollusca,* Vol. 2. New York: Academic Press, 1966. Pp. 387-454.

Watanabe, A., Obara, S., & Akiyama, T. Acceleratory synapses on pacemaker neurons in the heart ganglion of a stomatopod, *Squilla oratoria. Journal of General Physiology,* 1969, 54, 212-231.

Yarmizina, A., Sokolov, E. N., & Arakelov, G. G. Identification of neurons of the left parietal ganglion of *Limnaea stagnalis. Neuroscience Translations,* 1969-1970, No.10, 1384-1389. (Originally appeared in *Tsitologiya,* 1968, 10 (11), 1384-1389.)

TRACE PHENOMENA IN SINGLE NEURONS
OF HIPPOCAMPUS AND MAMMILIARY BODIES

O. S. VINOGRADOVA
T. P. SEMYONOVA
V. Ph. KONOVALOV
Department of Memory Problems
Academy Center for Biological Research
Puschino-on-the Oka, USSR

Among the numerous hypotheses concerning the physiological bases of memory, the majority accepts as an axiom that at least the first stage of a trace formation is based upon some changes of the neuronal activity in the CNS. Even the theories that regard glial elements (Galambos, 1962, p. 52; Roitbak, 1969) or coherent oscillations in the neuronal networks (John, 1967) as the basis of the memory processes are not incompatible with the idea that the elements which code the information should somehow participate in the retention of this information, changing their patterns of activity. Until now we have not known much about the changes in neuronal reactions which represent the trace formation. Even the much discussed idea of reverberation in closed neuronal circuits is experimentally supported only by Verzeano's works (Verzeano & Negishi, 1961). In the last years many attempts to investigate different types of classical conditioning on the neuronal level were made, but the effect of conditioning, involving interaction of two different stimuli is often difficult to interpret. That is why the observation of the possible changes of the neuronal activity during repeated single stimulus presentations seems a justified approach to the problem.

In the light of the recent experimental and clinical data, we scarcely need to explain why limbic system structures were chosen by us as a major locus of investigation of trace phenomena. The data on relative rarity of plastic phenomena in the neurons of specific sensory relays and primary areas of the neocortex (Galeano, 1963; Sokolov, 1968) were also taken into account. For demonstration of the specificity of the obtained facts for the limbic structures, other areas of the brain were investigated by the same methods.

191

MATERIALS AND METHODS

The experiments were performed on 32 adult rabbits. Prior to the experiments, rabbits were operated on under Nembutal anesthesia in a stereotaxic apparatus (for the deep structures) or without drugs (for more superficial ones). In the skull, a trephine opening 5 mm. in diameter was made over the structure to be investigated. The dura was cut off and the opening filled with agar. A plastic plug was mounted over the opening with the help of dental cement. The reference electrode was placed on the nasal bone. Two days after the surgery, the experiments started. During the experiment, the animal was placed in a special box, restricting gross movements, but allowing a comfortable and natural position. The box with the animal was placed in a screened semidark and sound-proofed chamber. Each experiment lasted for 4 to 8 hours; from 5 to 10 experiments were performed with each animal.

For registration of single unit activity, extracellular tungsten microelectrodes with a tip diameter of 1 to 3 μm and with resistance in saline of 4 to 8 MΩ were used. Electrodes were inserted with the help of a distance hydraulic micro-drive (Hubel type). An amplifier with cathode follower (UBP-1-02) was used. The neuronal activity and stimulus artifacts were registrated on a two-channel tape recorder. Later some of the magnetic tape records were photographed from the screen of a two-beam cathode-ray oscilloscope.

During the experiments, different sensory stimuli were used: flashes of light, general illumination, clicks, pure tones, and air puffs. The stimuli could be varied in intensity, pitch, and duration. The interval between the stimuli usually was 5 sec.; it was changed only in some special conditions for special reasons.

The analysis of neuronal activity was performed by counting averaged post-stimulus time histograms with an interval counter for 100 or 200 msec. Individual PST histograms or block PST histograms (for blocks of 2 to 5 successive stimulus presentations) were used for evaluation of plastic changes of neuronal activity. In some cases an electronic analyzer "Neuron-1" was used for processing of the data.

RESULTS

The data presented in the paper were obtained from the extracellular records of the units in dorsal hippocampus (103), ventral hippocampus (98), and mammillary bodies (40). For comparison, in order to show relative specificity of the observed phenomena to the limbic structures, the data obtained by us earlier in other brain regions were used (visual cortex, Vinogradova & Lindsley, 1963; motor cortex, Vinogradova, 1966; caudate nucleus, Vinogradova, 1968a; a midbrain reticular formation, Konovalov & Vinogradova, 1970). The majority of units of dorsal and ventral hippocampus were recorded in the field CA_3 (Lorente de No, 1934).

I. General Characteristics of the Neuronal Activity in Hippocampus and Mammillary Bodies

The highest level of spontaneous firing was observed in dorsal hippocampus (averaged value 15-30 spikes per sec., with the maximal values 70-90). The firing was extremely irregular and consisted of long and short bursts intermingled with random single spikes and long silent periods. In ventral hippocampus, the mean firing frequency was lower (10-20 per sec.); some cells were almost devoid of spontaneous activity, in others activity was more regular than in dorsal hippocampus. In many mammillary body cells spontaneous firing of cells was completely absent; in others, it was typically very low (2-6 per sec.). Several neurons were observed with high and very regular spike activity (pacemaker type).

The level of responsiveness to the stimuli used in the experiments was approximately equal in all three structures (62% in dorsal hippocampus, 64% in ventral hippocampus, and 58% in mammillary bodies). Later we shall regard only these responsive units and all numbers will be given with respect to the responsive population.

The type of sensory input to these cells was also rather uniform. The majority of the cells were at least bimodal (responding to light and sound stimuli), though reactions to light were usually less prominent. All units responsive to pure tones showed absence of any selectivity ("optimal" or "characteristic" frequency), responding by the same reaction to the tones from .1 kcps up to 10 kcps. This was equally true for all three structures.

On the contrary, types of output reactions were very different in different structures. In both dorsal and ventral hippocampus, reactions were of a diffuse, tonic type, with the slight dominance (55 and 54%, correspondingly) of tonic inhibition over tonic excitation (48 and 32%). Only a small group of neurons had reactions of the patterned phasic type (7 and 16%). In the mammillary bodies, reactions as a rule were strictly phasic, without aftereffects, and usually of an excitatory type.

It is clear that a great similarity in basic features exists between the neuronal activity of dorsal and ventral hippocampus. Reactions in the mammillary neurons were also multimodal and had, as we shall show later, many common features in dynamics, but were nevertheless very different. Later we shall return to the discussion of the significance of these facts.

II. Types of Trace Phenomena in
Hippocampal and Mammillary Neurons

The facts that we are going to describe below are very different in manifestations, dynamics, and, most probably, in mechanisms. Still it seems to us that they all deserve some attention as possible expressions of the lasting changes within the nervous system which may be connected (or may not be) with the formation of the memory traces.

1. Long-Lasting Effects of a Single Stimulus Presentation

As was mentioned above, reactions of hippocampal neurons are of atonic type. Many of the units respond to a short stimulus (flash or click, 1-3 msec.) by an activation or by a pure inhibitory response lasting for 12 to 15 sec. Effect of longer stimuli (such as pure tones 300-500 msec. long and more) can be maintained up to 3 to 5 min. This type of event is very characteristic of dorsal hippocampus and of some units in ventral hippocampus (Fig. 1). But in the last structure, an important difference exists. In many cases neurons are not responsive to the short stimuli at all. Presentation of the single flashes, clicks, or pure tones up to 250 to 500 msec. produce almost no effect. For some neurons even longer stimuli are necessary to evoke a response (1 sec.). But as soon as the critical duration of a stimulus is reached, reaction reaches maximal value and is tonic in nature with a long-lasting aftereffect. This can be demonstrated by Fig. 2 where short signals (tone 60 cps, 140 msec.) remain inactive while the same tone 2 sec. long evokes an intense reaction with aftereffect. The length of the aftereffect depends approximately upon the stimulus duration, though some other dynamic effects (e.g., habituation) make this correlation not strictly obvious. Counting the average frequency of spikes per second during stimulus presentation and aftereffect shows that the constant level of spike activity is maintained throughout this time; only very slowly does it return to the prestimulus level. It is necessary to mention that the reactions of these neurons have very long latencies (equal to the duration of inactivity of the stimuli, i.e., 300-1000 msec.), at least during the few first presentations of the stimulus. Subsequent presentations, given sometimes after rather long intervals (several minutes—after the return of the cell activity to the prestimulus level), are able to evoke reactions with much shorter latencies.

It is possible that in the case of neurons with long-lasting reactions we observe a very strong effect of potentiation. From the work of Kandel & Spencer (1961), Andersen & Lomo (1967), and Andersen, Blackstad, & Lomo (1966) it is known that hippocampal pyramids display quite different reactivity to single electrical impulses than to repetitive stimulation (trains of impulses). The duration of this post-tetanic potentiation (or "frequency potentiation," Andersen & Lomo, 1967) lasts about 3 to 5 min., about the same values we observe in chronic experiments during the action of long sensory stimuli. So, synaptic

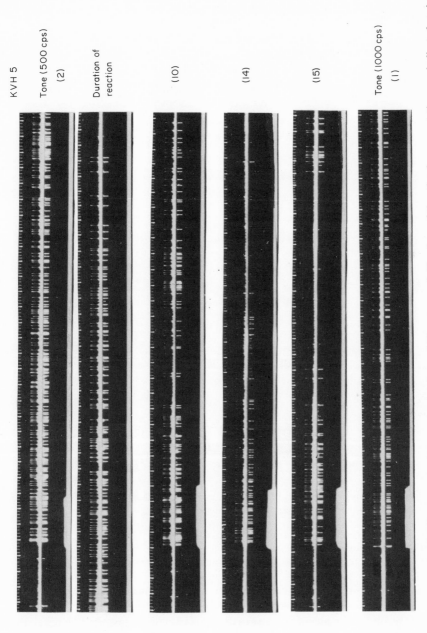

FIG. 1. An example of diffuse tonic excitatory reaction (ventral hippocampus). Numbers of the stimulus presentations are indicated at right. Stimulus (tone 500 Hz) is indicated at the lower part of the record. The second record is the direct continuation of the first. The last record represents the introduction of the changed stimulus (tone 1000 Hz). Time—200 msec.

potentiation may be considered as a mechanism of the long-lasting reactions, but a somewhat different explanation may also be added. The tonic nature of the hippocampal reactions was noticed already in the first microelectrode study of the hippocampus (Renshaw, Forbes, & Morison, 1940). It was supposed at this

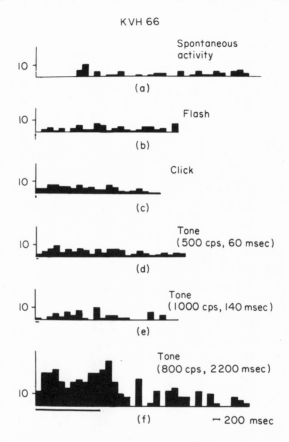

FIG. 2. Action of stimuli of different duration upon a cell of the ventral hippocampus. Averaged PST histograms for 10 successive stimuli presentations.

(a) spontaneous activity,   (d) tone 500 cps (60 msec),
(b) light flash (1 msec),   (e) tone 1000 cps (140 msec),
(c) click (3 msec),   (f) tone 800 cps (2200 msec. Period of counting–200 msec.

time that reverberation in closed circuits might be responsible for the effect. We want to underline that in some cases during the long-lasting effects it is possible to see regular groupings of spike activity. This rhythmic burst activity develops gradually in the course of a stimulus presentation and in the same way gradually disintegrates in the aftereffect. This can be seen in Fig. 3. This cell of ventral

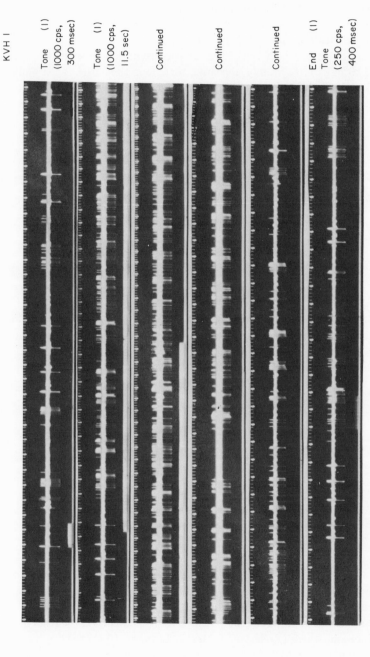

KVH 1

Tone (1)
(1000 cps,
300 msec)

Tone (1)
(1000 cps,
11.5 sec)

Continued

Continued

Continued

End (1)
Tone
(250 cps,
400 msec)

FIG. 3. Action of stimuli of different duration upon a cell of the ventral hippocampus. Appearance of rhythmic bursts during stimulation and in aftereffect. All records are continuous. The stimuli (tone—1000 cps, 300 msec and 11.5 sec; and tone—250 cps, 400 msec) are indicated below the records of spike activity. Time—200 msec.

hippocampus had irregular background activity of medium level with the signs of inactivation process (appearance of the "doublets," collated pairs of spikes with the pauses between them, regarded by some authors as a manifestation of inactivation, Creutzfeldt & Jung, 1961, p. 131). Application of a stimulus, after a long latent period, evoked high level burst activity (duration of a burst is approximately 110 msec.), recurrently appearing for a long time after the stimulus. At the end of the activation random spikes appear after which activity again stabilizes at a low level with occasional "doubles." The gradually developing periodic activity can be also demonstrated on neurons of dorsal hippocampus (Fig. 4),

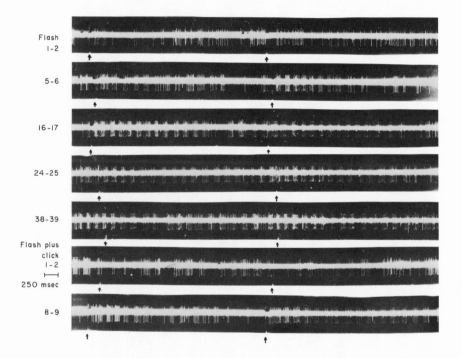

FIG. 4. Gradual formation of tonic responses with rhythmic bursts in a neuron of dorsal hippocampus. Stimulus (click) is indicated below the spike record. Numbers of presentations are indicated at the left. In the last two records, the stimulus is changed (click plus tone of 500 Hz; tone is not indicated in the record). Time calibration–250 msec.

where an initially nonactivating stimulus with each later presentation evokes more pronounced rhythmic activity which disappears after the stimulus change and then gradually reappears again.

Of course, this rhythmic activity can be explained also on the basis of recurrent inhibition, which (Andersen, Eccles, & Loyning, 1964a,b) is represented in hippocampus by the basket cell system and may play an important role in the hippocampal rhythmic processes. Still, the reverberation hypothesis also finds support in the anatomical structure of intra-hippocampal and extra-hippocampal connections. Presumably the combined explanation by post-tetanic potentiation in multisynaptic reverberating closed chains is the most probable explanation of the hippocampal long-lasting reactions.

2. Reaction Transformation during Repeated Presentations of the Stimuli

In our previous works, it was shown that the "novelty" of a stimulus is the special quality adequate for evocation and restoration of reactions in hippocampal neurons (Vinogradova, 1965, 1968b). During repeated presentations of the same stimulus in stable conditions, reaction to novelty became habituated. By the presence of this reaction, we may be able to differentiate "new" information from "old." In this context, "old" information is such information that has already formed its trace in the nervous system. Thus, the persistence of the reaction to a given "novelty" may be regarded as the measure of the speed of registration process, and habituation itself is seen as a negative manifestation of a memory trace formation.

The percentage of the neurons displaying habituation effects in the limbic system is high: 80% in dorsal hippocampus, 65% in ventral hippocampus, and about 50% in mammillary bodies.

a. The basic type of habituation process. The first presentation of a stimulus usually evokes the longest reaction. In the course of the following presentations of the same stimulus, the reaction becomes shorter, finishing closer to the onset of the stimulus; gradually it completely disappears. As a rule, latency of response increases at the same time only slightly. The initial intensity of the reaction also remains relatively stable, so that habituation consists primarily in shortening the response and not in the attenuation of the initial level of reaction (Fig. 1).

The average number of stimulus presentations (with the interval 3-5 sec.) sufficient for complete extinction of the response is about 10-15. There exists another group of neurons with a longer course of habituation—in these neurons habituation occurs only after 20 to 35 stimulus presentations. In a few cases, habituation was obtained after 3 to 5 stimuli. In one mammillary neuron, a reaction appeared only once, at the first presentation of stimulus. To evoke its reaction again, it was necessary to change the stimulus; after that a single reaction appeared again. It seemed that this neuron just marked the introduction of a new class of stimuli, but did not display real habituation to individual stimuli.

The basic feature of neuronal habituation − the gradual shortening of response—is equally characteristic of excitatory and inhibitory types of reaction. The critical test for habituation (against exhaustion, lowering of neuronal reactivity as a result of injury, etc.,) is the change of some single parameter of a stimulus while others remain constant. As a rule, any change of a stimulus produces restoration of the initial type of reaction. The restoration of the reaction is more complete, the greater the difference between stimuli, but even small changes have quite obvious dishabituating effects (Fig. 5).

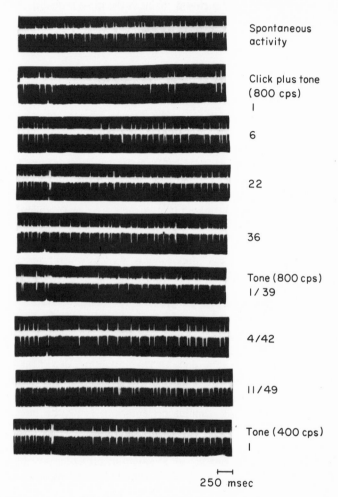

FIG. 5. Recovery of an inhibitory reaction after a stimulus change in a cell of dorsal hippocampus. (1) spontaneous activity, (2)-(5) presentation of a complex stimulus (click plus tone 800 cps), (6)-(8) tone 800 cps alone, and (9) first presentation of tone 400 cps. Time calibration–250 msec.

Specific features of the habituation process make it necessary to regard the shortening of neuronal reactions in the course of repeated presentations of a stimulus as an active inhibitory process with gradual potentiation. The mechanism of this phenomenon may be regarded as "collateral" or "parallel" inhibition (Eccles, 1964; Sokolov, 1966), though other mechanisms may also be taken into account (Horn, 1967).

The fact of immediate restoration of the reaction after a minor change of a stimulus together with the concept of the coding of different stimulus paramenters by different neuronal inputs (frequency-specific neurons, intensity-specific neurons, etc.,) was the basis of a hypothesis regarding the membrane of habituating neuron as a matrix of synaptic inputs (Sokolov, 1966; Horn, 1967). These inputs, representing different qualities of the stimulus, may be blocked or activated relatively independently. After habituation to one stimulus, the new one will activate the cell proportionally to the number of new synapses coming into action and inhibit it proportionally to the number of synapses shared with the first stimulus.

In this case, the degree to which the habituation of one stimulus influences the reaction to the next one may be regarded as a measure of the number of common shared synapses. In our experiments, it was possible to see that the level of such synaptic convergence of the same stimuli is different for different neurons (different level of "stimulus generalization"). While the majority of neurons responded to a change of stimulus by immediate brisk restoration of response, some of them showed a continuous tendency to habituation in spite of some stimulus change. The last case was more typical of ventral hippocampus neurons. The limits of these diffusely habituating stimuli varied widely with different neurons. In the case of generalized habituation, it was possible to show initially equal neuronal reactivity to all diffusely habituated stimuli by the intro-duction of long intervals between the series of different stimuli (Fig. 6).

b. Habituation with a backward shift of the reaction. As was described above, usually habituation consists of a progressive limiting of reaction duration. This type of habituation dominates in dorsal hippocampus and was observed also in some neurons of ventral hippocampus and mammillary bodies.

But in the last two structures, another type of dynamic was also observed. In terms of neuronal activity, where latency of response has very specific signifi-cance, the segregation of this type of habituation as a special form seems to be justified. Figure 7 represents the gradual changes in a tonic excitatory reaction (ventral hippocampus) during repeated presentations of the stimulus (pure tone–700 cps, 2 sec). The initial reaction appears with a latency of about 300 msec and continues for approximately 5 sec. Then, from one presentation to another, the reaction not only finishes earlier but also starts later, so that by the eighth presentation of the tone, the "latency" of the response reaches the value 1050 msec. Thus, the reaction becomes shifted towards the end of the stimulus. For convenience, we call this change of reaction "V-type habituation." The same effect is even more striking in the mammillary neurons with their phasic re-sponse type, where the reaction gradually seems to transform from "on-effect" to "off-effect" (Fig. 8). The change of the stimulus brings about in these

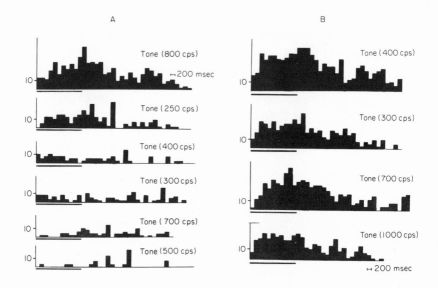

FIG. 6. Generalized habituation to tones in a cell of ventral hippocampus. Averaged PST histograms for 10 successive presentations of different pure tones (2 sec). Histograms are represented in order of application.

(A) intervals between series—30 sec., (B) intervals between series—5 min. Period of counting—200 msec.

neurons a double change of the reaction: sharp shortening of the initial inactive period and the prolongation of response. The opposite changes of these two reaction parameters are shown in Fig. 9.

The question arises about the nature of the observed reaction transformation. It is obvious that the dramatic increase of the initial delay of reaction cannot be explained on the basis of the usual increase of latency. The dynamics of the process with the radical decrease of the initial silent period after a change of stimulus indicates that this temporary delay is the result of an active inhibitory process, gradually potentiated during the repeated stimuli presentation. From the graphs of Fig. 9, it can be seen that initial inhibition (measured as "latency" duration) and final inhibition (inversely proportional to the length of reaction) are to some extent correlated, but their changes are not always parallel. Above we described the usual type of habituation with the increase of the final inhibitory process. In some cases (especially in mammillary neurons), it was possible to see the opposite effect: increase of the initial inhibitory process without expressed shortening of the reaction. This together with the different time characteristics of the described effects make us believe that we observe here two

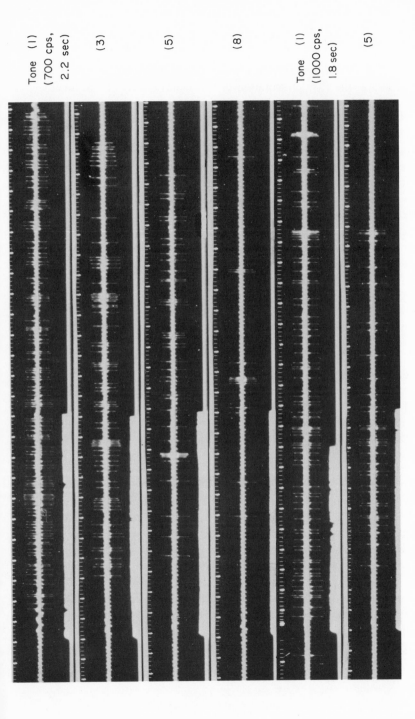

Tone (1)
(700 cps,
2.2 sec)

(3)

(5)

(8)

Tone (1)
(1000 cps,
1.8 sec)

(5)

FIG. 7. "V-type" habituation in a cell of ventral hippocampus. Stimulus (tone 700 cps) is indicated below the record of the spike activity. In the last two records, the stimulus is changed (tone 1000 cps). Time—200 msec.

different correlated inhibitory processes rather than only one. In this case a hypothetical inhibitory interneuron must gradually be building up its reaction, simultaneously introducing a time delay in the activity of the registered unit.

c. Habituation with an initial absence of reaction. In both types of neurons described above, the first presentation of a stimulus evokes the maximal reaction. A group of neurons was encountered both in ventral hippocampus and mammillary bodies in which the development of habituation was more complicated.

During the first presentations of a stimulus, reactions in these neurons were absent or scarcely noticeable and disorganized. Reaction developed gradually and then stabilized at maximal level for some time. In mammillary neurons, the full development of the reaction usually occurred by the third to fourth stimulus presentation. In the ventral hippocampus the formation of the reaction was longer; it appeared only after 7 to 12 repetitions of the stimulus. After that, the reaction persisted in ventral hippocampus neurons for 5 to 10 times, in mammillary neurons sometimes for longer periods, and then gradually declined toward zero. If during this period the stimulus is changed, there is no obvious effect: The reaction is still absent, but after a while it builds up again and undergoes the same course of extinction (Fig. 10a). The biphasic development of this process is represented graphically (Fig. 10b). The whole cycle of events in these neurons is completed in 2 to 3 min.

It is possible to explain the first stage of development of the reaction as a simple effect of potentiation and summation phenomena. This is also suggested by the fact that sometimes these effects were observed during repeated presentations of initially inactive short stimuli (250-500 msec.) in those neurons of ventral hippocampus which displayed "the critical time effect" (appearance of tonic effect after the sufficient duration of a stimulus). It was further noticed that in some cases after the introduction of a new series of stimuli of the same class (different pure tones), the appearance of the reactions occurred earlier with each new series (Fig. 11). But it is not easily explainable why this "summation" vanishes with subsequent presentations of the stimuli. Probably inhibitory processes with slower potentiation develop or those with higher thresholds are superimposed over initial exictatory events.

In the mammillary bodies, as we mentioned above, reaction formation occurs earlier and the late stage of habituation is more prolonged. In some cases, once they are formed, reactions show almost no tendency toward habituation. The course of events in these neurons with their phasic reactions resembles more a "stabilization" effect, observed in the neurons of specific sensory systems (Sokolov, 1968). It is possible that the group of neurons with an initial absence of reaction may include quite different types of units.

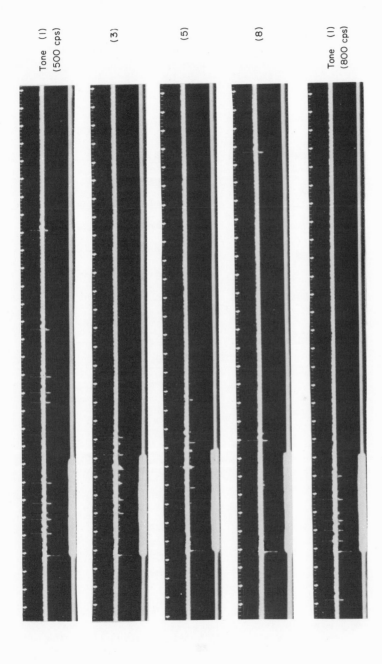

FIG. 8. "V-type" habituation in a cell of mammillary bodies. In the first four records—presentations of the tone 500 cps. In the last record, the stimulus is changed (800 cps). Time—200 msec.

3. Time-Conditioned Trace Effects

In recent years many papers have appeared describing the plastic effects of conditioned reflex elaboration on the neuronal level. Many different events have been described under this name. These experiments showed the possibility of the

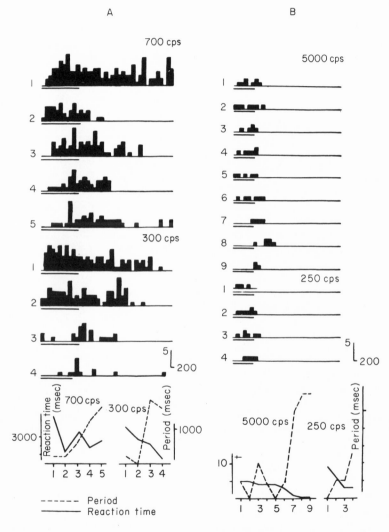

FIG. 9. Graphical representation of "V-type" habituation in ventral hippocampus (A) and mammillary bodies (B). Top: individual serial PST histograms. The changes of the stimuli are indicated for both cells (A–300 Hz after 700 Hz; B–250 Hz after 5000 Hz). Bottom: Graphs of "latency" durations and reaction duration for successive stimuli presentations and after the change of the initial stimulus.

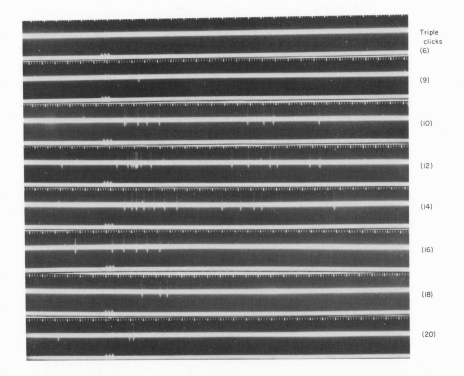

Triple
clicks
(6)

(9)

(10)

(12)

(14)

(16)

(18)

(20)

FIG. 10. Habituation with an initial inhibition of reaction in a cell of ventral hippocampus. Repeated triple click presentations; number of stimulus is indicated at the right. Time−200 msec.

plastic transformation of neuronal reactions, but events by no means can be regarded as usual and widely distributed in the observed neuronal populations (e.g., Bures & Buresova, 1967; Shulgina, 1967, p. 296; Gerbrandt, Skrebitsky, Buresova, & Bures, 1968).

We shall describe here only time-dependent trace-effects which were observed, without classical reinforcement procedures, in the course of repeated presentations of single stimuli with a constant interval between them.

a. Extrapolation phenomenon. During the investigation of the neurons in dorsal hippocampus (Vinogradova, 1965), it was shown that in approximately 10% of units the PST histograms reveal a very special "saucer-like" pattern of spike distribution. After the initial increase of firing, activity returned to the background level; then a new rise of activity occurred just before the moment of the next stimulus application. Analysis of individual spike distribution patterns revealed no such type of reaction or showed its existence only as a phasic event. In fact, the shift of the initial excitatory reaction occurred, so that it was

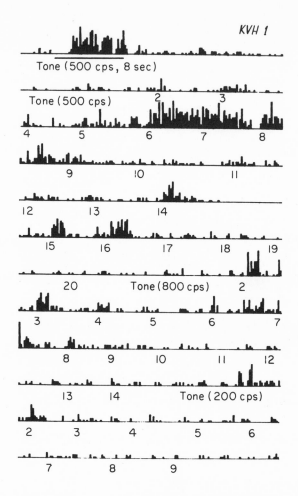

FIG. 11. "Running" histogram for a cell of ventral hippocampus, showing gradual reaction formation and extinction for consecutive series of stimuli. Period of counting—200 msec. Stimulus duration and number is indicated below the histograms. Notice the earlier appearance and habituation of the excitatory response with each subsequent series of stimuli. Before the sixth tone, 500 cps and during its seventh and eighth presentations, spontaneous activation with motor excitation of the animal occurred.

initiated before the next stimulus was applied; at the same time, the initial reaction became reduced, so that the number of spikes remained relatively constant, but the moment of the reaction initiation changed (Fig. 12). In some cases the development of the extrapolatory response occurred without the reduction of the initial response, as an additional prereaction. We were not able to find the same phenomenon in ventral hippocampus neurons. Maybe, at least partially, this was because of the extreme tonic reactions in this structure, so that the interval used (5 sec.) was not sufficient for demonstrating extrapolation in clear form.

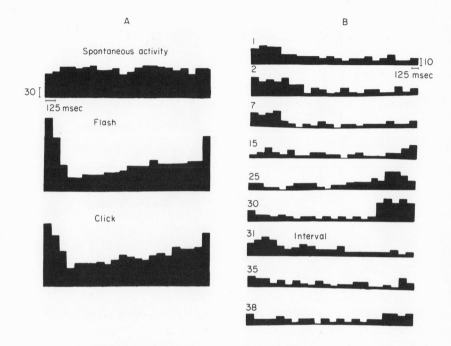

FIG. 12. Extrapolation phenomenon in the dorsal hippocampus cells. (a) Averaged PST histograms for spontaneous activity, flash, and click action, (B) individual PST histograms for another cell, showing gradual formation of extrapolatory response and its deterioration after unusual interval (before the seventh histogram). Period of counting–125 msec.

But in mammillary neurons with their low level or absent spontaneous activity and strictly phasic type reactions, the extrapolation phenomenon was even more clearly displayed. The counting of the PST histograms for blocks of five successive stimulus presentations showed quite convincingly the gradual development of extrapolatory reactions (Fig. 13). It is important to notice that the first signs of the extrapolatory reaction already appear after the first 3 to 5 stimuli followed by the constant interval. After a change of the interval, or the introduction of some extraneous stimulus, the extrapolatory effect deteriorates and then develops again.

Extrapolatory effects were observed in approximately 30% of mammillary units. It is interesting to note that in spite of the high number of neurons with inhibitory responses in the hippocampus, we never observed extrapolatory inhibitory effects. The same is true for the mammillary neurons, although the number

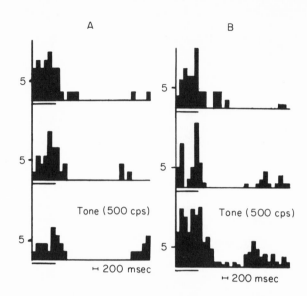

FIG. 13. Formation of extrapolatory effect in two cells (A and B) of the mammillary bodies. PST histograms for successive blocks of 5 stimuli (tone 500 cps, 1 sec). Period of counting–200 msec.

of neurons with inhibitory responses was much lower here. The cause of such differences between neurons with excitatory and inhibitory types of response is not clear.

b. Reproduction of the time characteristics of stimuli. In mammillary neurons where reactions usually reflect almost exactly the duration of a stimulus, it is possible to observe the trace reproduction of the time characteristics of the stimuli. If the stimulus is applied several times with constant duration (for example, 5 sec.) and then, without a change of the interval, the duration is altered, the evoked reaction is usually equal not to the current stimulus, but to the one applied before. This is equally true for a sudden decrease and a sudden increase of stimulus duration.

An example of the stability of the reaction duration in spite of a prolongation of the stimulus is showed in Fig. 14. After the application of a stimulus 1 sec. long, it was suddenly increased to 2 sec. As a result, only the first half of the stimulus evoked a reaction, while during the second the neuron remained inactive, although this was atypical for this phasic neuron. The second presentation evoked spikes throughout all of the 2-sec. period of stimulation, but even for several presentations following, the gap in grouping of the spikes after the first second of the stimulation could be noticed. In other cases, if after several presentations of a tone 1-sec. long, the stimulus is shortened to 200 or 300 msec., spikes appeared at the place of the absent end of the stimulus.

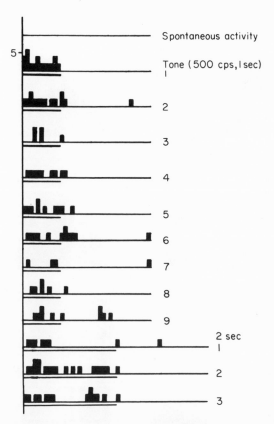

FIG. 14. Reproduction of the initial stimulus duration by a cell of the mammillary bodies. Individual PST histograms. Stimulus (tone 500 cps, first 1 sec., then 2 sec. long) is indicated below the histograms. Period of counting—200 msec.

The case of perseverance of the reaction length in spite of the stimulus shortening can be explained as a kind of extrapolatory activation phenomenon where reaction is determined by the preexisting excitation developed during previous presentations of a constant stimulus and released by the shortened stimulus. In the case of the shortening of a reaction on the background of a prolonged stimulus, it is necessary to suppose the existence of an extrapolating limiting inhibitory process, because interruption of the reaction occurs during continuous synaptic bombardment; but that means that such a limiting inhibitory process exists normally and participates in the formation and limitation of any phasic reaction.

c. *Perseverance of the reaction after the end of a stimulus series.* To some extent these effects resemble those described in the previous section. The differ-

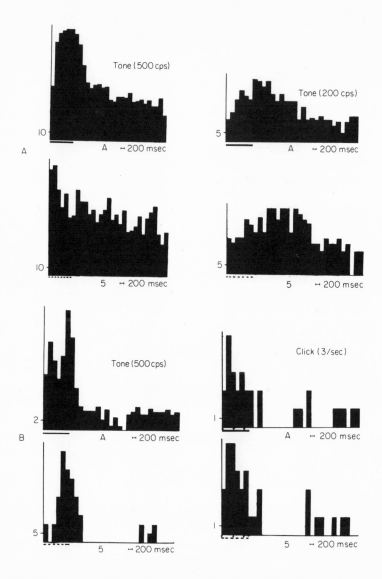

FIG. 15. Perseverance of a reaction pattern after the end of a stimulus series. (A) Two cells of the midbrain reticular formation, (B) two cells of the mammillary bodies. Averaged PST histograms for stimulation periods and equal number of postserial activity periods. For each cell, the upper histogram is the reaction to the actual stimulus (solid line below the histogram), the lower histogram represents the perseverance of the response (broken line below the histogram corresponds to the usual place and duration of the absent stimulus). Period of counting—200 msec.

ence consists in the fact of reaction reproduction without any stimulus presentation when only time remains as a releasing condition.

In these experiments, stimuli were applied as usual with a stable interval of 5
sec. After the end of a series, spike distribution was counted for periods equal to
the time from the beginning of one stimulus to the beginning of the next one.
The PST histograms obtained in this way revealed a persistence of the initial
reaction patterns after switching off the stimulus. This fact is shown in Fig. 15A
and B. Figure 15B demonstrates the reproduction of the pattern of the phasic
reactions by two neurons in the mammillary bodies. It is possible to observe the
same fact in some units of the midbrain reticular formation. Figure 15A shows,
for comparison, the reproduction of the tonic excitatory reactions by two reticular neurons: one with early and another one with late augmentation of activity.
Such effects were observed also in some neurons of dorsal and ventral hippocampus. It is important that in studying poststimulus neuronal activity, not only
general increase of firing, but also duration and exact shape of the reaction is
reproduced.

In the two ventral hippocampus neurons, reproduction of the inhibitory reactions was observed. In one of them, an inhibitory effect was observed after
switching off the click (Fig. 16). In another case, series of different stimuli were

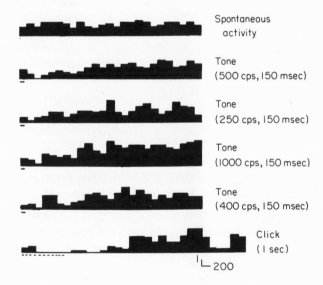

FIG. 16. Perseverance of the inhibitory response in a cell of ventral hippocampus. After
several series of stimuli, onset is increased. Note the reproduction of the inhibitory reaction
at the usual place of the stimulus beginning. Consecutive averaged PST histograms. Period of
counting–200 msec.

used with a standard interval of 5 sec. After that the interval was increased up to 6 sec. The definite period of inhibition was reproduced exactly after the end of the 5-sec. period.

In a few rare cases, where we tried to elaborate a classical conditioned reflex while pairing sensory stimuli, inactive and active for a given cell as was described by several authors, we did not see the conditioned effect. The first inactive ("conditioned") stimulus never acquired the ability to reproduce the effect of the following active ("reinforcement") stimulus. But it was possible to see that an active stimulus preceding an inactive one facilitates the display of the time-dependent effects. An example is the exact reproduction of the pattern evoked by the tone 500 cps after it was switched off, when only the triple light flash usually given before the tone remained, shown in Fig. 17. In such cases, the initial stimulus is acting as an additional marker of time and facilitates the appearance of the time-dependent effect.

The described effects can be observed for as long as 7 to 10 times in the background activity. Sometimes they persist even longer (for 2-3 min.). The uppermost limit of such continuing phenomena has not yet been evaluated in our experiments. It is important to note that these continuing reactions appear after a few presentations of the stimuli (5-10). The effect is less expressed or completely absent if the serial application of the stimuli is stopped later, after 30-50 presentations. This is easily explained for neurons with habituating reactions, but it is equally true for neurons with stable reactions. Maybe it is a result of an excitatory mechanism blockade which becomes developed by this time. Perhaps these mechanisms are necessary for the circulation of excitation or for the realization of otherwise subthreshold time-dependent processes.

DISCUSSION

I. Comparison between the General Type of Neuronal Reactions in the Limbic System and in Other Brain Structures

From the description above it is obvious that, judging by the general type of activity, the dorsal hippocampus and ventral hippocampus constitute an entity. They are both characterized by high and irregular spontaneous activity, by reactions of multimodal, diffuse, and tonic type without any specific and stable pattern, and by slight dominance of inhibitory reactions over excitatory ones. From the data available in the literature, it is possible to conclude that the closest resemblance exists between hippocampal and amygdalar neuronal activity (Gloor, 1961, p. 1; Sawa & Delgado, 1963; Machne & Segundo, 1956; Creutzfeldt, Bell, & Adey, 1963). This is not surprising, considering the close relations between these two limbic structures. Resemblance exists also between hippo-

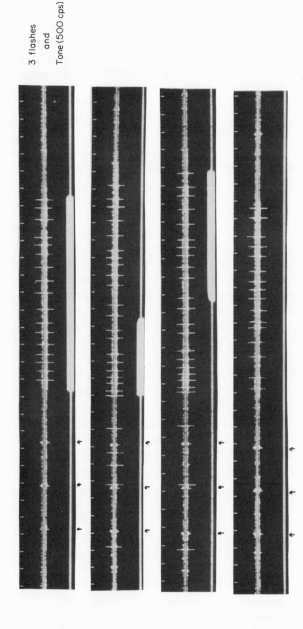

3 flashes
and
Tone (500 cps)

FIG. 17. Reproduction of the reaction pattern by a cell of the mammillary bodies. The cell does not respond to a triple light flash (indicated by the artifacts on the line of record); it responds to the tone (500 cps, 1 sec. indicated below the record) by phasic activation. Pairing of flashes and tone does not lead to elaboration of conditioned effect to flash, but after shortening or switching-off of the tone, reaction is steadily reproduced at the usual place of the absent tone after flashes. Time—200 msec.

campal activity and that of the midbrain reticular formation (Hill & Horn, 1964; Bell, Sierra, Buendia, & Segundo, 1964). According to our own observations, spontaneous activity of the reticular neurons is even higher (average frequency 20-80 per sec.) and in comparison with hippocampus is more stabilized and regular. The general type of reactions to sensory stimuli is also close to the hippocampal ones, although here an inverse relation exists between the number of excitatory and inhibitory reactions. This similarity is also understandable because of the significant anatomical connections of these structures and their suspected functional antagonism.

In spite of great similarity of activity in dorsal and ventral hippocampus, some differences should also be mentioned. These differences can be summarized as follows: The latencies of the reactions in ventral hippocampus, their duration, and some peculiarities of the dynamics (more generalized habituation, prolonged time of the reactions' recovery, etc.) seem to indicate more multisynaptic connections for the ventral hippocampus as compared to the dorsal one. Maybe this shows the secondary nature of the processes in the ventral hippocampus; this is compatible with data on the course of the spreading of seizure activity in hippocampus (Elul, 1964; Psatta & Ungher, 1965).

The lack of resemblance between hippocampal and mammillary reactions was for us rather unexpected. Low-level or absent spontaneous activity, strictly phasic, stimulus-bound type reactions, resemble more closely those of some specific sensory relays (such as colliculi, for example). It is known that the mammillary nuclei have an origin different from other limbic structures. It was shown also that neurons in the mammillary bodies histologically resemble those of specific sensory nuclei (Leontovich, 1968). Nevertheless, the main inputs to this structure are the massive fornix system from hippocampus and mammillary peduncle from the tegmental nuclei of the reticular formation, i.e., from the two structures with expressed unspecific (diffuse and tonic) type of activity. It is difficult to imagine how it is possible that the output of mammillary neurons does not reflect the features of the input; or if we accept this possibility, what the significance of such recoding might be.

Of course, there are certain characteristics of mammillary neurons that are unusual for specific structures. We showed that they are characterized by a high degree of sensory convergence. In complete accordance with the hippocampal mode of reactivity, mammillary neurons respond to all elements of the tonal scale without any "optimal" frequency or band of frequencies. Reactions of mammillary neurons are phasic, but they are not patterned in the strict sense of the word, as reactions of the specific sensory neurons usually are. We did not observe in the reactions of mammillary neurons typical alternations of excitatory and inhibitory phases-reactions. Rather uniform spiking throughout the stimulus duration or in inhibition of spontaneous discharge occurred. It is also worth mentioning that though mammillary neurons respond to short stimuli (flashes and clicks), the optimal responses are usually obtained with more prolonged (up to 500 to 1000 msec.) stimuli. These features, together with the strongly expressed dynamic aspect of activity (habituation, extrapolatory effects, time-dependent trace reactions) show that mammillary neurons occupy an intermediate place between the limbic and the specific sensory systems of the brain.

II. Evaluation of the Described Trace Phenomena

The common feature of hippocampal and mammillary neurons is the high number of units displaying trace phenomena (60-80%). We described several forms of them, different in manifestations and possible underlying mechanisms. From the description given above it may be seen that different trace phenomena are to a different degree expressed in the three limbic structures: The long-lasting reactions depending upon stimulus duration are proper for ventral hippocampus; habituation processes are best expressed in dorsal hippocampus; and conditioned time-dependent effects are encountered primarly in the mammillary bodies. We would not make any special conclusions on this basis just because the real significance of each of these effects and their relevance to the memory processes is not as yet clear. But as we mentioned at the beginning, the almost complete absence of knowlege about the form of expression of the functional stage of memory makes us regard without prejudice all neuronal effects that outlast the time of a stimulus. It is necessary to keep in mind that all these events develop simultaneously in the course of a stimulus presentation and that complicated forms of integration should exist between them. Their final integration possibly participates in some special forms of information processing and memory trace formation.

We are not enthusiastic about superficial analogies, but comparison of some different sets of facts may be relevant to the problem under discussion.

The comparison of reaction latencies and duration resulting from sensory stimulation given in the current literature for neurons of different brain regions, shows the special place occupied by the limbico-reticular system. Both latencies and reaction durations are maximal for hippocampus, amygdala, and reticular formation; mammillary bodies are equal to them in latencies, although different in reaction duration. Using available data on the parameters of neuronal reactions to adequate stimuli in specific sensory structures, it is possible to see that the mean latency of the neuronal reactions is about 10 to 60 msec. (with the maximal values for visual cortex of 100 to 300 msec.) and mean reaction duration about 70 to 300 msec. For the limbic structures, the corresponding values are 60-300 msec. and more than 1000 msec. This means that here information processing only starts when it is almost finished in specific sensory structures and greatly outlasts all residual events in them.

If this secondary processing of information is (at least partly) relevant to memory trace formation, a comparison with data on short-term memory may be interesting. The great discrepancies in the evaluation of the period of short-term memory are well known. In the last decade, experimental psychology has presented evidence for the length of the vulnerable stage of memory ranging from a few seconds to several days. Now it is clear that not only the differences in methods and criteria used, but also the complex nature of the preconsolidatory stage, which includes more than one process, is responsible for this discrepancy. Still the evidence accumulates that the earliest ("reverberatory") functional stage lasts for several minutes. For example, Albert (1966) experimentally evaluates this initial stage as equal to 3 min. It may be worthwhile to recall that the effects described in this paper have approximately the same time values. The maximal duration of the long-lasting reaction of the habituation process (i.e., negative expression of the trace formation), and of time-dependent reaction perseverances are approximately 2-3 min. long. It is possible that this is not mere coincidence. If the described phenomena (or some of them) may be regarded as potention participants in the early stage of the trace formation, their widespread presence in the limbic structures confirms on the neuronal level the long-suspected participation of these structures in the processes of learning and memory.

III. Concluding Remarks on the Dynamic Processes in Limbic Structures

At the present stage of the development of neurophysiology, it is possible to ascertain the existence of the two great systems of information processing in the brain. The first, dealing with reception and primary processing of sensory information, may be regarded as the system of objective reflection of the relatively stable sensory environment. The functioning of this system (which includes sensory relays up to the highest levels of the primary cortical areas) is within wide limits independent of the influences of the present level of activity, emotional state, or influence of the past experience of an organism. With some exceptions, described in the current literature (e.g., Horn & Hill, 1966; Spinelli & Weingarten, 1966), neuronal reactions in these structures are characterized by high stability of the pattern. These reactions, as a rule, do not habituate in the course of the repeated stimulus presentations; on the contrary, they became stabilized (Sokolov, 1968). Only late components, presumably dependent upon unspecific activating influences, undergo reduction and may disappear. It should be mentioned that, as our experiments showed, the same type of activity is characteristic of caudate nucleus neurons (Vinogradova, 1968).

The evidence supporting the fact that the quality of novelty of the stimulus and not any other physical parameters serves as the special stimulus for the hippocampal neuronal reactions is discussed by us elsewhere (Vinogradova, 1965, 1968b). Analysis of the hippocampal reactions to novelty, together with other anatomical and physiological data, makes us support the concept of the hippocampus as a comparator of signals, as it is regarded by a number of authors

(McLardy, 1959; Adey, 1962, p. 203; Pickenhein & Klinberg, 1967). The hippo-campus may provide for comparison between current stimuli and corresponding traces through selective filtering of "old" or irrelevant information. This would be possible through the mechanism of blocking the orienting reflex, presumably by hippocampal antagonistic inhibitory influences upon the midbrain reticular formation. On the other hand, by producing long-lasting tonic pulses, hippocampus may increase the time of poststimulus activity, acting as a mechanism for augmenting the dynamic processes predetermining the stage of consolidation. But the diffuse, unpatterned, and generalized characteristics of the hippocampal reaction prevents us from making the hypothesis of a direct participation of the hippocampus in the registration of the discrete memory traces. It is more proba-ble, that in the process of memory trace formation, the hippocampus plays a necessary but auxillary role.

At any rate, hippocampal neuronal reactions more closely resemble para-meters of the orienting reflex, appearing as a powerful and continuous control-ling signal. Reactions of mammillary neurons are more stimulus-bound and pre-serve at least the time-dependent characteristics of the stimuli. This suggests that the mammillo-thalamic system may be more intimately connected with the spe-cific content of the registered information.

SUMMARY

Neuronal activity was registered by extracellular microelectrodes in the dorsal hippocampus, ventral hippocampus, and mammillary bodies of unanesthetized rabbits. Different trace phenomena, observed during repeated presentations of sensory stimuli were described: tonic reactions with long-lasting aftereffects, different types of habituation, and conditioned time-dependent effects (extra-polation, reproduction of stimulus duration, perseverance of the reaction pattern in background activity). The number of responsive units displaying different types of trace phenomena was very high (from 60 to 80%) in the investigated limbic structures.

In both dorsal and ventral areas of hippocampus, reactions were very much alike (multimodal, diffuse, and tonic), but reactions in ventral hippocampus seem to be more multisynaptic. Hippocampal reaction characteristics were close to orienting reflex parameters, and presumably were involved in its regulation through controlling inhibitory influences upon midbrain reticular formation. Reactions of mammillary neurons were quite different: phasic and stimulus-bound. They occupied an intermediate place between reactions of specific and unspecific systems and were more intimately connected with registered information.

ACKNOWLEDGMENT

We acknowledge our gratitude to Dr. Kristi Kultas for her valuable and continuous help in histological analysis of the data.

REFERENCES

Adey, W. R. EEG studies of hippocampal system in the learning process. In *Physiologie de la hippocampe*, Montpellier: 1962.

Albert, D. J. The effect of spreading depression on the consolidation of learning. *Neuropsychologia*, 1966, 4, 65.

Andersen, P., Blackstad, T. W., & Lømo, T. Localization and identification of excitatory synapses on hippocampal pyramidal cells. *Experimental Brain Research*, 1966, 1, 236.

Andersen, P., Eccles, J. C., & Loyning, P. Localization of postsynaptic inhibitory synapses on hippocampal pyramids. *Journal of Neurophysiology*, 1964, 17, 592. (a)

Andersen, P., Eccles, J. C., & Loyning, P. Pathway of postsynaptic inhibition in the hippocampus. *Journal of Neurophysiology*, 1964, 27, 608. (b)

Andersen, P., & Lomo, T. Control of hippocampal output by afferent volley frequency. *Progress in Brain Research*, 1967, 27, 400.

Bell, C., Sierra, G., Buendia, N., & Segundo, J. P. Sensory properties of units in mesencephalic reticular formation. *Journal of Neurophysiology*, 1964, 27, 961.

Bureš, J., & Burešová, O. Plastic changes of unit activity based on reinforcing properties of extracellular stimulation of single neurons. *Journal of Neurophysiology*, 1967, 30, 98.

Creutzfeldt, O., Bell, F. R., & Adey, W. R. The activity of neurons in the amygdala of the cat following afferent stimulation. *Progress in Brain Research*, 1963, 3, 31.

Creutzfeldt, O., & Jung, R. Neuronal discharge in the cat's motor cortex during sleep and arousal. In G. E. Wolstenholme (Ed.), *The nature of sleep,* Ciba Foundation Symposium. London: Churchill, 1961.

Eccles, J. C. The Physiology of synapses. Berlin: Springer, 1964.

Elul, R. Regional differences in the hippocampus of the cat. *Electroencephalography and Clinical Neurophysiology*, 1964, 16, 470.

Galambos, R. Glia, neurons and information storage. In P. O. Schmitt (Ed.), *Macromolecular specificity and biological memory,* Cambridge, Mass.: M. I. T. Press, 1962.

Galeano, G. Electrophysiological aspects of brain activity during conditioning: A review. *Acta Neurologia Latinoamericana*, 1963, 9, 395.

Gerbrandt, L. K., Skrebitsky, V. G., Burešová, O., & Bureš, J. Plastic changes of unit activity induced by tactile stimuli followed by electrical stimulation of single hippocampal and reticular neurons. *Neuropsychologia*, 1968, 6, 3.

Gloor, P. Etudes electrographiques de certaines connexions rhinencephaliques. In T. Alajouanine (Ed.), *Physiologie et patologie du rhinencephale,* Vol. 2. □ □: □ □, 1961.

Hill, R. M., & Horn, G. Responsiveness to sensory stimulation of cells in the rabbit midbrain. *Journal of Physiology (London)*, 1964, 175, 40P,

Horn, G. Neuronal mechanisms of habituation. *Nature*, 1967, 215, 707.

Horn, G. A neural basis for the novelty response. In E. N. Sokolov & O. S. Vinogradova (Eds.), *Neuronal mechanisms of the orienting reflex.* Moscow: Univ. Press, 1968.

Horn, G., & Hill, R. M. Responsiveness to sensory stimulation of units in the superior colliculus and subjacent tecto-tegmental regions of the rabbit. *Experiemtnal Neurology*, 1966, 14, 199.

John, E. R. *Mechanisms of memory.* New York: Academic Press, 1967.

Kandel, E. R., & Spencer, W. A. Electrophysiological properties of an archicortical neuron. *Annals of the New York Academy of Sciences,* 1961, **94**, 570.

Konovalov, V. Ph., & Vinogradova, O. S. Trace phenomena in reactions of neurons in mammillary bodies. *Zh. Vyss. Nervn. Deyat.,* 1970, **20**, 215.

Leontovich, T. P. On the problem of emotions. *Uspekhi Sovrem. Biol.,* 1968, **65**, 35.

Lorente de No, R. Studies on the structure of the cerebral cortex. II. Continuation of the study of the Ammonic system. *Journal fur Psychologie und Neurologie,* 1934, **46**, 113.

McLardy, T. Hippocampal formation of brain as detector-coder of temporal patterns of information. *Perspectives in Biology and Medicine,* 1959, **2**, 443.

Machne, X., & Segundo, J. P. Unitary responses to afferent volleys in amygdaloid complex. *Journal of Neurophysiology,* 1956, **19**, 232.

Pickenhein, L., & Klinberg, F. Hippocampal slow wave activity as a correlate of basic behavioral mechanisms in the rat. *Progress in Brain Research,* 1967, **27**, 218.

Psatta, D., & Ungher, J. Electro-anatomo-clinical correlations in seizures determined by hippocampal lesions. *Electroencephalography and Clinical Neurophysiology,* 1965, **18**, 643.

Renshaw, B., Forbes, A., & Morison, B. R. Activity of isocortex and hippocampus. Electrical study with micro-electrodes. *Journal of Neurophysiology,* 1940, **7**, 74.

Roitbak, A. I. A hypothesis about the mechanism of temporary connection formed during elaboration of conditioned reflex. Gagrskye Besedy, 1969.

Sawa, M., & Delgado, J. M. R. Amygdala unitary activity in the unrestrained cat. *Electroencephalography and Clinical Neurophysiology,* 1963, **15**, 637.

Shulgina, G. I. Investigation of the activity of neurons in the cerebral cortex at early stages of a conditioned reflex elaboration. In V. S. Rusinov (Ed.), *The modern problems of the electrophysiology of CNS.* Moscow: 1967.

Sokolov, E. N. Neuronal mechanisms of the orienting reflex. *18th International Congress of Psychology, Symposium, Moscow,* 1966, Vol. 5, p. 31.

Sokolov, E. N. Investigation of the memory on neuronal level. *Zhurnal Vysshei Nervnoi Deiatelnosti,* 1967, **17**, 909.

Sokolov, E. N. Neuronal mechanisms of the orienting reflex. In *Neuronal mechanisms of the orienting reflex,* Moscow: Univ. Press, 1968.

Spinelli, D. N., & Weingarten, M. Afferent and efferent activity in single units of the cat's optic nerve. *Experimental Neurology,* 1966, **15**, 347.

Verzeano, M., & Negishi, K. Neuronal activity in wakefulness and sleep. In G. E. Wolstenholme (Ed.), *The nature of sleep, Ciba Foundation Symposium.* London: Churchill, 1961.

Vinogradova, O. S. Dynamic classification of responses to sensory stimuli in the hippocampal neurons of the rabbit. *Zhurnal Vysshei Nervnoi Deiatelnosti,* 1965, **15**, 501.

Vinogradova, O. S. Habituation of neuronal reactions in different structures of brain with the special reference to hippocampus. *18th International Congress of Psychology, Symposium, Moscow,* 1966. Vol. 5, p. 55.

Vinogradova, O. S. Investigation of habituation in the caudate neurons of the rabbit. *Zhurnal Vysshei Nervnoi Deiatelnosti,* 1968, **18**. (a)

Vinogradova, O. S. Hippocampus and the orienting reflex. In *Neuronal mechanisms of the orienting reflex,* Moscow: Univ. Press, 1968. (b)

Vinogradova, O. S. & Lindsley, D. F. Extinction of reactions to sensory stimuli in single neurons of the visual cortex of the unanesthetized rabbit. *Zhurnal Vysshei Nervnoi Deiatelnosti,* 1963, **13**, 48.

INVESTIGATIONS OF PLASTICITY
IN SINGLE UNITS
IN THE MAMMALIAN BRAIN

L. GERBRANDT,[1] J. BUREŠ, AND O. BUREŠOVÁ
Institute of Physiology
Prague, Czechoslovakia

Two questions are legitimately asked of the physiological psychologist who wishes to study learning processes with microtechniques. First, it is questionable whether any current microelectrode preparations involve learning, since an important feature of learning is its permanence, and it is presently difficult to record from the same cell for more than a few hours. Also, when confronted with such examples as the development and maintenance of epileptic mirror foci in the cerebral cortex (Morrell, 1961), the setting and pacing of diurnal rhythms in the abdominal ganglion of the sea slug (Strumwasser, 1965), or the "acquisition and discrimination" of heterosynaptic facilitation in the same abdominal ganglion (Kandel & Tauc, 1965), to ask "Is this learning?" is justified. Or to avoid the usual semantic cul-de-sac, "Is this what we commonly understand as learning?" Second, when confronted with the degree of connectivity in the brain as is evidenced by Lashley's mass action findings (1950) or the finding by Norton, Frommer, & Galambos (1966) that 2% of the optic nerve is sufficient for pattern discrimination, it is necessary to ask, "How do you know that your electrode is not simply picking up the consequences of learning in another area?"

These two questions are illuminating because they characterize the extremes in the *family* of learning, which has one parent of common sense and another of scientific rigor. With such a heterozygous background, it is not surprising that each offspring has its own set of biases, methods, and techniques for the study of learning processes. Our bias, which is typical of many physiological psychologists, is that greater distances from the inputs and outputs of an active system necessitate the disadvantage of greater inferences about, and less control over,

[1] Present address: Neuropsychology Laboratory, Veterans Administration Hospital, West Haven, Connecticut.

the system of concern. Some investigators prefer such great control over the system that the risk that they are not studying common learning processes is of little concern. Other investigators wish to maximize the learning phenomena to the extent that an attempt to locate and study the learning system (other than in the organism) is of little concern. Our goal is to move the microelectrode as close as possible to the active learning system while ensuring the likelihood that a familiar form of learning is occurring. How can we have our learning and study it too?

In order to maximize the chance that our preparations are related to the learning process of concern to the field of psychology, our experiments use a mammal commonly recognized as capable of learning (hooded rat), use paradigms common in investigations of learning (classical conditioning, habituation), and explore brain structures often suspected of participating in the learning process (cerebral cortex, reticular formation, medial thalamus, and hippocampus). In addition, the experiments are formulated and the results are assessed by a matrix of characteristics common to learning phenomena. We assess learning[2] by the following criteria:

(1) Acquisition: A change in input-output functions away from a baseline must occur as a result of new input exposure (reinforcement, habituation, matching).

(2) Reversibility: A reversal back to a baseline input-output function must occur as a result of withdrawal of the new input condition that produced the acquisition (extinction, dishabituation, mismatch).

(3) Representation: Some configurational isomorphism of what is learned and what is an input or output to the system should be evident in the learning system (stimulus and response generalization gradients, discrimination, and differentiations).

(4) Permanence: That a system has "learned" something requires that at a later time it "remember" something (the more lasting the trace, the better).

Finally, to assess whether our preparation has been "classically conditioned" or "habituated," an evaluation by an even greater number of criteria (cf. Kimble, 1961; Thompson & Spencer, 1966) is required.

The microelectrode technique is especially susceptible to the difficulty that the unit being recorded from, although showing a change away from baseline, has not learned anything but is merely reflecting a change in another system. Connectivity within and between brain structures is sufficient that the many claims for location of active learning units must be regarded sceptically. In order to lessen this difficulty, we have used the recording microelectrode itself as a

[2]In common sense usage, "learning" refers to the acquisition of knowledge or skill. Learning to know or to do, however, involves the prerequisite acquisition of basic "what, where, and when" information before any knowledge or skill can be demonstrated. We therefore include these sources of increments in performance in the phenomena of learning.

source of the "information" to be learned. In the classical conditioning para-digm, for example, after delivery of a sensory CS (acoustic or tactile), the UCS may be delivered to the single unit by an extremely small polarization current applied to the micropipette. The polarization can be used either to excite or inhibit unit firing by making the voltage anodal or cathodal. Tests of the revers-ibility of the process can be made by withdrawing the paired polarization. Al-though the polarization "information" can be delivered in several ways (as a CS, a reinforcer, or a dishabituator), we report here our results where microelectrode polarization serves as an UCS in a classical conditioning paradigm. In addition, studies are reported which show the "unconditioned" effect of microelectrode polarization on unit firing to sensory input.

UNLEARNED (UNCONDITIONED) PHENOMENA

All experiments were performed on unanesthetized, curarized rats aged 3 months. Capillary microelectrodes filled with 3 M KCl or saturated sodium glutamate were used for both extracellular recording and stimulation. The ampli-fied activity was fed into an electronic analyzer programmed for plotting post-stimulus histograms (PSHs). Unit activity was counted in each of nine successive decade counters, the counting time of which could be programmed from .3 to 1.0 sec. Usually 6-60 trials were accumulated to make one PSH. The polarizing current, usually anodal and between 10 and 40 nA, and the peripheral sensory stimulus could be programmed to occur during any of the nine sampling inter-vals on a trial. Either an acoustic (2000 Hz.) or a tactile (puff of air to eye-cheek area) stimulus was used as sensory input.

Two sets of experiments were run that were intended to produce "unlearned" reactions. In the first experiment (Bureš & Burešová, 1965), the acoustic stimu-lus was simply imbedded on a background of polarization, and the unit activity in the inferior colliculus was studied as a function of increased anodal or cath-odal polarization current, and hence altered "background" firing rate. Essential-ly two classes of reaction were observed during current polarization in the acous-tically responsive neurons. In some units (40%), the sensory input incremented (Fig. 1) by the same amount, in spite of large increases in background firing rates. These additive units comply with the conventional model of a nerve cell based on the electrophysiological properties of spinal motoneurons (Granit, Kernell, & Lamarre, 1966). If residual alterations in firing rates carried over from the UCS of one trial to the pre-CS and CS periods of the next trial, these unconditioned reactions would not be mistaken for conditioning. The reactivity to the input is not changed and could be detected by testing for pre-CS and CS effects before the conditioning period. A second group of units (40%) incre-

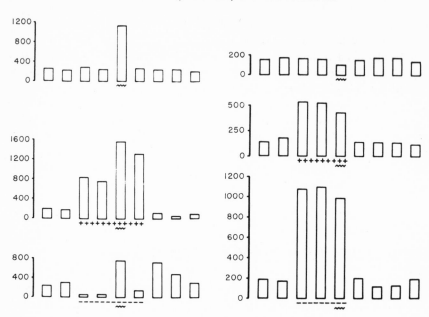

FIG. 1. Additive reactions of collicular units to acoustic stimulus (wavy line). Above: control recording; middle and below: background activity changed by positive (+ + + +) or negative (– –·– –) voltage applied to the microelectrode. Left: excitatory reactions; right: inhibitory reactions.

mented or decremented their reaction to the acoustic input in a multiplicative fashion (Fig. 2) as background activity was changed. Most commonly, the response increased or decreased proportionally to the background activity in such a way that the incremented firing rate to background firing rate ratio remained essentially constant. If the firing rates during the subsequent CS presentation were altered by the previous UCS presentation, these unconditioned multiplicative effects could be confused with conditioned effects. Fortunately, alterations in the firing rate during the pre-CS sampling period could be used to detect such effects. Two additional classes were distinguished in neurons initially unresponsive to tone. One group (50%) began responding to tone while the background polarization was applied (Fig. 3). Increases and decreases in the background firing rate had the same initiating effect. Similar effects have been reported in stimulated cortical neurons by Spehlmann & Kapp (1964) and by Voronin (1966). If intertrial intervals in a conditioning paradigm were short enough, a spread of effect from the UCS to the subsequent CS period could be confused with a conditioned reaction. In order to preclude such a possibility, the units should ideally be tested for such unconditioned effects before the conditioning paradigm is initiated. These effects could also be reduced by using longer intertrial intervals. In the last class of collicular unit effects, background polar-

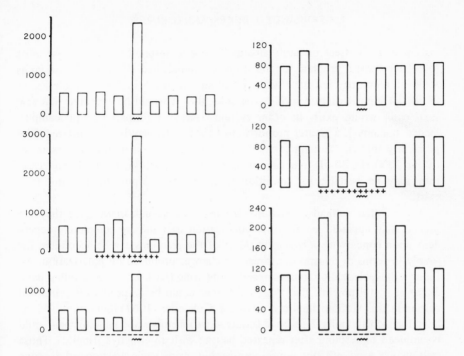

FIG. 2. Multiplicative reactions of collicular units to acoustic stimulus (wavy line). Above, middle, and below as in Fig. 1. Left: excitatory reaction; Right: inhibitory reaction.

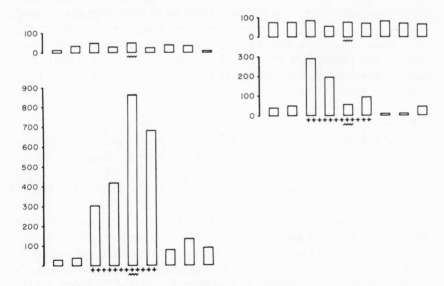

FIG. 3. Examples of two collicular units which do not react to the acoustic stimulus under no polarization conditions (upper figures). During polarization (lower figure, + + + +) the acoustic stimulus evoked excitatory (left) or inhibitory (right) reactions.

ization had no effect on units already failing to respond to tone. These units (50%) represent a problem for the study of conditioned effects only in so far as some of them may not have sufficient inputs for conditioning to take place at all. In an input structure such as the colliculus, it would be expected that few such cases would exist. In other systems (reticular formation, hippocampus, medial thalamus), a greater proportion of these cells may be encountered. The possibility that the "tuning curve" of these units was too narrow for responses to our 2000 Hz, 80 dB tone cannot be ruled out (Katsuki, 1961). In this case, they may be available for conditioning effects since inputs to the units may exist.

These initial collicular reactions are regarded as unlearned since they are immediately apparent on the first polarization trial and are completely dependent upon concurrent polarization. Most of the reactions can be accounted for simply in terms of nonspecific threshold changes produced by polarization. Although the polarization onset precedes the tone (backward conditioning paradigm), it is still possible that a plastic change could be induced with continued pairing in this fashion. Lindsley, Chow, & Gollender (1967) found that in some lateral geniculate units the second (nonreactive) member of a stimulus pair could be induced to respond after repeated pairing with an effective stimulus. Those cells which were initially nonresponsive but were made to respond to tone during polarization might also be relevant to a demonstration of plasticity (acquisition and extinction), and perhaps of learning (acquisition, extinction, representation, permanence). Typically several cells are recorded from and the tone is presented repeatedly in an experiment on each animal. At least some of these "unresponsive" collicular units could have been habituated prior to their study. Horn & Hill (1966) have reported habituation of single cell activity in the superior colliculus. Background polarization could have "dishabituated" this habituated reaction. The fact that either an increase or a decrease in background firing (induced by polarization) could initiate reactivity to tone might indicate that the polarization produced a mismatch from the neural representation of the input, and dishabituation resulted. These results are not simply explained as a decrease in threshold, since both increased and decreased firing rates are associated with the increase in reactivity to inputs.

In the second experiment (Gerbrandt, Skrebitsky, Burešová, & Bureš, 1968), the unit activity of the reticular formation was studied in 70 units as a function of repeated presentations of tactile stimuli with background polarization superimposed on later trials. Out of the 32 initially unresponsive units, 6 cells (19%) could be induced to fire to a tactile stimulus if background polarization was superimposed (Fig. 4). In 27 initially responding units, rapid habituation of response to the tactile stimulus occurred in most cases (Fig. 5). In one case (Fig. 6), we managed to "dishabituate" a previously habituated tactile reaction. During background polarization, the unit again resumed firing to the sensory input. These results reinforce the previous suggestion that "unresponsive" collicular

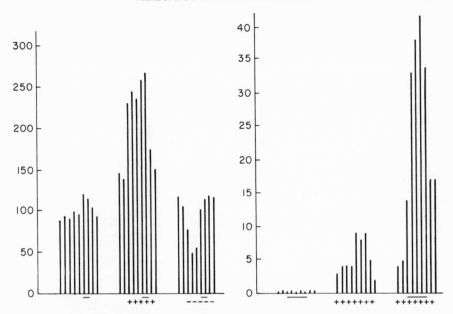

FIG. 4. Examples of two reticular units which do not react to the tactile stimulus significantly without polarization. During background polarization (+ + + + or – – – –) the reaction to the tone (————) was increased significantly. Analyzing interval–1 sec. Left: summation of 4 trials; right: summation of 1 trial in each histogram.

units could have been dishabituated by the polarization. If this initiation of reactivity persisted beyond the polarization and habituated again with repetition of the tactile stimulus plus polarization, a stronger case would be made for this conclusion. "Rehabituation" during polarization was observed in some of the reticular units. The possibility that background polarization can dishabituate single units then at least deserves further consideration. If so, one would have a way os studying an environmentally induced habituation at the cellular level with some assurance that the microelectrode is near the active learning network.

PLASTIC PHENOMENA

The technique of directly influencing a learning network with microelectrode polarization in order to differentiate units actively engaged from those only passively involved has been used in several studies on classical conditioning in our laboratory (Bureš & Burešová, 1965, 1967; Gerbrandt et al., 1968). The apparatus and methods used were the same as described previously. Intertrial intervals were varied from 0 to 60 sec. in order to see if plastic reactions could develop in units "conditioned" when the spread of effect from the UCS was

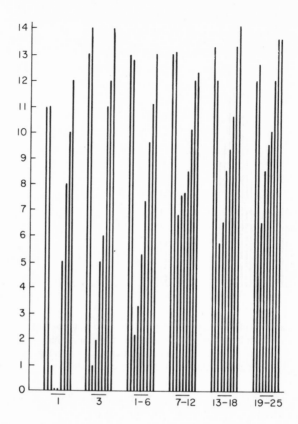

FIG. 5. Initial rapid habituation of a tactile response in a reticular neuron. Analyzing interval–1 sec; no polarization. First two histograms are trials 1 and 3. Subsequent histograms are sums of each 6 sequential trials.

displaced in time from the subsequent CS presentation. From 6 to 30 trials were usually accumulated into blocks of trials for automatic plotting of poststimulus histograms (PSHs). Shorter blocks of trials were occasionally used to test for short-term effects such as habituation to the CS. A PSH consisted of nine successive time intervals, each interval from .3 to 1.0 sec. Either an acoustic signal (2000 Hz) or a tactile stimulus (puff of air to the face) was used as the CS during intervals 3-7. Typically, the UCS (anodal dc voltage) overlapped the CS during intervals 6 and 7. In the cortical, hippocampal, nonspecific thalamic, and reticular formation areas, the acoustic CS elicited a low percentage of plastic reactions (Bureš & Burešová, 1965, 1967). Only 17% (4 out of 29) of the hippocampal units and 12% (4 out of 33) of the reticular units could display acquisition and extinction (Fig. 7). The incidence of plastic reactions in cortical neurons was still lower. The tactile CS also elicited a low percentage of plastic reactions in the hippocampus and reticular formation (Gerbrandt *et al.*, 1968). Only 12% (7 out of 57) of hippocampal units and 8% (4 out of 50) of reticular units could display acquisition and extinction (Fig. 8). The occurrence of a plastic reaction in any area studied with either CS usually was not associated with either a decrease or increase in spontaneous or UCS elicited activity over trials. Spontaneous activity was sampled in the period preceding CS onset. The strength of the UCS elicited activity was sampled by spike frequency during the UCS delivery in each block of trials. Since spontaneous firing rates were not associated with the plastic reactions, the unconditioned "artifacts" which were seen previously in the colliculus did not appear to have entered into these results. Since conditioning under long intertrial intervals did not produce any lesser or greater yield of plastic reactions, it is not likely that "dishabituation" of a previously habituated reaction can account for all of the plastic reactions. If any nonspecific change (plastic, but not capable of representation or permanence) accounts for the plastic reactions, it does not consistently alter spontaneous or UCS elicited firing rates and yet persists several minutes beyond the last UCS presentation (during extinction tests). Whether the plastic change will be shown to be specific (capable of discrimination) or nonspecific, and what its mechanisms may be, is purely conjectural at this point.

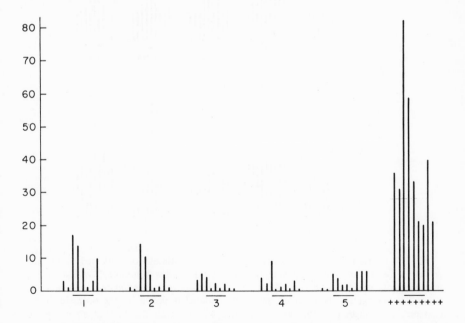

FIG. 6. Example of a reticular neuron in which the habituated tactile reaction is "dishabituated" by positive polarization voltage.

SUMMARY AND CONCLUSIONS

It is our aim to investigate the processes of learning in mammals even though we confine these studies to the cellular level. In order to reduce the risk that cellular preparations usually run, i.e., that one is not studying learning at all, we have used an intact mammal commonly used in learning studies, we have selected classical conditioning and habituation for study, and our results are evaluated by a set of criteria representative of learning processes. Another risk in cellular investigations of learning is that it is difficult to tell whether or not the single unit showing the change is merely passively involved in the sets of

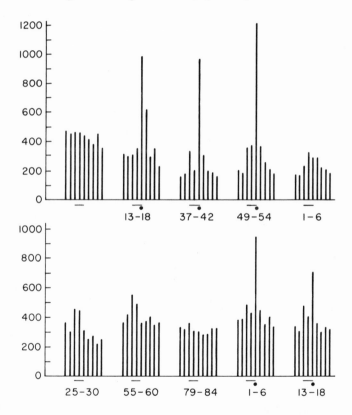

FIG. 7. Plastic reaction in a reticular neuron. Sound stimulation indicated by the horizontal bar below Columns 3-5; polarizing current by dot below Column 5. The first block of measurements constitutes a control set. Serial numbers of the integrated trials are given below the histograms. Number of spikes accumulated is shown on the ordinate. In this example, the acoustic CS, followed by a positive, 40 nA current for the UCS, elicits a plastic reaction after 30 paired trials, disappears after 50 extinction trials, and is restored immediately with "retraining."

pathways from input to output. To reduce this risk, we have used the recording microelectrode also to stimulate (UCS) the single unit under study. It might be said that the micropipette is used to inject additional information into the system. If the cell recorded from is part of a learning network, then it should eventually be modified in its reaction to the added information.

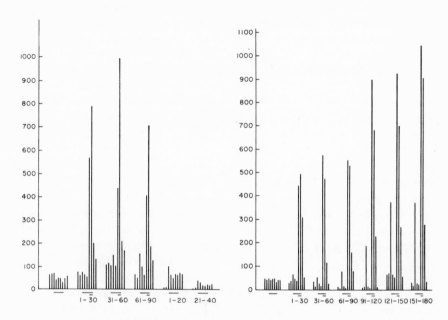

FIG. 8. Plastic reaction in hippocampal (left) and reticular (right) neurons elicited by a tactile CS (upper horizontal bar, Columns 3-7) which is followed by a positive 30 nA current for the UCS (lower horizontal bar). The first block constitutes a set of 10 trials with tactile CS and without UCS. Extinction is shown for the hippocampal neuron.

In experiments where background polarization modified collicular and reticular formation unit reactions to tone in an "unlearned" fashion, several possibilities could be seen for future investigation of plastic reactions. It is conceivable that "backward conditioning" of the sort described by Lindsley, Chow, & Gollender (1967) could have occurred had training trials been continued. Even more promising is the possibility that the microelectrode could be used to inject a "novel stimulus" into a habituated network. "Nonresponsive" collicular units were found to be activated by background polarization that either increased or *decreased* the rate of unit firing. Reticular units which were habituated by repeated presentation of the tactile stimulus were "dishabituated" by polarization and rapidly "rehabituated" again during background polarization. Hopefully, the restoration of unit activity would occur in some units for a few trials even after the polarization is turned off. If so, this technique may prove valuable in locating networks and brain areas active in habituation learning.

The plastic reactions in units studied in the classical conditioning and extinction paradigm pose several problems for future study. First, a way is needed to increase the number of units showing plasticity. If the absolute number of plastic units in the nervous system is low, as suggested by Chow in this volume, nothing can be done to increase the yield; hence further research will be slowed to 10% of the pace that might occur otherwise (approximately 10% of cells seem to be plastic). Several other possibilities remain, however. Plasticity may normally involve larger networks than are involved as a result of our microelectrode polarization of a single unit. If this is the case, then the CS could be delivered as polarization through the microelectrode, and the UCS could be made more effective by stimulating through a semi-microelectrode nearby. This would be a more localized version of the study by Doty (1961). Another possibility is that the sensory CS is not adequate in the areas under study (cerebral cortex, medial thalamus, reticular formation, hippocampus). Although the percentage of plastic reactions was not any higher for units which initially responded to the CS, the "responsiveness" could have habituated away from the network being studied. A more adequate CS could be provided by a double microelectrode preparation, where both the CS and UCS information is induced by nearby microelectrode polarizations. Of course the CS could be improved by attempting the "conditioning" of primary afferent systems such as the inferior or superior colliculi or the striate cortex. Although these systems are usually conceived of as lacking, or at least having minimal plasticity (cf. Chow, this volume), the possibility that appreciable learning occurs in these areas should not be overlooked. In yet another paper in this volume, Spinelli is concerned with a model where "string memories" (e.g., classical conditioning) can be addressed in parallel in primary sensory receiving areas.

Finally, future studies should also be devoted to increasing the rigor of the microelectrode technique, the number of learning criteria, and the variety of types of learning used for evaluation of the single unit preparation. Intracellular recording would avoid delivering the UCS directly to the presynaptic inputs, it would allow detection of EPSP and IPSP events which might be crucial to the learning which occurs, and it would provide knowledge about whether the CS has inputs to the cell under study. If a sinusoidal rather than a dc microstimulation were used, accumulation of ions due to electrophoresis could be reduced. Discrimination testing could also be done in order to extend the number of criteria used to evaluate the changes in each unit. Habituations and reinforcement paradigms should be tested by these techniques. Eventually, chronic micropipettes will have to be developed so that permanent cellular changes can be tested for days. Hopefully, some of these approaches will bring us closer to our goal of recording and influencing a single *learning* brain cell.

REFERENCES

Bureš, J., & Burešová, O. Relationship between spontaneous and evoked activity in the inferior colliculus of rats. *Journal of Neurophysiology,* 1965, **28**, 641-654.

Bureš, J., & Burešová, O. Plastic changes of unit activity based on reinforcing properties of extracellular stimulation of single neurons. *Journal of Neurophysiology,* 1967, **30**, 98-113.

Doty, R. W. Conditioned reflexes formed and evoked by brain stimulation. In D. E. Sheer (Ed.), *Electrical stimulation of the brain.* Austin, Texas: University of Texas Press, 1961. Pp. 397-412.

Gerbrandt, L. K., Skrebitsky, V. G., Burešová, O., & Bureš, J. Plastic changes of unit activity induced by tactile stimuli followed by electrical stimulation of single hippocampal and reticular neurons. *Neuropsychologia,* 1968, **6**, 3-10.

Granit, R., Kernell, D., & Lamarre, Y. Algebraic summation in synaptic activation of motoneurons firing within primary range to injected currents. *Journal of Physiology (London),* 1966, **187**, 379.

Horn, G., & Hill, R. M. Responsiveness to sensory stimulation of units in superior colliculus and subjacent tectotegmental regions of the rabbit. *Experimental Neurology,* 1966, **14**, 199-223.

Kandel, E. R., & Tauc, L. Heterosynaptic facilitation in neurones of the abdominal ganglion of *Aplysia depilans. Journal of Physiology (London),* 1965, **181**, 1-27.

Katsuki, Y. Neural mechanisms of auditory sensation in cats. In W. A. Rosenblith (Ed.), *Sensory communication.* New York: Wiley, 1961. Pp. 561-583.

Kimble, G. A. *Conditioning and learning.* New York: Appleton-Century-Crofts, 1961.

Lashley, K. S. In search of the engram. *Symposia of the Society for Experimental Biology,* 1950, **4**, 454-482.

Lindsley, D. F., Chow, K. L., & Gollender, M. Dichoptic interactions of lateral geniculate neurons of cats to contralateral eye stimulation. *Journal of Neurophysiology,* 1967, **30**, 628-644.

Morrell, F. Lasting changes in synaptic organization produced by continuous neuronal bombardment. In J. F. Delafresnaye (Ed.), *Brain mechanisms and learning.* Oxford: Blackwell, 1961. Pp. 375-392.

Norton, T., Frommer, G., & Galambos, R. Effects of partial lesions of optic tract on visual discriminations in cats. *Federation Proceedings,* 1966, **25**, 2168.

Spehlmann, R. S., & Kapp, H. Direct extracellular polarization of cortical neurons with multibarreled microelectrodes. *Archives Italiennes de Biologie,* 1964, **102**, 74-94.

Strumwasser, F. The demonstration and manipulation of a circadian rhythm in a single neuron. In J. Aschoff (Ed.), *Circadian clocks,* Amsterdam: North-Holland Pub., 1965. Pp. 442-462.

Thompson, R. F., & Spencer, W. A. Habituation: A model phenomenon for the study of neuronal substrates of behavior. *Psychological Review,* 1966, **73**, 16-43.

Voronin, L. L. Influence of extracellular polarization of single units of the sensorimotor cerebral cortex of the rabbit on their evoked activity. *Zhurnal Vysshei Nervnoi Deyatel'nosti imeni Pavlova,* 1966, **16**, 667-677.

Part V

REALIZING THE MODELS

THE ACTIVITY OF NEURONAL NETWORKS
IN THE THALAMUS OF THE MONKEY[1]

M. VERZEANO,[2] M. LAUFER,[3] PHYLLIS SPEAR,
and SHARON McDONALD

Department of Biophysics and Nuclear Medicine
University of California, Los Angeles, California

INTRODUCTION

In order to explain the processes that occur in short-term memory and in the consolidation phase of learning, Verzeano (1965) presented a hypothesis according to which activity that circulates, spontaneously, in the neuronal networks of the cortex and of the thalamus, would function as a "carrier" that would be "modulated" by the incoming sensory information. This modulated carrier would continue to circulate through the networks for some time, functioning as a short-term storage mechanism and achieving consolidation by repeated passages of the information over the elements implicated in the formation of the permanent engram.

To be viable, this hypothesis requires the existence of a process of spontaneous circulation of activity through the neuronal networks of cortical and subcortical structures, and of a mechanism for the modulation of such spontaneous activity.

The existence and the characteristics of activity that circulates through the neuronal networks of the cortex and of the thalamus, have been described in several papers, between 1954 and the present time, by Verzeano and his collaborators (see references in this publication). More recently (Verzeano, Dill, Vallecalle, Groves, & Thomas, 1968; Dill, Vallecalle, & Verzeano, 1968; Verze-

[1] Aided by grant NB-00649 from the National Institute of Health.
[2] Present Address: Department of Psychobiology, University of California, Irvine, California.
[3] Fellow of the Instituto Venezolano de Investigaciones Cientificas, Caracas.

ano, 1970), studies of the relations between gross evoked responses and neuronal activity, simultaneously recorded from the visual system in response to sensory stimulation, have shown that the spontaneous neuronal activity increases and decreases in magnitude, in relation to the time derivative (slope) of the gross response. Changes in the characteristics of the visual stimulus result in changes in the waveform, amplitude, and slopes of the gross response, that are reflected in the simultaneous neuronal activity, which becomes a mirror image of the first derivative of the gross response. By this process, the spontaneous activity is "modulated" by the incoming sensory information. Thus, the existence of both processes required by the theory, the spontaneous circulation of neuronal activity and its modulation by the incoming sensory information, can be demonstrated by experimental findings. Much remains to be done in order to elucidate the mechanisms which are at the basis of these processes of circulation and modulation of activity, and to ascertain whether or not they may be implicated in perception and learning.

The study of the circulation of neuronal activity in the thalamus and in the cortex of the monkey has provided an exceptionally clear picture of its characteristics and has elucidated some of the mechanisms by which it is generated and distributed through the brain. This study was published in 1965 in the "Actualites Neurophysiologiques," in French. The editors of this volume have suggested that an English translation be presented here.

PRELIMINARIES

Studies conducted on the brain of the cat, in recent years, have shown that, under certain conditions of "synchronization" of the gross waves, a circulation of impulses develops spontaneously in the neuronal networks of the cortex and thalamus. The experimental evidence for such circulation has been obtained, at first, by recording extracellularly, with a single microelectrode, the activity of several neurons and considering the relations between the amplitudes of their action potentials (Verzeano & Calma, 1954; Verzeano, 1955) and, later, by recording, simultaneously, with several microelectrodes, the activity of several neurons and considering the temporal and spatial distribution of their action potentials (Verzeano, 1956; Verzeano & Negishi, 1960, 1961).

The principles on which these methods are based will be briefly mentioned here. The amplitude of the neuronal spikes recorded by a microelectrode is related to the distance between the tip of the microelectrode and the active neuron. When the activity of a neuronal network is recorded, simultaneously, with an array of extracellular microelectrodes whose tips are separated by distances of the order of 30 to 200 μ the neuronal territories "seen" by the microelectrodes overlap. Under such conditions the activity of some neurons may be recorded by one microelectrode, the activity of other neurons may be recorded by another microelectrode, and the activity of some neurons may be recorded, simultaneously, by several microelectrodes.

Thus, by considering the tracings on which the neuronal spikes are recorded, their amplitudes and their time of occurrence, some information can be derived about the temporal and spatial distribution of activity in the network. Figure 1

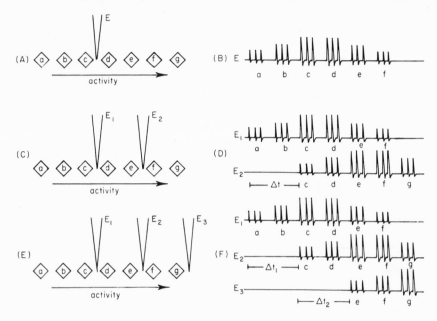

FIG. 1. Diagrammatic representation of results obtained by recording, simultaneously, the activity of several neurons, by means of arrays of microelectrodes whose tips are located along a straight line (see text). In order to simplify the diagram (in this figure as well as in Fig. 3), successive neuronal discharges are represented as groups containing equal numbers of spikes. Actually, the number of spikes in the successive groups is variable.

illustrates, diagrammatically, the application of these methods. In A and B, as activity approaches, reaches, and goes beyond the tip of microelectrode E, the latter records spikes of progressively increasing and decreasing amplitudes. In C and D, the tracings obtained with two microelectrodes (E_1, E_2) which record the activity of overlapping territories show similar sequences of progressively increasing and decreasing amplitudes and show a delay (Δt) between the appearance of activity first at the tip of E_1 and later at the tip of E_2. Furthermore, the spikes generated by neurons c, d, e, and f, located within the overlapping sections of the two territories, are recorded simultaneously by the two microelectrodes. In E and F similar relations between spike amplitudes and similar delays (Δt_1; Δt_2) in the successive appearance of activity can be seen in tracings

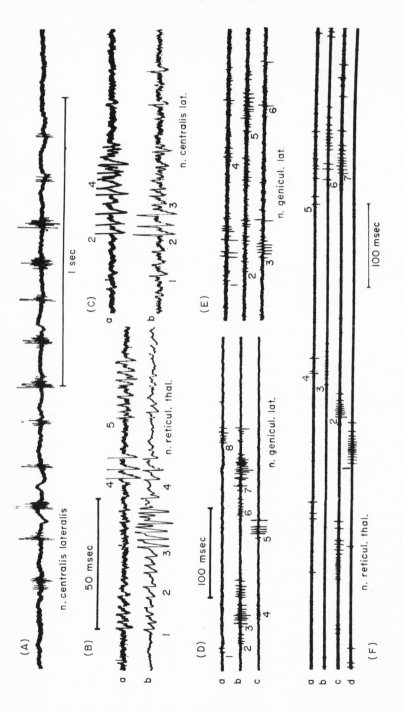

FIG. 2.

obtained simultaneously with three microelectrodes E_1, E_2, E_3, displayed along a straight line. Actual records from the cat's brain exhibiting such characteristic activity are shown in Fig. 2.

Against the hypothesis that such phenomena are related to circulation of activity through the neuronal network, two objections might be raised: one, that spikes generated locally by a single neuron might, under certain conditions, appear on the tracing as increasing and decreasing in amplitude; two, that the appearance of activity, in succession, at the tips of several microelectrodes displayed along a straight line, might represent the propagation of this activity along one and the same neuron, from dendrites through soma to axon.

The first objection can be tested by recording the activity, at one point of the network, with a microelectrode whose tip is so small that it may detect the activity of only one neuron. If the changes in spike amplitude are generated locally, at one point, by a single neuron, the very small microelectrode should still record them. It the changes in spike amplitude are not generated at one point, the very small microelectrode, recording at that point, should not detect them but should provide a tracing in which all spikes are of the same amplitude. Figure 2F shows several such recordings, obtained with an array of small microelectrodes, displayed along a straight line. Each one of the microelectrodes, recording from one or two neurons only, shows spikes of one or two amplitudes only. Progressive increases and decreases in amplitude cannot be seen. However, the appearance of activity, in succession, at the tips of the microelectrodes is still present. The first objection can, thus, be eliminated.

The second objection can be eliminated on the basis of the following considerations:

(1) If the changes in the amplitude of successive groups of spikes were due to propagation of activity along one and the same neuron, each successive group should contain the same number of spikes. As can be seen in Fig. 2, this is very seldom the case.

FIG. 2. Circulation of activity in the neuronal networks of the thalamus of the cat. A: Low-speed record, obtained with a single microelectrode, showing periodic occurrence of activity near its tip; B and C: high-speed records, obtained with two microelectrodes (a and b), showing that each periodic occurrence of A corresponds to the sequential activation of several neurons (1, 2, 3, . . . ,etc.); D and E: high-speed records obtained with three microelectrodes (a, b, c) with tips displayed along a straight line, showing, in D, propagation of activity in the direction a-b-c (at 1, 2, 3, 4), followed by propagation in the opposite direction c-b-a (at 5, 6, 7, 8) and, in E, propagation of activity twice in the same direction (at 1, 2, 3, and 4, 5, 6); F: record obtained with four microelectrodes (a, b, c, d), with tips displayed along a straight line, each tip recording the activity of no more than one or two neurons and showing propagation of activity first in the direction d-c-b-a (at 1, 2, 3, 4), then in the opposite direction a-b-c-d (at 5, 6, 7). The thalamic nucleus from which the data were obtained is indicated next to each record. Anesthetic: pentobarbital in all cases (from Verzeano & Negishi, 1961).

(2) No "dendritic" potentials such as have been defined in the few cases in which they have been recorded with microelectrodes (Tasaki, Polley, & Orrego, 1954; Hild & Tasaki, 1962) can be seen in the records. All potentials, by their waveforms, durations, and amplitudes are typical action potentials of neuron somata.

(3) In some cases several hundred milliseconds elapse between the times at which activity appears in succession, at the tips of two microelectrodes separated by a distance of 200 μ. No action potentials are known to propagate along a single neuron at such low velocities.

(4) When activity appears in succession at the tips of several microelectrodes displayed along a straight line, there are frequent reversals in the order of appearance (Fig. 2D and F). These reversals cannot be explained on the basis of activity propagating along a single neuron for, in that case, the activity would have to consist of a series of spontaneous alternations of orthodromic-antidromic propagation of action potentials in the same neuron, an occurrence of which it is difficult to conceive on the basis of present-day neurophysiological knowledge.

Results obtained by other workers give strong support to the view that activity circulates in neuronal networks. Creutzfeldt & Jung (1961) obtained simultaneous recordings with two microelectrodes from the cat's motor cortex and, frequently, found neurons discharging in regular succession at the two microelectrode tips. Mescherskii (1961), in his studies of the temporal and spatial characteristics of the spontaneous activity in small regions of the rabbit's cortex, found that, during the development of such activity, groups of neurons, different in their composition and distribution, are successively activated. Andersen, Andersson, and Lømo (1966), using arrays of microelectrodes similar to those developed by Verzeano and his collaborators, demonstrated the spread of neuronal as well as gross wave activity, through extensive regions of the thalamus. The relations of this spread of activity to the generation of rhythmic patterns in the thalamus and in the cortex is further discussed in a more recent work by the same authors (Andersen & Andersson, 1968).

The configuration of the pathways of circulation of activity could not be accurately determined with the experimental methods available at present. However, by varying, in successive experiments, the distances between the tips of the microelectrodes in rectilinear arrays and by using triangular microelectrode arrangements (Verzeano & Negishi, 1960, 1961), it has been determined that the pathways of circulation are curvilinear and follow a series of loops whose "locus" constantly displaces itself through the neuronal networks.

Since the distance between two consecutive microelectrode tips is known and the time which elapses between the appearance of activity, first at one tip and later at the next, can be measured, the velocity of circulation has been estimated to vary from .5 to 9 mm/sec, depending upon the region of the brain under study and upon the conditions of wakefulness, sleep, or anesthesia of the animal. This estimate, however, is that of an "apparent" velocity, established by noting the time of arrival of activity at consecutive microelectrode tips. Since at the present time the pathway of circulation from one tip to the next is not exactly known, the "true" velocity cannot be determined.

The characteristics of the circulation of activity through the cortical and the thalamic networks of the cat and the patterns of discharge of the neurons involved in it have been found to be related to the degree of "synchronization" of the gross cortical or thalamic waves (Verzeano, 1956, 1961, 1963). The increasing "synchronization" of the gross waves corresponds to: a larger number of neurons involved in the pathway of circulation and an increasing frequency and clustering of their spike discharge; an increasing apparent velocity of circulation; a lengthened period of silence between successive passages of circulating activity through the network; a decrease in the activity of neurons located outside the pathway of circulation (Fig. 3).

From the results obtained in these investigations in the cat, it has been concluded that the "synchronization" of brain waves is not based on the activity of individual neurons discharging sporadically nor on the activity of many neurons discharging all at once, but on the activity of neurons and groups of neurons discharging in sequence and in characteristic patterns.

Recent investigations have shown that the development and the distribution of gross waves in the brain of the chimpanzee and of the monkey are more complex than they are in the cat (Adey, Kado, & Rhodes, 1963; Verzeano, Laufer & Spear, 1964; Reite, Rhodes, Kavan & Adey, 1965) and that, in the human brain, the gross waves and the neuronal activity exhibit patterns which are characteristic of the region of the brain in which they develop (Albe-Fessard, Arfel, & Guiot, 1963). The question arises whether the circulation of neuronal activity and its relations with the "synchronization" of gross waves, which were found in the brain of the cat, have greater complexity in a more evolved brain, such as that of the monkey. A series of experiments has been conducted in order to investigate these phenomena in the brain of the monkey. The results are presented in this report.

METHODS

Experiments were conducted in adult macaque and squirrel monkeys (*Macaca mulatta* and *Saimiri sciureus*). Some animals were anesthetized with pentobarbital. Others were anesthetized with ether during a brief period, sufficient for tracheotomy and craniotomy, after which they were paralyzed with gallamine triethiodide ("flaxedil") and maintained with artificial respiration. Local anesthesia was administered to incision and pressure regions.

Microelectrodes were made of metallic rods (70% platinum, 30% iridium) electrolitically sharpened to a diameter of 1 to 3 μ and insulated with a glass

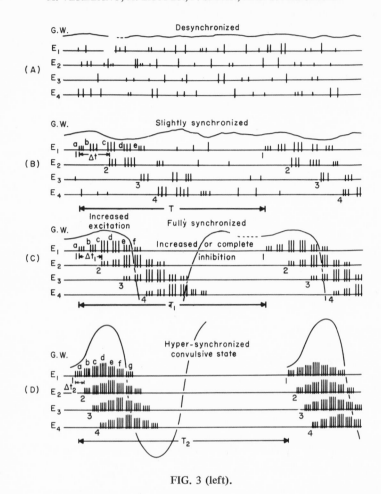

FIG. 3 (left).

FIG. 3. Relations between neuronal discharge, circulation of neuronal activity, and synchronization of the gross waves, as they appear when recorded simultaneously with four microelectrodes with tips separated by 100 to 150 μ. Left: Diagrammatic representation of oscilloscope tracings, showing the progressive changes which take place from the desynchronized to the hypersynchronized state. Right: Diagrammatic two-dimensional representation of neuronal fields, showing the neuronal activity corresponding to each successive state. E_1, E_2, E_3, E_4 represent the microelectrodes through which oscilloscope tracings E_1, E_2, E_3, E_4 (at left) would be obtained; the circles represent neurons in the field of the microelectrodes; the degree of darkness in each circle represents the degree of excitation of that particular neuron; the arrow represents the direction of the circulation of neuronal activity. A: Oscilloscope: infrequent clustering of the spikes, no circulation of neuronal activity, no synchronization of the gross waves. Neuronal field: scattered, sporadic neuronal activity, at low level of excitation; no circulation of neuronal activity. B: Oscilloscope: increased clustering of spikes; occurrence of neuronal activity in regular succession at

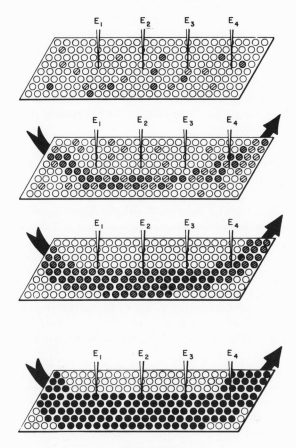

FIG. 3 (right).

each one of the tips of the microelectrodes, indicating circulation through the neuronal network; decreased activity in the interval between successive passages of circulating activity through the network; gross waves slightly synchronized. Neuronal field: neuronal activity at higher level of excitation, concentrated mostly in the pathway of circulation (arrow); decreased activity outside this pathway. C: Oscilloscope: high degree of clustering of spikes; increase in the velocity of circulating activity ($\Delta t_1 < \Delta t$); activity abolished in an increased interval between successive passages of circulating activity through the network; gross waves fully synchronized. Neuronal field: neuronal activity at high level of excitation in the pathway of circulation; no activity outside the pathway. D: Oscilloscope: extreme degree of clustering of spikes; high velocity of circulation ($\Delta t_2 < \Delta t_1$); further increase in the interval between successive passages of circulating activity through the network; neuronal activity in this interval abolished; hypersynchronized gross waves of high amplitude. Neuronal field: neuronal activity at very high level of excitation concentrated exclusively in an enlarged, multilane pathway of circulation; completely abolished outside this pathway (from Verzeano, 1963).

coating (Wolbarsht, MacNichol, & Wagner, 1960). Arrays of microelectrodes were made by bringing together, with micromanipulators, the tips of several microelectrodes, maintaining them at the desired distance (100-300 μ), and joining the stems with an acrylic cement.

The microelectrodes were introduced into the brain stereotaxically and the location of the recording points was checked histologically after each experiment, using stereotaxic atlases of the thalamus of the monkey (Olszewski, 1952; Gergen & MacLean, 1962).

The microelectrodes were connected to amplifiers of high input impedance and low grid current (Verzeano & Negishi, 1960). The output of the amplifiers was recorded on magnetic tape through frequency modulating devices in order to provide adequate frequency response for the recording of gross waves as well as of neuronal spikes. The tape was "read" either on cathode ray oscilloscopes or on oscillographs provided with high-speed galvanometers. The overall frequency response of the system was flat from 3 to 5000 Hz.

In most cases each microelectrode in the array recorded the activity of several neurons and therefore, the corresponding magnetic track on the tape contained spikes of different amplitudes. By means of a pulse-height analyzer, the different amplitudes were separated and recorded, again, on separate channels. In this way each channel exhibited either the activity of a single neuron or the activity of a restricted group of neurons whose spikes were contained within a limited range of amplitudes.

The pulse-height analyzer, of the "stacked discriminator" type, was especially designed to handle the type of pulses and the range of amplitudes and repetition rates encountered in the study of neuronal spikes. Similar pulse-height analyzers have been constructed by other authors (Van Rennes, 1952; Littauer & Walcott, 1959). The advantages of the instrument described here are its simplicity and compactness, its high resolution, and its capability of providing, in one operation, either directly from the microelectrodes during the experiment or directly from the original magnetic tracks on which the primary data have been recorded, the complete amplitude spectrum of the neuronal spikes encountered.

The instrument consists essentially of: a preamplifier and filter which eliminate much of the high frequency and low frequency noise (Fig. 4A, B), an amplifier of adjustable gain, which provides easily adjustable resolution, and an inverter, which can be set to pass either the positive or the negative phase of the original spikes (Fig. 4C); a series of amplitude discriminators of the "Schmitt-trigger" type (N, $N-1$, $N-2$, etc.), delay circuits, and gates (Figs. 4 and 5).

It operates as follows: The spectrum of amplitudes is divided into a number of ranges, from $N-2$ to $N-1$, from $N-1$ to N, from N to $N+1$ μV, etc. (from lower to higher). The discriminators are preset to be triggered successively as the rising phase of the incoming pulse reaches the successive range boundaries, $N-2$, $N-1$, N, etc. When the rising phase of the incoming pulse reaches a boundary,

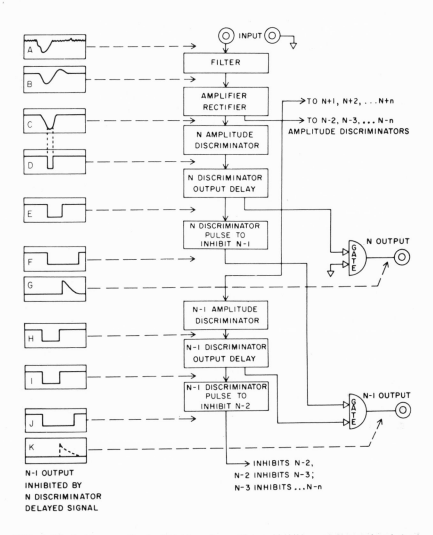

FIG. 4. Block diagram of pulse-height analyzer. Neuronal spikes are separated and classified in a series of amplitude ranges whose extension and limits are determined by the settings of a series of amplitude discriminators (see text).

say $N - 1$ μV, the $N - 1$ discriminator generates a brief pulse (Fig. 4H). This pulse triggers two multivibrators. The first multivibrator ($N - 1$ discriminator output delay) provides a brief pulse (Fig. 4I) at the end of which the $N - 1$ output gate should be activated. The second multivibrator ("Inhibit $N - 2$") generates a pulse

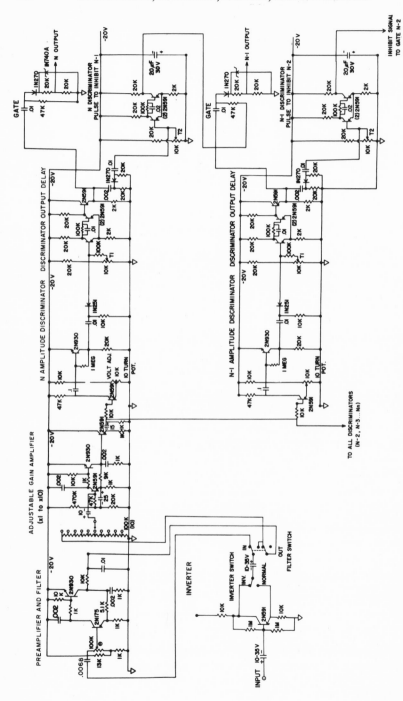

FIG. 5. Wiring diagram of pulse-height analyzer.

(Fig. 4J) which is transmitted to the $N-2$ gate to "inhibit" the pulse resulting from the previous triggering of discriminator $N-2$ by the rising phase of the incoming pulse, which has reached boundary $N-2$ before reaching $N-1$. If the rising phase of the incoming pulse does not reach the N boundary, the gate of $N-1$ remains open and a pulse (Fig. 4K) is registered in the channel destined to record the amplitudes ranging from $N-1$ to N. If the rising phase of the incoming pulse goes beyond boundary $N-1$ to reach boundary N, it triggers discriminator N. This discriminator triggers its two multivibrators: "Inhibit $N-1$" transmits a pulse (Fig. 4F) to the gate of $N-1$ and inhibits it; "N output delay" provides a pulse through gate N (Fig. 4E). If the rising phase of the incoming pulse does not reach $N+1$, gate N remains open and a pulse is registered in the channel destined to record the amplitudes ranging from N to $N+1$ (Fig. 4G).

Thus, the rising phase of the incoming pulse goes through the successive range boundaries and, when it reaches its peak, it is automatically classified in the range to which it belongs and recorded on the oscillograph channel reserved for

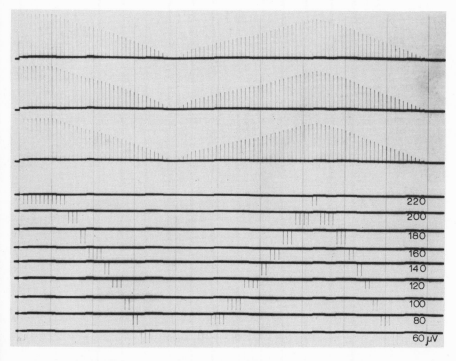

FIG. 6. Classification of pulses by the pulse-height analyzer into amplitude ranges of 20 μV width. Line 60 contains all pulses whose amplitudes fall into the 60 to 80 μV range; line 80 contains all pulses whose amplitudes fall into the 80 to 100 μV range, etc.; line 220 contains all pulses whose amplitudes go beyond 220 μV.

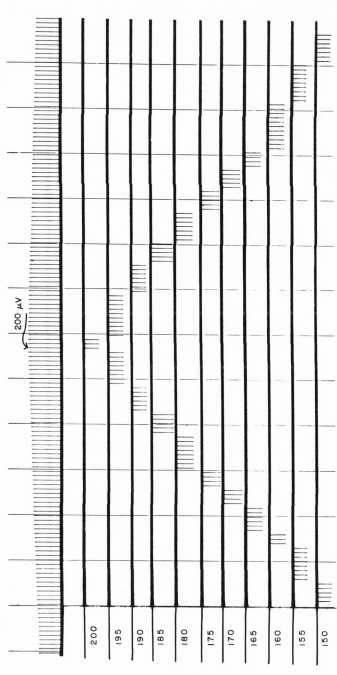

FIG. 7. Classification of pulses by the pulse-height analyzer into amplitude ranges of 5 μV width.

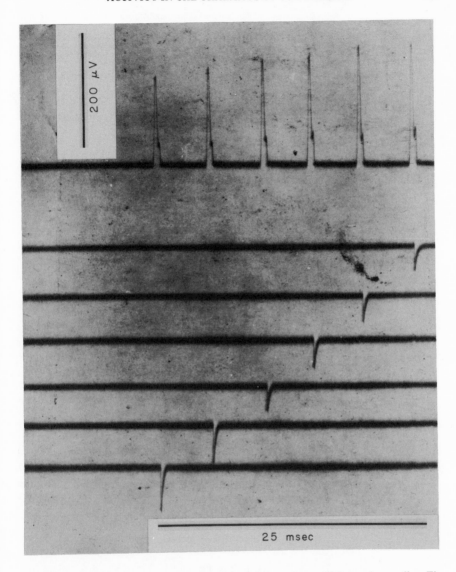

FIG. 8. Classification of pulses by the pulse-height analyzer. High-speed recording. The pulses shown on the top line of Figs. 6-8, were produced by a pulse generator.

spikes in that particular range (Fig. 6). The extension of each range can be specified by adjusting the potentiometer whose setting determines the bias of the Schmitt triggers in the discriminators ("ten turn pot," Fig. 5). In its present form the instrument provides a maximum amplitude resolution of 5 μV and time resolution of 1 msec (Figs. 7, 8, and 13). In addition to the automatic separation

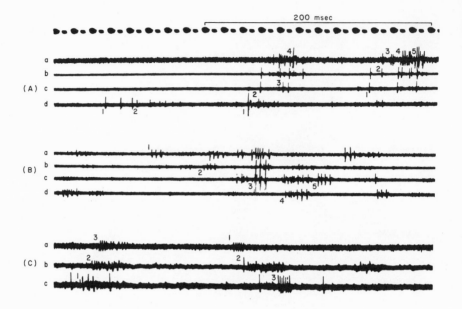

FIG. 9. Circulation of neuronal activity in the brain of the Macaque, during light barbiturate anesthesia. Recordings obtained, simultaneously, with four microelectrodes (a, b, c, d), from the cingulate gyrus (A), the nucleus ventralis anterior of the thalamus (B), and the pulvinar (C). Activity appears in regular succession at the tips of the microelectrodes, at 1, 2, 3, 4, etc. In C, activity circulates first in the direction c-b-a, later in the direction a-b-c. Distances between the tips of the microelectrodes: in A and B, 140 μ; in C, 110 μ.

and classification of pulses according to their amplitudes, the instrument can be used to extract only one or a specific number of amplitudes from the totality of available amplitudes. This is done by forming one or several "windows" with one or several pairs of discriminators: one discriminator determining the lower limit and the other discriminator the upper limit of each window.

RESULTS

The results obtained in this series of experiments indicate that: circulation of neuronal activity occurs in the cortex and in the thalamus of the monkey; its relations with the patterns of neuronal discharge and of "synchronization" of gross waves is similar to those which have been found in the cat (Fig. 9); in the nucleus ventralis anterior of the monkey, the features of neuronal activity and its relations with the gross waves are characteristic of that particular nucleus

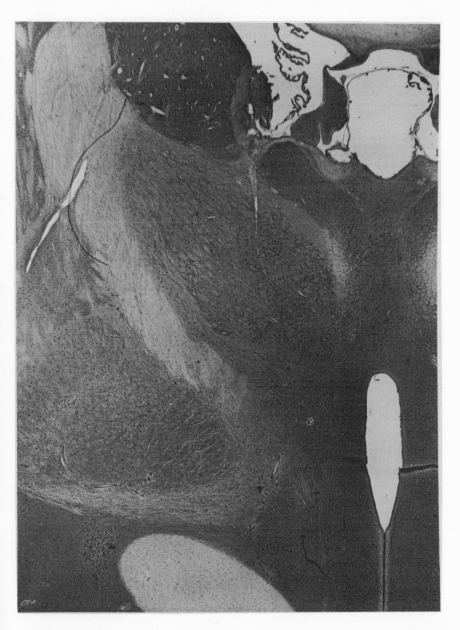

FIG. 10. Transversal section of the thalamus of the squirrel monkey, showing, in the nucleus ventralis anterior, a microelectrode track, left by one of the four microelectrodes of the longitudinal array which was used in the recording of the tracings shown in Fig. 12. Nissl stain.

FIG. 11.

(Figs. 10-12). The data presented below deal, specifically, with the characteristic activity of the nucleus ventralis anterior in various states of wakefulness, sleep, or anesthesia, and with its relations with the activity of neighboring nuclei.

1. Activity in the Nucleus Ventralis Anterior in Sleep

Figure 11 shows recordings of neuronal activity and gross waves obtained, simultaneously, with four microelectrodes (a, b, c, d) from the nucleus ventralis anterior of the macaque monkey under light barbiturate anesthesia. Microelectrodes b, c, and d record only neuronal spikes; microelectrode a records both neuronal spikes and gross waves. Recordings begin in the upper left hand corner of the picture (A) and continue, uninterrupted, to te lower right hand corner (B). At the beginning, the neuronal spikes are clustered and activity appears, in succession, at the tips of the four microelectrodes (as in the example 1, 2, 3, 4); as time goes on, the frequency of discharge and the clustering of the spikes of each neuron increase, the delays between the appearance of activity at the successive microelectrode tips become shorter, new neurons are activated, and a larger number of neurons is progressively implicated in this process. At the end of this period, which lasts for 8 to 12 sec., the frequency of discharge, the degree of clustering of the spikes, and the number of neurons involved reach a maximum. During this period of maximal activity, which lasts from 2 to 4 sec. (y to z), the delays between the appearance of activity at consecutive microelectrode tips are very short, the neuronal discharge is highly periodic, groups of high amplitude spikes alternate regularly with groups of low amplitude spikes, one group of amplitudes being recorded by one set of microelectrodes, the other group by another set of microelectrodes (s, x). There follows a period of complete silence, which lasts from 3 to 5 sec., after which the whole sequence of events (from A to B) repeats itself in the same order, indefinitely, as long as the animal remains at a specific level of light sleep or anesthesia. A similar sequence of events, developing in the nucleus ventralis anterior of the squirrel monkey in the state of natural sleep and recorded, simultaneously, with four microelectrodes (A, B, C, D) displayed along a straight line, is illustrated in Fig. 12. In this

FIG. 11. Neuronal and wave activity in the nucleus ventralis anterior of the thalamus of the Macaque, in light barbiturate anesthesia. Recordings obtained, simultaneously, with four microelectrodes (a, b, c, d), whose tips were located along a straight line; microelectrode a recorded spikes as well as slow waves; microelectrodes b, c, and d recorded neuronal spikes only. The tracings are continuous, from A to B. The appearance of activity in succession, at the tips of microelectrodes, indicating circulation of neuronal activity through the neuronal network, is shown at 1, 2, 3, 4. The period of progressive development of activity extends from A to y; the period of maximum activity extends from y to z and the slow waves which develop during this period can be seen on tracing a; the alternations of groups of high amplitude and low amplitude spikes are designated s-x; the period of silence extends from z to B (see text). Distances between the tips of the microelectrodes: 140 μ.

case, the period of maximal activity is seen to appear in regular succession at the tips of the four microelectrodes (at 1, 2, 3, 4), then to disappear in the same order.

During the period of maximal activity and alternation of amplitudes, each group of spikes is associated with a gross wave (Fig. 13): the higher amplitude spikes with higher amplitude waves, the lower amplitude spikes with lower amplitude waves (Fig. 14). During this period, each microelectrode in a longitu-

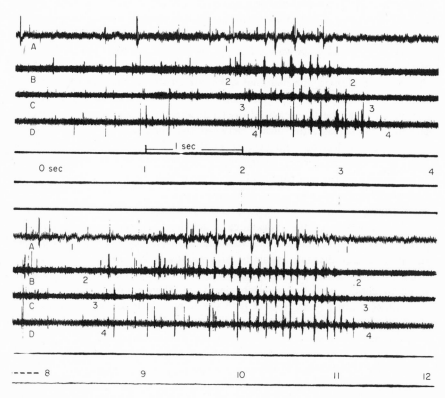

FIG. 12. Activity in the nucleus ventralis anterior of the squirrel monkey in light natural sleep. Recordings obtained, simultaneously, with four microelectrodes (A, B, C, D), whose tips were located along a straight line. Microelectrode A recorded neuronal spikes as well as slow waves; microelectrodes B, C, and D recorded neuronal spikes only. Two complete episodes are shown, with their progressive developments and their periods of maximum activity, between time 0 and time 12. The first progressive development extends from 0 to 2, the first period of maximum activity extends from 2 to 3, the first period of silence (shown only in part) extends from 4 to 7. The second episode, similar to the first, extends from 7 to 12. During the periods of maximum activity, groups of high amplitude spikes alternate with groups of low amplitude spikes, on all four tracings. These periods of maximum activity enter and leave the territory surveyed by the microelectrodes in regular succession (1, 2, 3, 4). Distance between the tips of the microelectrodes: 170 μ.

dinal array may record a different set of alternations, as in the example of Fig. 14. The anterior microelectrode (A) shows little or no alternation either in the amplitudes of the spikes or in that of the waves. The middle microelectrode (B) shows an alternation of amplitudes: one group of high amplitude spikes associated with a high amplitude wave alternates, at equal intervals, with a group of low amplitude spikes associated with a low amplitude wave. The posterior electrode (C) shows a different alternation of amplitudes: Each group of high amplitude spikes associated with a high amplitude wave is followed, at equal intervals, by two or three groups of low amplitude spikes associated with low amplitude waves.

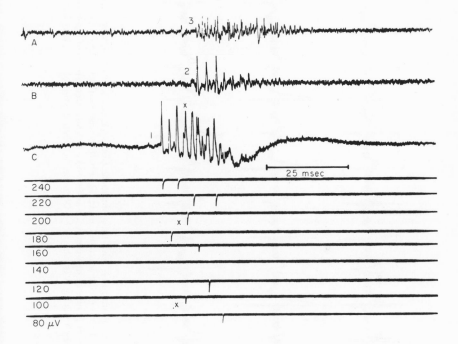

FIG. 13. Recordings obtained, simultaneously, with three microelectrodes (A, B, C), whose tips were located along a straight line, from the thalamus of the Macaque, under light barbiturate anesthesia. Microelectrode A recorded neuronal spikes from the nucleus reticularis. Microelectrodes B and C recorded neuronal spikes as well as slow waves from the nucleus ventralis anterior. The activity in the nucleus reticularis (3, in tracing A) follows the activity in the nucleus ventralis anterior (1 and 2, in tracing B and C). The time scale is expanded so that individual spikes may be distinguished. Tracing C shows a single group of spikes, accompanied by a single slow wave (similar to groups a, b, c, etc., in Fig. 14). The amplitudes of the spikes of this group are properly classified by the pulse-height analyzer, despite the variations of the base line. The spikes designated x, are classified in the amplitude ranges to which they belong, even though they are separated by an extremely short interval. Distances between the tips of the microelectrodes: 180 μ.

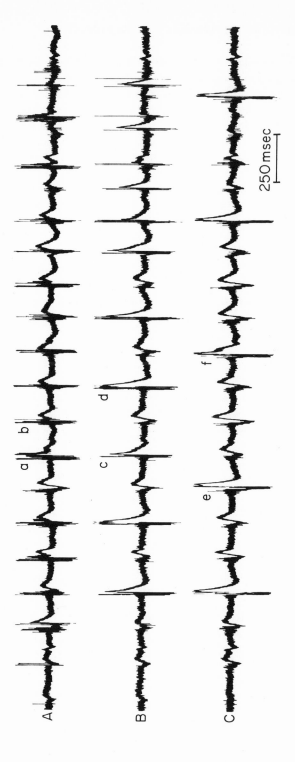

FIG. 14. Recordings obtained, simultaneously, with three microelectrodes (A, B, C), whose tips were located along a straight line, from the nucleus ventralis anterior of the thalamus of the Macaque, under light barbiturate anesthesia, during the period of development of slow waves. Tracings B and C show the activity of groups of neurons (such as c-d and e-f) whose frequencies of discharge are submultiples of the frequency of discharge of the groups recorded on tracing A (such as a-b). Distances between the tips of the microelectrodes: A to B, 200 μ; B to C, 175 μ.

The alternation of groups of high amplitude and low amplitude spikes indicates that several groups of neurons participate in the development of these processes in the nucleus ventralis anterior. Separation of the amplitudes by the pulse-height analyzer provides a clearer picture of the relations between the activities of these various groups of neurons. Tracing C, of the upper part of Fig. 15, shows a recording obtained from the nucleus ventralis anterior of the thalamus of the macaque monkey. Three complete episodes of progressive development can be seen in this tracing (x-y, j-k, o-s), reaching periods of maximum activity at y-z, k-l, s-p. The classification, by the pulse-height analyzer, of the amplitudes of the spikes present on tracing C, is shown in the lower part of Fig. 15. The time scale is highly compressed so that each vertical line on the original tracing C as well as on the analyzer channels may represent several neuronal spikes. The amplitudes are classified into a series of ranges, each one of which is 20 μV wide: line 80 records all spikes whose amplitudes range from 80 to 100μV, line 100 records all spikes whose amplitudes range from 100 to 120 μV, and so on to line 240, which records all spikes whose amplitudes go beyond 240 μV. In examining the distribution of spikes in these ranges, it can be seen that at least two groups of neurons participate in each of the episodes of progressive developments of activity (such as xyz, jkl, osp): One group represented by the spikes classified in the high amplitude ranges from 180 to 240 μV, another represented by spikes classified in the low amplitude ranges, from 80 to 160 μV. In the episode jkl, for example, the activity of one group begins at m, the activity of the other at j; new neurons are progressively brought into action by each group so that new spikes are classified in the different amplitude ranges, until a maximum number of neurons in both groups are active in the period of maximum activity (kln). A similar distribution can be seen in the episode osp: the activity of one group of neurons begins at q, the activity of the other at o, and a maximum number of neurons in both groups are active during the period of maximum activity (spr).

2. Activity in the Nucleus Ventralis Anterior, in the State of Wakefulness

The sequence of episodes of progressive development leading to periods of maximum activity can be seen in natural sleep or in sleep induced by barbiturates. They show the greatest consistency and regularity in the state which coincides with the presence, in the electrocorticogram, of trains of waves of 10 to 12 Hz. As sleep becomes lighter and the animal comes closer to the state of wakefulness, these episodes become less frequent, their periodicity becomes less regular, and the intermediate periods of silence become shorter. In the state of wakefulness, the patterns of activity change: The microelectrode located in the nucleus ventralis anterior records sequences of spikes of periodically increasing and decreasing amplitudes (Fig. 16A, a to b) interrupted by spikes of irregularly

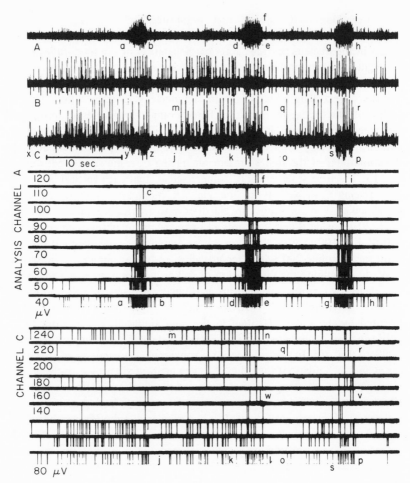

FIG. 15. Recordings obtained, simultaneously, with three microelectrodes (A, B, C), whose tips were located along a straight line, from the thalamus of the Macaque, under light barbiturate anesthesia. Microelectrode A recorded the activity in the nucleus reticularis. Microelectrodes B and C recorded the activity in the nucleus ventralis anterior. Tracings B and C show two complete episodes of progressive development, maximum activity, and silence (xyz; jkl, osp). Each period of maximum activity (y-z; k-l; s-p) in the nucleus ventralis anterior is concomitant with the development of activity in the nucleus reticularis (a-b; d-e; g-h). The amplitudes of the neuronal spikes in tracing A are separated and classified by the pulse-height analyzer in a-c-b, d-f-e, g-i-h; these classifications show the progressive increases and decreases in the amplitudes of the spikes in the groups a-b, d-e, g-h. The amplitudes of the spikes in tracing C are separated and classified below; this classification shows the activity of two groups of neurons which participate in the development of the activities xyz, jkl, osp: one group whose neuronal spikes are distributed within the high amplitude ranges (such as m-w-n or q-v-r), another group whose neuronal spikes are distributed within the low amplitude ranges (such as j-w-l or o-v-p). Distances between the tips of the microelectrodes: 180 μ.

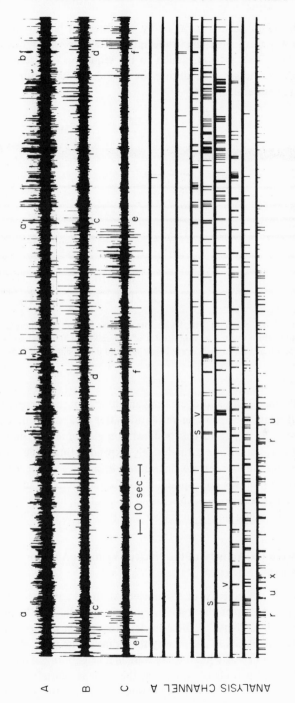

FIG. 16. Recordings obtained, simultaneously, with three microelectrodes (A, B, C), whose tips were located along a straight line, from the thalamus of the Macaque, in the waking state. The tip of microelectrode A was in the nucleus ventralis anterior, the tip of microelectrode C was in the ventralis medialis, and the tip of microelectrode B was at an intermediate point between the two nuclei. Periods of activity in the ventralis anterior, characterized by progressive increases and decreases in the amplitude of the neuronal spikes (a-b, on tracing A), correspond to periods of silence in the ventralis medialis (e-f, on tracing C). The amplitudes of the spikes in tracing A are separated and classified, by the pulse-height analyzer, into progressively increasing and decreasing amplitude ranges (r-s-u-v-x). Distances between the tips of the microelectrodes: 210 μ.

varying amplitudes (Fig. 16A, b to a) or by sequences of high frequency discharges in which groups of high amplitude spikes alternate with groups of low amplitude spikes (Fig. 18c, y to z), similar to the sequences of alternating high and low amplitude discharges seen during the periods of maximum activity in light sleep or light anesthesia.

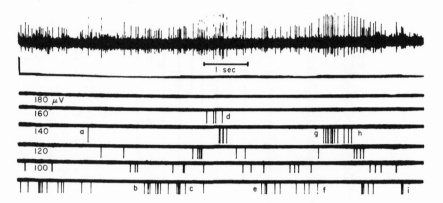

FIG. 17. Section of tracing A of Fig. 16 and its analysis by the pulse-height analyzer, shown on an expanded time scale. The amplitudes of the spikes in the original tracing (A) are separated and classified into progressively increasing and decreasing amplitude ranges (a, b, c, d, etc.).

The periodically increasing and decreasing amplitudes of the spikes in tracing 16A, a to b, are displayed with better resolution after separation and classification by the pulse-height analyzer. This is shown, on a compressed time scale, in the lower part of Fig. 16 and, on a moderately expanded time scale, in Fig. 17. In both examples the amplitudes are distributed in a series of successively increasing and decreasing ranges corresponding to the variations of amplitudes in the original tracing (increasing to a, decreasing from a to b; increasing from c to d, decreasing to e; increasing from e to g, decreasing from h to i, in Fig. 17).

3. Relations between the Activity of the Nucleus Ventralis Anterior and That of Neighboring Nuclei

Relations between the activity of the nucleus ventralis anterior, that of the nucleus reticularis, and that of the nucleus ventralis medialis have been investigated by recording the activity of these nuclei, simultaneously, with arrays of several microelectrodes placed in such a way that some of the microelectrodes in the array were in one nucleus while others were in a neighboring nucleus. It has been found that certain periods of activity in the nucleus ventralis anterior are related to the development of activity occurring rostrally, in the nucleus reticu-

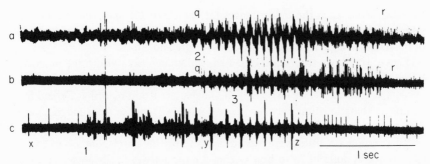

FIG. 18. Recordings obtained, simultaneously, with three microelectrodes (a, b, c), whose tips were located along a straight line, from the thalamus of the squirrel monkey, in the waking state. The tips of microelectrodes a and b were in the nucleus reticularis, the tip of microelectrode c was in the ventralis anterior. Tracing c shows a period of progressive development of activity (x-y), followed by a period of maximum activity (y-z). The different periodicities of the groups of spikes of different amplitudes which occur during the period x-y became coordinated (lock-in) during the period of maximum activity y-z. A period of activity in the nucleus reticularis (q-r), follows a period of activity in the nucleus ventralis anterior. Distances between the tips of the microelectrodes: a-b, 215 μ; b-c, 280 μ.

laris, and to the cessation of activity occurring caudally, in the nucleus ventralis medialis.

Such relations can be seen in Figs. 15, 16, and 18. Figure 15 shows recordings obtained, simultaneously, with three microelectrodes (A, B, C) displayed antero-posteriorly along a straight line, from the nucleus reticularis (A) and from the nucleus ventralis anterior (B and C) of the macaque monkey under light barbiturate anesthesia. While periods of maximum activity develop in the nucleus ventralis anterior (such as y-z, k-l, and s-p in tracing C), bursts of spikes of progressively increasing and decreasing amplitudes appear on the tracing corresponding to the nucleus reticularis (at a-b, d-e, and g-h in tracing A). Similar relations between the activity of these two nuclei can be seen in Fig. 18, which shows recordings obtained, simultanously, with three microelectrodes (a, b, c), displayed antero-posteriorly along a straight line, from the nucleus reticularis (a and b) and from the nucleus ventralis anterior (c) of the squirrel monkey in the waking state. While sequences of high frequencey neuronal discharges in which groups of high amplitude spikes alternate with groups of low amplitude spikes appear on the tracing corresponding to the nucleus ventralis anterior (c) bursts of spikes of progressively increasing and decreasing amplitudes appear on the tracing corresponding to the nucleus reticularis (a and b).

The progressively increasing and decreasing amplitudes of the spikes in each burst which develops in the nucleus reticularis (Fig. 15A) are displayed in the middle part of Fig. 15, after separation and classification by the pulse-height analyzer. The spikes of lowest amplitudes of burst a-b appear first (at a, on the 40 μV line), spikes of progressively higher amplitudes appear in succession on the next lines, reach the higher ranges (at c, on 110 μV line), and disappear in inverse order (from c to b). Similar classifications of the amplitudes of the spikes of bursts d-e and g-h of tracing A, are seen at dfe and gih.

Figure 16 shows recordings obtained, simultaneously, with three microelectrodes (A, B, C), displayed antero-posteriorly along a straight line, from the nucleus ventralis anterior (A), from the nucleus ventralis medialis (C), and from an intermediate location between the two nuclei (B), of the macaque monkey in the state of wakefulness. While sequences of spikes of progressively increasing and decreasing amplitudes are recorded in the tracing corresponding to the nucleus ventralis anterior (a to b in tracing A), the activity in the nucleus ventralis medialis is silenced (e to f in tracing C). During the same period, the activity at the intermediate location between the two nuclei (c to d in tracing B) shows an intermediate pattern.

DISCUSSION

The basic patterns of neuronal discharge and of circulation of neuronal activity associated with the "synchronization" of the gross waves (summarized earlier and in Fig. 3 in this paper) are common to the cat and the monkey.

However, in some of the thalamic nuclei of the monkey, these patterns show a degree of complexity and interrelation with one another which, so far, has not been found in the cat. Several features characterize the neuronal activity in the thalamic nuclei whose activity has been investigated in the monkey:

1. Differences between the patterns of activity in various nuclei are greater than in the cat. Some patterns of neuronal activity and their association with the gross waves are typical of certain nuclei and have not been found in others.

2. Several groups of neurons participate in the kind of activity which has been found to be typical of the nucleus ventralis anterior. At the beginning of the periods of progressive development, the various groups of neurons discharge at irregular intervals; as the development goes on, the discharge of each group becomes more frequent and more regularly periodic, and each group develops its own periodicity of discharge; finally, when the period of maximum activity is reached, the periodicities of discharge of the different groups are related to one another: One group of neurons discharges with the same periodicity as the gross waves while the other groups discharge with periodicities which are submultiples of it.

When this is seen with a single microelectrode, a tracing is obtained in which the occurrence of a sequence of two or three groups of spikes of low amplitude, generated by neurons distant from the tip of the microelectrode, alternates with the occurrence of groups of spikes of high amplitude, generated by neurons close to the tip of the microelectrode (Fig. 18c). The progressive involvement of several groups of neurons in these phenomena is confirmed when the amplitudes of the spikes on such a recording are separated and classified with the pulse-height analyzer (Fig. 15, lower part).

When this is seen with an array of microelectrodes displayed along an antero-posterior line, the anterior microelectrode records the activity of one group of neurons, whose discharge is concomitant with every gross wave, the middle electrode records the activity of another group of neurons whose discharge is concomitant with every other gross wave, and the posterior microelectrode records the activity of a third group of neurons whose discharge is concomitant with every third or fourth gross wave (Fig. 14).

These temporal and spatial relations between the discharge of the several groups of neurons involved in the development of such sequences of events suggest that the activities of several regions of the neuronal networks of the nucleus ventralis anterior became progressively coordinated, in frequency and in phase, until a resonance-like state is achieved during which the neuronal activity reaches a maximum, and gross waves develop.

This resonance-like state, which occurs in the nucleus ventralis anterior, is temporally related to the development of neuronal discharge in the nucleus reticularis and to the cessation of discharge in the nucleus ventralis medialis (Fig. 15, 16, 18). In the nucleus reticularis, the discharge is either concomitant with (Fig. 15) or follows (Fig. 18) the activity in the nucleus ventralis anterior, and the rhythmicity of the groups of spikes and of the associated gross waves is the same in both nuclei.

The possibility that the anterior regions of the thalamus may influence the rhythmicity of other regions of the brain has been frequently discussed in the literature (Morison & Dempsey, 1942; Hunter & Jasper, 1949; Verzeano, Lindsley & Magoun, 1953; Hess, 1954, 1957). Because of their relations with the activity of neighboring nuclei, the question arises whether the sequences of progressive development and resonance-like states which occur in the nucleus ventralis anterior may constitute the basis of a neuronal mechanism by which such influences on other regions of the brain might be exerted.

For this reason the temporal relations between thalamic and cortical activities, in both hemispheres, were studied by recording, simultaneously, the activities of the nucleus ventralis anterior and of the cortex on the right and on the left sides. These simultaneous recordings show that the temporal relations between these regions are variable (Fig. 19). In some cases, the neuronal activities in the nucleus ventralis anterior on the right and on the left are synchronous; in other cases the right leads the left or vice versa. In some cases the period of maximum neuronal activity in the nucleus ventralis anterior precedes the development of a train of gross waves in the cortex or vice versa (Fig. 20).

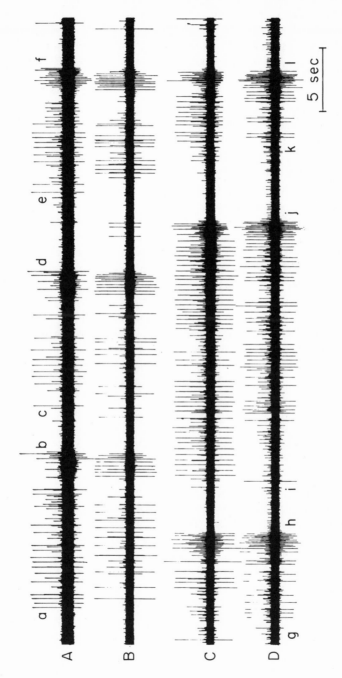

FIG. 19. Recordings obtained, simultaneously, with four microelectrodes (A, B, C, D), from the thalamus of the Macaque, in light barbiturate anesthesia. Microelectrodes A and B were in the right nucleus ventralis anterior, C and D in the left ventralis anterior. Three episodes of progressive development and maximum activity were recorded from the right side (a-b, c-d, e-f) and three from the left side (g-h, i-j, k-l). The temporal relations between periods of maximum activity on the two sides are variable: the left side precedes the right side at g-h and a-b; the right side precedes the left side at i-j and c-d, and the periods of maximum activity are synchronous at e-f and k-l. Distances between the tips of the microelectrodes: A-B, 245 μ; C-D, 350 μ.

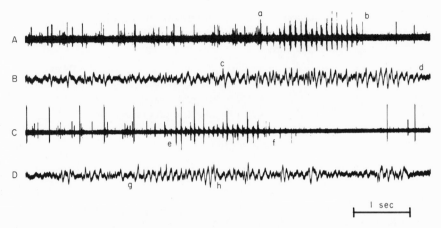

FIG. 20. Recordings obtained, simultaneously, with two microelectrodes (A and C) and two macroelectrodes (B and D), from the thalamus and the cortex of the Macaque, in light barbiturate anesthesia. Microelectrodes A and C were in the nuclei ventralis anterior, right and left, respectively. Macroelectrodes B and D were on the surface of the right and left parietal cortex, respectively. A period of maximum neuronal activity is shown in each of the thalamic tracings (a-b and e-f). A train of cortical slow waves is shown in each of the cortical tracings (c-d and g-h). The temporal relations between the thalamus and the cortex are variable: A train of cortical slow waves corresponds to each period of maximum neuronal activity in the ventralis anterior, but it may either precede or follow this period, by several seconds.

Because of the variability of these relations, several possibilities have to be considered:

1. The activity of the nucleus ventralis anterior may have only an influence limited to its immediate vicinity, such as the nucleus reticularis and the nucleus ventralis medialis, without relation to the activity of the cerebral cortex.

2. The activity of the nucleus ventralis anterior may have an influence on the activity of a limited region of the cortex. In such case, full synchrony between the thalamic and cortical activities could be found only if, by exhaustive exploration of the cortex, this limited region could be determined.

3. The activity of the nucleus ventralis anterior may have an influence on the activity of wide cortical regions but this influence may be mediated by other thalamic nuclei. In such case, these thalamic nuclei may influence different cortical regions at different times and, therefore, full synchrony between the activity in the nucleus ventralis anterior and the activity of the cortex would occur only occasionally.

It is possible that the circulation of neuronal activity in the nucleus ventralis anterior and its relations with the neuronal activity of other thalamic nuclei may be only one of several subcortical mechanisms which influence the rhythmicity of the electrical activity of the brain. Certain structures in the medulla (Moruzzi,

1960) and certain structures in the basal forebrain (Sterman & Clemente, 1962; Hernandez-Peon, 1963) have also been shown to influence the "synchronization" of the electrocorticogram.

It is therefore conceivable that synchrony or lack of synchrony between the electrical activity of several cortical and subcortical regions of the brain may depend on the degree of coordination between the activities of these various structures. And it is equally conceivable that the processes in which the circulation of neuronal activity leads to the building up of resonance-like states may be at the basis of these mechanisms of coordination.

REFERENCES

Adey, W. R., Kado, R., & Rhodes, J. M. Sleep: Cortical and subcortical recordings in chimpanzee. *Science,* 1963, **141**, 932-933.

Albe-Fessard, D., Arfel, G., & Guiot, G. Activites electriques caracteristiques de quelques structures cerebrales chez l'homme. *Annales de Chirurgie.* 1963, **17**, 1185-1214.

Andersen, P., Andersson, S. A., & Lømo, T. Patterns of spontaneous rhythmic activity within various thalamic nuclei. *Nature*, 1966, **211**, 888-889.

Andersen P., & Andersson, S. A. *Physiological basis of the alpha rhythm.* New York: Appleton, 1968.

Creutzfeldt, O., & Jung, R. Neuronal discharge in the cat's motor cortex during sleep and arousal. In G. E. W. Wolstenholme & M. O'Connor (Eds.), *The nature of sleep,* Ciba Symposium, London: Churchill, 1961. Pp. 131-170.

Dill, R. C., Vallecalle, E., & Verzeano, M. Evoked potentials, neuronal activity and stimulus intensity in the visual system. *Physiology and Behavior,* 1968, **3**, 797-801.

Gergen, J. A., & MacLean, P. D. A stereotaxic atlas of the squirrel monkey's brain. *U. S. Public Health Service, Publication,* 1962, **933**.

Hernandez-Peon, R. Sleep induced by localized electrical, or chemical stimulation of the forebrain. In R. Hernandez-Peon (Ed.), *The physiological basis of mental activity. Electroencephalography and Clinical Neurophysiology, Supplement*, 1963, **24**, 188-198.

Hess, W. R. The diencephalic sleep centre. In J. F. Delafresnaye (Ed.), *Brain mechanisms and consciousness,* Springfield, Ill.: Thomas, 1954. Pp. 117-125.

Hess, W. R. *The functional organization of the diencephalon.* New York: Grune & Stratton, 1957.

Hild, W., & Tasaki, I. Morphological and physiological properties of neurons and glial cells in tissue culture. *Journal of Neurophysiology,* 1962, **25**, 277-304.

Hunter, J., & Jasper, H. H. Effects of thalamic stimulation in unanaesthetized animals. *Electroencephalography and Clinical Neurophysiology,* 1949, **1**, 305-324.

Littauer, R. M., & Walcott, C. Pulse-height analyzer for neuro-physiological applications. *Review Scientific Instruments,* 1959, **30**, 1102-1106.

Mescherskii, R. M., The vectorgraphical characteristic of spontaneous rabbit brain cortex activity. *Sechenov Physiological Journal of the USSR (English Translation),* 1961, **47**, 419-426.

Morison, R. S., & Dempsey, E. W. A study of thalamo-cortical relations. *American Journal of Physiology,* 1942, **135**, 281-292.

Moruzzi, G. Synchronizing influences of the brain stem and the inhibitory mechanisms underlying the production of sleep by sensory stimulation. In H. H. Jasper & G. D. Smirnov (Eds.), *The Moscow colloquium on electroencephalography of higher nervous activity*. *Electroencephalography and Clinical Neurophysiology, Supplement*, 1960, **13**, 232-252.

Olszewski, J. *The thalamus of the Macaca mulatta*. Basel: Karger, 1952.

Reite, M. L., Rhodes, J. M., Kavan, E., & Adey, W. R. Normal sleep patterns in Macaque monkey. *Archives of Neurology*, 1965, **12**, 133-144.

Sterman, M. B., & Clemente, C. D. Forebrain inhibitory mechanisms: Cortical synchronization induced by basal forebrain stimulation. *Experimental Neurology*, 1962, **6**, 91-102.

Tasaki, I., Polley, E. H., & Orrego, H. Action potentials from individual elements in cat geniculate and striate cortex. *Journal of Neurophysiology*, 1954, **17**, 454-474.

Van Rennes, A. B. Pulse-amplitude analysis in nuclear research, Parts I to IV. *Nucleonics*, 1952, **10**, No. 7, 20-27; No. 8, 22-28; No. 9, 32-38; No. 10, 50-56.

Verzeano, M., Sequential activity of cerebral neurons. *Archives Internationales de Physiologie et de Biochimie*, 1955, **63**, 458-476.

Verzeano, M. Activity of cerebral neurons in the transition from wakefulness to sleep. *Science*, 1956, **124**, 366-367.

Verzeano, M. Neuronal interaction and synchronization of the EEG. Fifth International Congress, EEG and Clinical Neurophysiology, Rome, 1961. *Excerpta Medica International Congress Series*, 1961, **37**, 49-54.

Verzeano, M. The synchronization of brain waves. *Acta Neurologica Latinoamericana*, 1963, **9**, 307.

Verzeano, M. *Proceedings of the 3rd Conference on Learning, Princeton, N. J., 1965* (unpublished).

Verzeano, M. Evoked responses and network dynamics. In R. E. Whalen, R. F. Thompson, M. Verzeano, and N. M. Weinberger (Eds.), *The neural control of behavior*. New York: Academic Press, 1970 (to be published).

Verzeano, M., & Calma, I. Unit-activity in spindle bursts. *Journal of Neurophysiology*, 1954, **17**, 417-428.

Verzeano, M., Dill, R. C., Vallecalle, E., Groves, P., & Thomas, J. Evoked responses and neuronal activity in the lateral geniculate. *Experientia*, 1968, **24**, 696-697.

Verzeano, M., Laufer, M., & Spear, P. Neuronal activity in the brain of the monkey. Meeting of the Biophysical Society, Chicago, 1964 (Abstr.).

Verzeano, M., Lindsley, D. B., & Magoun, H. W. Nature of recruiting response. *Journal of Neurophysiology*, 1953, **16**, 183-195.

Verzeano, M., & Negishi, K. Neuronal activity in cortical and thalamic networks. *Journal General Physiology*, 1960, **43**, Pt. 2, 177-195.

Verzeano, M., & Negishi, K. Neuronal activity in wakefulness and in sleep. In G. E. W. Wolstenholme & M. O'Connor (Eds.), *The nature of sleep*. Ciba Symposium, London: Churchill, 1961, pp. 108-130.

Wolbarsht, M. L., MacNichol, E. F., Jr., & Wagner, H. G. Glass insulated platinum microelectrodes. *Science*, 1960, **132**, 1309-1310.

INTEGRATIVE FUNCTIONS OF THE THALAMOCORTICAL VISUAL SYSTEM OF CAT[1]

KAO LIANG CHOW

Division of Neurology
Stanford University School of Medicine
Stanford, California

The major portion of the optic nerve fibers of cat make synaptic contacts on neurons in the dorsal nucleus of the lateral geniculate body (LGD). Collaterals from some of these fibers together with others coming directly from the retina pass on to the superior colliculi and the pretectal region (Glees, 1941; Barris, Ingram, & Ranson, 1935; O'Leary, 1940; Hayhow, 1958). The LGD cells send axons to the visual cortex, area 17 (as defined by Otsuka & Hassler, 1962), and axons and collaterals to area 18 (Meikle & Sprague, 1964; Glickstein, King, Miller, & Berkley, 1967). Behaviorally, cat's ability to react differentially to different visual forms, its pattern vision, depends largely on the integrity of the geniculate-cortical system. The midbrain optic centers do not project directly to the visual cortices. Destruction of the superior colliculi has little effect on the animal's visual learning (Urbaitis & Meikle, 1968) but causes various defects of visual field and visuo-motor reflexes (Sprague, 1966, pp. 391-414). A normal cat's responses to visual patterns probably do not involve critically the activities of the midbrain centers. They will not be considered further.

Either by placing lesions in the retina or in the LGD in order to trace the antegrade axonal degenerations (Polyak, 1927; Laties & Sprague, 1966; O'Leary, 1940; Hayhow, 1958; Glees, 1941; Glickstein *et al.*, 1967) or by placing lesions in area 17, 18, or in the LGD to detect the retrograde cell degenerations (Sprague, 1966, pp. 391-414; Stone, 1966; Chow & Dewson, 1966), anatomists have obtained data to show an orderly projection of the retina to the LGD and of the LGD to the visual cortices. Neurons in adjacent retinal loci send their axons to adjacent regions of the nucleus, which cells in turn project to adjacent

[1] Supported by N.I.H. Grant NB 3816 and 5K6, NB 18512. I thank Dr. David F. Lindsley, Dr. James Dewson, and Dr. Morten Gollender for their collaboration on some of these experiments.

273

cortical loci. Although the spatial relationships of the retinal points are maintained throughout the system, these topographically organized pathways are not
discrete but overlapping. Stone & Hansen (1966) showed by Nauta stain that
even in the central retina, ganglion cells within a range of .5 to .7 mm. could
impinge on the same LGD region and that at the peripheral retina this distance
increased to about 2.5 mm. Using the retrograde degeneration method, Dewson
and I (Chow & Dewson, 1966) also observed an intermediate zone of about .5
mm. between the normal number of cells in the unaffected region and few
neurons in the degenerated part of the cat's LGD after visual cortical lesions.
The latter finding is in contrast to the sharp boundary of less than .05 mm. in
width between the normal and degenerated areas in the LGD of rat (Lashley,
1941), rabbit (Chow & Dewson, 1966), and monkey (Chow, unpublished).

The physiology of the neurons in the retino-geniculato-cortical system has
been intensively studied by many workers using the microelectrode recording
technique. From these results (Kuffler, 1953; Hubel & Wiesel, 1959, 1961,
1962, 1965; Baumgartner, Brown, & Schutz, 1965; Jung, 1961, pp. 627-674;
and others) emerged a picture of a hierarchical organization with increasing
complexity at successive levels which presumably is based on the increase of
anatomical circuitry. Thus, the retinal cells have a concentric on-off receptive
field which is further elaborated by the cells in LGD. Most cortical cells are not
easily activated by simple light stimuli but are responsive to a line oriented in a
certain direction, or to a moving light in one direction, and so on. The response
properties of these neurons develop successively more complexly from areas 17
to 18 and 19. Spinelli (1966) and Weingarten & Spinelli (1966) have recently
taken exception to this schema. They pointed out that even at the retinal level
the receptive field organization of some cells could be complex and could be
altered by auditory or somatic stimuli. I feel that these may be further adaptive
variations of some neurons added to the basic functional architecture of the
system which is by and large, invariant and exquisitely organized.

Another aspect of the physiology of the visual cells is the temporal characteristics of their spike discharges. Bishop (1964, 1967), Rodieck (1965, 1967),
and others have emphasized the dynamics of the spike discharge patterns, and
have studied the spike interval histograms (IH) of maintained baseline discharge
of retina ganglion cells and the poststimulus time histograms (PSTH) of their
evoked response patterns. The power of these analytic methods to provide new
information has begun to be explored. For example, when a light spot is moved
across the receptive field of a ganglion cell, the shape of the summed response
histograms is not static but varies as the size of the spot and the moving speed
changes (Kozak, Rodieck, & Bishop, 1965). Also, almost all LGD neurons respond to light stimulation of one eye only. However, their response patterns
(e.g., PSTH) to one-eye stimulation could be altered by another light stimulating
the second eye, even though this light given to the second eye by itself would
not evoke spike discharges (Lindsley, Chow, & Gollender, 1967). Therefore, the

behavior of single cells in the system is not exhausted by a "yes" or "no" answer to its most "preferred" stimulus.

These then, as we know them now, are the basic anatomical and physiological substrates making up the cat's retino-geniculate-cortical system which underlies its visually guided behavior. The following are some of our attempts to understand the workings of this system by way of either manipulating the structurally fixed but overlapping pathways or modifying the response properties of single cells.

EFFECTS OF LESIONS OF EITHER OPTIC TRACT OR VISUAL CORTEX

The total number of fibers in one optic tract of cat is about 100,000 (Chang, 1961), containing either no or very few efferent fibers (Brindley & Hamasaki, 1966). After cutting about 98% of both optic tracts, the remaining 4000 or so are sufficient to sustain a cat's pattern vision including visual learning and memory (Galambos, Norton, & Frommer, 1967). These results showed a high degree of redundancy in the capacity of information transmission by these structurally separate paths. One model for explaining this redundancy is to have a small number of cell types, each responding to one specific feature of a patterned stimulus, and at the same time to have a large number of duplicates of them. Information is conveyed by a combination of these individual types of cell. This would be analogous to having alphabets which carry meaning by spelling them into words. As long as a few sets of the alphabets were intact (such as the 4000 or so optic fibers), there would be no difficulty in spelling out any words. The several categories of retinal ganglion cells revealed by the microelectrode recording technique may be viewed as equivalent to the alphabets. They are combined at successive levels into words. The question is where and how such words are completed and read out.

The cortical visual areas could be the *a priori* site for the word-completion task. If this is so, then a complete destruction of visual areas would eliminate the cat's capability to react differentially to visual patterns. (Parenthetically, since their ability to discriminate differences in brightness appeared not to depend on the visual cortices, the following discussion pertains only to cat's pattern vision.) Experimental studies on this problem are inconclusive. Winans (1967) recently reported that after "complete" ablation of areas 17 and 18, cats still performed a visual form discrimination, i.e., discriminated between an upright and an inverted isosceles triangle. However, her conclusion was challenged on the ground that the material used to test discrimination did not exclude the possibility of differentiation based on brightness cues. Also, only one out of four of her cats' brains has been studied histologically; the completeness of the other cats' lesions remained unknown. For an unequivocal solution to this problem, the visual cortical lesion not only has to be complete but also should be confined to areas 17 and 18 with minimum involvement of area 19, suprasylvian, and ectosylvian gyri. A lesion covering most parts of the posterior brain produces complex behavioral defects which are not exclusively visual (Sprague, 1966, pp. 391-414; Doty, 1961, pp. 228-243).

In a similar attempt I have tried to test cats with complete visual cortical lesions restricted to areas 17 and 18. Preoperatively, seven cats were trained on two successive visual discriminations: (1) to choose a gray door for food reward rather than a black door; (2) to choose a black disk against a black cross of the same area. They were tested for retention after the surgery and in addition they were tested for original learning on a third discrimination: to choose a black-white horizontal against vertical situation (see Chow, 1968, for detail). The lesions of five cats were restricted to the visual areas, with none of them "complete." Four of the cats showed perfect postoperative retention of the two discriminations and also acquired the third task at a normal rate. The amount of destroyed visual areas, as estimated from the percent degeneration of the lateral geniculate body (Chow & Dewson, 1966) ranged from 65 to 80%. A fifth animal remembered the black-gray discrimination, but failed to retain the disk-cross discriminations and took more than preoperative trials to reacquire them. The learning curves of this cat (N-9) are shown in Fig. 1. It also took about double

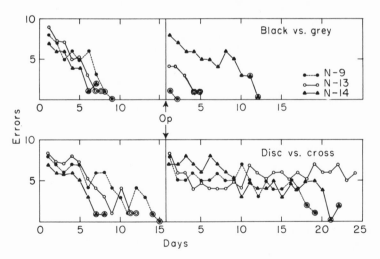

FIG. 1. Learning curves for visual discrimination problems showing the effects of lesions.

the normal rate to learn the horizontal-vertical striations discrimination. Figure 2 shows the extent of cortical lesions and LGD degenerations of N-9. Only about 5% normal LGD remained in the antero-ventral tip of this nucleus. The remaining two cats had large lesions covering the posterior brain that resulted in a complete degeneration of LGD plus widespread cell-atrophy of other thalamic nuclei. They became irritable and refused to be tested.

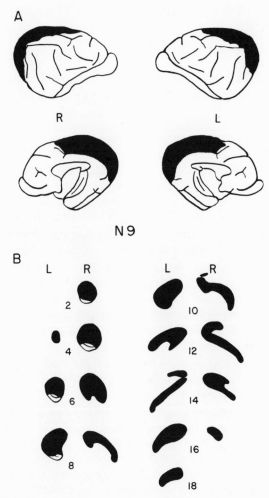

FIG. 2. Extent of cortical lesions (A) and LGD degenerations (B) in cat N-9.

Because of the difficulty of destroying only visual areas 17 and 18 without damaging other parts of the posterior brain, these results are not conclusive. That pattern vision is not likely to be present in cats without visual cortices was suggested by the difficulty in remembering and relearning pattern discriminations already displayed by cats left with about 5% of intact visual areas. A complete lesion may increase these defects and render pattern vision impossible.

This minimum of 5% cortex needed to sustain visual learning and memory is slightly larger than the minimum of 2% for optic nerves. This difference may be due to the fact that afferent fibers partially overlap both at the LGD and at the visual cortex. These results add new evidence to the capability of small remnants to substitute for the function of the whole at the two ends of a structurally fixed retino-cortical system.

EFFECTS OF COMBINED LESIONS OF OPTIC TRACT AND VISUAL CORTEX

This small percentage of optic nerves or visual cortices could be considered as the smallest subset of visual cell types (e.g., like the letters of the alphabet) needed to spell out all aspects of patterned vision (e.g., to form words). From this point of view, each cell type must be represented by a through path and should not switch randomly to another type en route from the retina to the cortex. To test this implied invariance of information transmitted by each of the more or less parallel lines, I have studied cat's vision after destroying large parts of both optic tracts and visual cortices. Such overlapping lesions were used to intercept the through projections, preventing their formation into patterned inputs.

Seven cats were trained on the same two successive discriminations described in the preceding section. They were then subjected to one-stage ablation of large parts of both optic tracts and visual cortices. Care was taken to vary the size and loci of the lesions. Postoperatively five cats remembered these tasks almost perfectly. They also learned a new vertical-horizontal striation discrimination at a normal rate. The amount of lateral geniculate degeneration of these cats ranged from 42 to 84% and of one optic tract section from 82 to 100%. The other two cats, however, failed to remember these tasks. The learning curves of these two cats (Fig. 1) show that cat N-14 took longer than preoperative days to relearn the two tasks. Cat N-13 showed some retention on the black-gray problem but failed to reach criterion on the disk-cross discrimination. Both cats had difficulty in avoiding obstacles and showed pass-pointing in reaching and constricted visual field. The latter is shown by their head held in a bizarre closed-up position in viewing visual stimuli. The percentages of LGD degeneration were 85, 89% (N-13) and 92, 90% (N-14), and of optic tract cutting, 100, 90% (N-13), and 90, 96% (N-14). The histological findings of N-13 are shown in Fig. 3. Figure 4 is a Weil stained section showing the complete destruction of the left optic tract, optic chiasma, and 90% damage of the right tract.

It appears that cats could tolerate 85% damage of both ends of this topographically fixed system without impairment of their visual learning and memory. But when this percentage is increased to about 90, the remaining intact optic

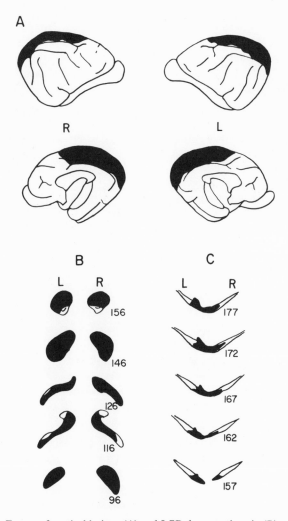

FIG. 3. Extent of cortical lesions (A) and LGD degenerations in (B) cat N-13.

nerves and visual areas are not sufficient to sustain visual memory although still adequate for the cat to relearn some visual discrimination. These results and the fact of N-13's failure to reacquire the disk-cross discrimination suggest that such large, combined lesions interrupted all through traffic. Otherwise, evidence cited in the last section would set the lower limit to 2% instead of the 10% for maintaining normal pattern vision. Even though a direct proof of the absence of through conduction is difficult, these results nonetheless suggest the possibility of reorganization of neural transmission at the lateral geniculate level. The long postoperative relearning may be based on this physiological process, provided of course, such relearning does not take place outside the geniculato-cortical system.

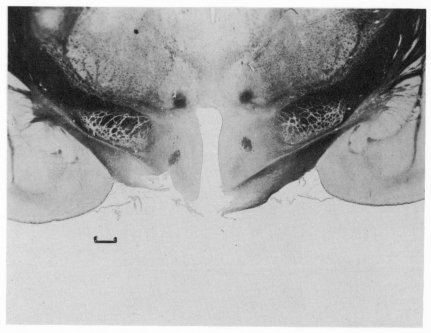

FIG. 4. Photograph showing the extent of optic nerve destruction in cat N-13, Weil stain.

RESIDUAL NEURONS IN THE DEGENERATED
LATERAL GENICULATE NUCLEUS

The dorsal nucleus of the lateral geniculate body occupies a pivotal position in this system. If neural reorganization does take place, it may be based partly on a switching of synaptic connections or an alteration of response properties of the LGD neurons. Extracellular recordings of single cells in normal LGD provide detailed information on their receptive field organization, spike discharge patterns (i.e., PSTH and IH), and the relative frequency of monocular, binocular, and dichoptic cells (Hubel & Wiesel, 1961; Lindsley et al., 1967). Therefore, one could begin to test this possibility of reorganization at this level by comparing the normative data with those obtained from cells in the degenerated LGD.

The neurons in the degenerated nucleus following partial ablation of visual areas were located either in a normal region spared by the incomplete lesion or inside the degenerated tissue. The presence of residual neurons within a cell-atrophied zone was a unique feature of cat's LGD. For in the LGD of rat, rabbit, monkey, and man, all neurons were eventually obliterated by visual cortical lesions. Dewson and I have determined the time course of retrograde degeneration in the LGD and found no neurons left in the rabbit nucleus 9-15 weeks after cortical lesion, but about 25% of the neurons remained in the cat nucleus during the 6-50 postoperative survival weeks (Chow & Dewson, 1966). Only small cells (diameter about 10 μ), but no large and medium-sized ones were left. Lindsley and I have recorded extracellularly these residual neurons in both the normal and degenerated portion of the cat's LGD 4-12 weeks after cortical ablation (Chow & Lindsley 1969).

We have used the following experimental procedures: (1) Large bilateral lesions were placed in visual areas of eleven cats; (2) two to 10 weeks later they were operated upon again and were prepared according to a special stereotaxic technique for semichronic, unanesthetized animal experimentation (Lindsley *et al.*, 1967); (3) during an experimental session, the cat was immobilized with Flaxidal (Abbott) plus d-tubocurarine chloride (Upjohn), intubated, and artificially respired; (4) at the end of each electrode penetration, direct current was passed through the microelectrode to mark the point of the last recorder unit; and (5) after the terminal experiment, the brain was cut and the sections stained to locate the position of each unit recorded either from the location of the marked spot or by calculating the distance back from the mark along the electrode track using the micrometer-drive readings corresponding to the unit. Single cells in both normal and degenerated LGD were recorded from 1 to 3 hrs.

Thirty-six neurons were located well inside the normal portion of the partially degenerated LGD. Four were dichoptic units, one was a binocular unit, and the rest were monocular units.[2] These frequencies were not significantly different from the 21 dichoptic units and 5 binocular units recorded by the same procedure applied to 145 LGD cells in normal cats. Furthermore, the receptive field, the baseline spike discharge pattern, and the poststimulus time histogram to light stimulation of the 36 neurons were indistinguishable from those of normal cells (Chow & Lindsley, unpublished data).

In contrast to the normal region, the residual neurons in the degenerated portion of the LGD were difficult to record. Many times no cells were encountered during an electrode penetration. Many cells had low amplitude and could be held for only a few minutes. However, when a cell could be recorded for many hours, it had all the characteristics of a normal LGD neuron, such as the usual positive-negative potentials with an inflection on the positive phase indicating discharges near the cell body. The receptive field of these cells showed the

[2]Dichoptic units refer to cells which respond only to light stimulation of one eye and not to the other eye, but its response patterns to one-eye stimulation can be altered by adding another light stimulation to the second eye. Binocular units are cells responding to light stimulation of either eye. Monocular units are cells responding to light stimulation to only one eye or the other.

usual center-surround organization. Also, their poststimulus time histogram remained unchanged after many hours of light stimulation.

Coincident with the normal behavior of individual residual neurons was a sharp increase in the number of binocular cells. Of the 19 neurons located well inside the degenerated zone, 8 could be activated by light stimulus given to either eye. This ratio was significantly higher than the 5 out of 145 cells in normal LGD. On the other hand, the two dichoptic units out of the remaining 11 cells represented the normal relative frequency of this cell-type. Figure 5 shows the PSTH's of 3 binocular units recorded during one electrode penetration. The upper trace of each pair was the cell's response to contralateral eye stimulations by a light spot placed at the center of its receptive field, and the lower trace is the same cell's response to a light flash shining on the ipsilateral eye. Each of the traces was the summed response of 20 light presentations. Figure 6A showed the position of the 3 binocular units located at the rostial part of the nucleus. At a higher power view, the region near the electrode mark showed severe cell depletion with only a few small cells scattered around (Fig. 6B). For comparison, a section through the anterior tip of a normal LGD was shown in Fig. 7. Note the striking difference in cell densities between Fig. 6B and 7B, and the absence of large and medium-sized cells in Fig. 6B.

These results revealed no definitive evidence of neural reorganization in the degenerated LGD. The small residual neurons probably do not send axons to the visual cortex, although their collaterals may leave the nucleus. Since they respond normally to light stimulation, the question of how and where they do transmit this afferent information remains to be explored. The increase of binocular units may mean some sort of shifting of cells from monocular to binocular functions. However, it is equally possible that these binocular cells were always present, but were now more easily recorded by the microelectrode amid the sparsely distributed cells. Moreover, one wonders how an increase of binocular units would counteract the effect of disrupting connections between the retina and the visual cortex on visual learning and memory.

MODIFICATION OF RESPONSE PATTERNS OF LGD NEURONS

The equivocal results obtained in degenerated LGD do not necessarily rule out the possibility of neural reorganization in the normal nucleus. We have tested whether the response pattern of a single cell is always invariant to its preferred stimulus or whether it could be modified by experience. Using the same semichronic preparation, we have recorded single neurons in normal awake cats and have attempted to "train" neurons to alter their response to visual stimulus (Chow, Lindsley, & Gollender, 1968).

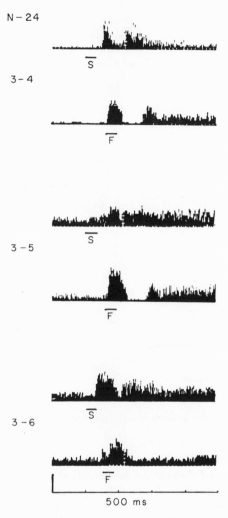

FIG. 5. PSTH's of three binocular units in cat N-24. Stimuli at S and F; vertical bar calibration, 10 spikes; bin size, 4 msec.

Nonvisual stimuli, such as clicks and cutaneous shocks, evoke no response of the LGD cells, except in a few cases, while such stimulation may transiently suppress the ongoing discharges. We were obliged to use separate stimulation of the two eyes, as a means to influence a cell's response. In order to control for factors, such as shifting levels of retinal adaptation, general arousal, and the occurrence of pseudo-conditioning which may influence a cell's discharge patterns, a rather stringent "training" method was used. Cats were immobilized with Flaxidal (Abbott) and held in a special stereotaxic frame without using ear

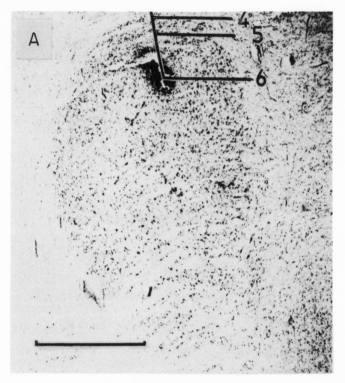

FIG. 6A.

FIG. 6. Photographs of the location of units that provided the PSTH's in Fig. 5. Calibration in A, 1 mm; in B, .1mm.

bar and eye bar and with no surgery or other medication. The receptive field of a LGD neuron was mapped through the appropriate eye on a translucent screen. A light spot of 30-msec. duration (diameter 1 cm), focused on the center of the field and presented on a dark screen, served as the test-spot (somewhat comparable to the conditioned stimulus in a sensory-sensory conditioning paradigm)and on a dimly-lighted screen as the control-spot (i.e., the differential stimulus). A light bulb attached to a contact lens was fitted into the second eye, covered with black tape to prevent any light leak. A light flash of 30-msec. duration delivered through this device was the training flash (i.e., unconditioned stimulus).

At the beginning of a training session, 20-30 trials of the test-spot were presented once every 2 to 10 sec. A poststimulus time histogram of a neuron's responses to the test-spot was computed. Other histograms of the units' responses to the control-spot and the training light were also obtained. These were the pretraining controls. The test-spot was then presented with the training flash at a fixed time interval. For dichoptic units, this interval is critical, and the flash was always given after the spot (Lindsley *et al.*, 1967). The pairing trials constituted

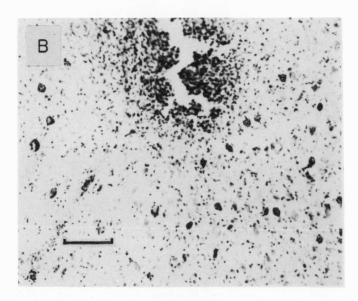

FIG. 6B.

the training process, and they were given at 2 to 10-sec. intervals for about 150 to 300 trials. Histograms of dichoptic and binocular units' responses to the pairing trials differed from the histogram of their responses to the test-spot alone. For monocular units, there were no differences. After the training trials, separate histograms of the units' responses to the test-spot alone, to the control-spot, and to the training flash were again computed. By comparing the pre- and post-training histograms, the following conclusions could be reached: (1) whether or not a cell's response pattern to the test-spot was modified as a result of the pairing trials; (2) if such modification occurred, whether it was specific to the pairing procedure and not generalized to the response evoked by the control-spot; and (3) whether the cell's general activity level remained the same as indicated by the light-flash histograms.

The histograms of monocular units were not affected by adding the light flash to the second eye. Therefore, one would not expect any modifications of their response to the test-spot after the training trials, and none was found. Since about 80% of the LGD cells are monocular units, this result stresses the invariant behavior of this nucleus in responding to many hours of light-spot stimulation at the early input stage of a specific sensory system. This stability contrasts with the gradual decrease of spike discharges of single neurons to repeated sensory stimuli in the midbrain and visual cortex of cats and rabbits (Bell, Sierra, Buendia, & Segundo, 1964; Horn & Hill, 1964; Hubel & Wiesel, 1965; Vinogradova & Lindsley, 1964). The latter phenomenon may be analogous to behavioral habituation. The majority of LGD neurons do not "habituate," and therefore, are secure in their role of always being ready to transmit information.

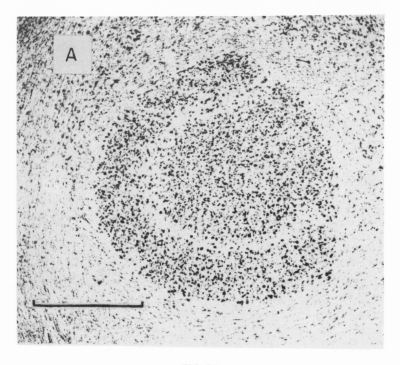

FIG. 7A.

FIG. 7. Photographs of the areas shown in Fig. 6 in a normal cat. Same calibrations as in Fig. 6.

Response modifications occurred in the post-training histograms of 7 out of 21 dichoptic units and 2 out of 5 binocular units. These modifications appeared only in the response histograms evoked by the spot presented in a dark screen that has been paired with light flash and not by the same spot in a lighted screen not paired with flashes. These differential results rule out factors not related to the training procedure as being effective in influencing the cell's responses. Figure 8 shows the poststimulus time histograms of a dichoptic cell. Each histogram is the summed response of 20 stimuli. The traces are presented in the same sequence as the experimental steps used. The first three are the pretraining controls. The flash (F) alone did not evoke any responses. The histograms evoked either by the test-spot (DS) or by the control-spot (LS) consisted of a single peak of discharges at 60 msec. after the onset of the stimuli. When the test-spot was paired with the flash (DSF), this peak broke into two and was followed by a long silent period. After about 150 training trials, the test-spot alone now evoked a double-peak response instead of the pretraining single-peak (compare DS to DS^1 and DS^2). The histograms of the control-spot did not show any changes (compare LS to LS^1 and LS^2). It should be noted that this response

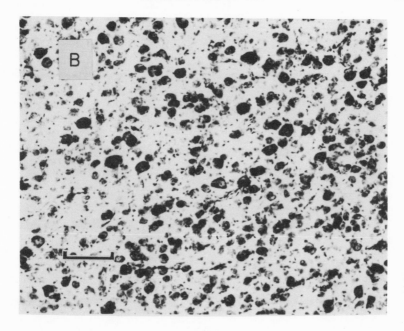

FIG. 7B.

modification was still present when the test-spot was given the third time around (DS^3). Since about 10 min. were needed to complete each histogram, this effect lasted about 50 min.

An example of the experimentally induced changes recorded from a binocular cell is shown in Fig. 9. In this case, the light flash alone evoked unit discharges after repeated stimulation (compare DF^1 to DF). Also, when the flash was paired with the test-spot (DSF), two new peaks appeared in the histogram; one was evoked by the flash alone, and the other at about 100 msec. preceding the onset of the flash. After the pairing trials, the test-spot alone now evoked a response pattern differing both from its pretraining and the paired-stimuli histograms (compare DS^1 to DS and DSF). This new pattern consisted of the initial peak as being evoked by test-spot before, plus a second peak at 100 msec. The third peak at 150 msec. evoked by the flash alone was not preserved. In this case, the two histograms in response to stimulating the two eyes are not simply added together; the resultant modification is nonlinear.

The stability of the great majority of LGD cells contrasts sharply with the nine neurons whose response patterns could be modified by experience. Since this training effect is differential, being present in response to the test stimulus, but not to the control stimulus, these results could be viewed as a neuronal analog of learning (Kandel & Spencer, 1968). That such "learning" is also characteristic of other groups of cells in cats' visual systems is demonstrated by

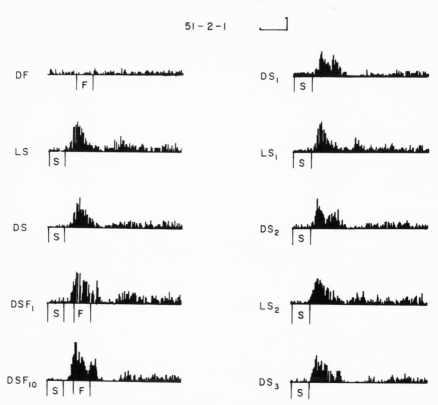

FIG. 8. PSTH's of a dichoptic cell. Calibration, 50 msec. and 10 spikes; bin size, 2 msec.

Morrell (1967, pp. 452-469). He found that some cells in visual area 19 could be conditioned. These visual cells differed from the LGD neurons in that they could be activated by nonvisual stimuli, such as clicks and cutaneous shocks. Morrell therefore used the conditioned reflex paradigm. By pairing clicks or shock to visual stimulus he observed that a cell's response to the visual stimulus was modified after the paired-trial experiences.

The number of modifiable cells in the LGD and in area 19 is comparable to the percentage of cells being conditioned in the hippocampus, reticular formation, and in specific thalamic nuclei (Bureš & Burešová, 1967; Kamikawa, McIlwain, & Adey, 1964; Gerbrandt, Skrebitsky, Burešová, & Bures, 1968). It seems that when an unselected population of neurons of the cat was tested, about 10% of them showed plastic changes following paired-trial experiences. This may indicate the emergence of a system of plastic cells in the neural axis parallel to the other 90% of cells having rigid input and output circuits. This system then could modulate the activity of the rest, thus providing the varying shades of functional plasticity. On philosophical ground, one may also ask about the adaptive value for the existence of such a system amid the great majority of other neurons whose connections and response properties are highly specific and invariant. If the plasticity of these cells signifies a higher level of evolutionary development, then their proportion should increase in the higher centers of the brain, such as the association center. Or, considering the LGD, such a notion

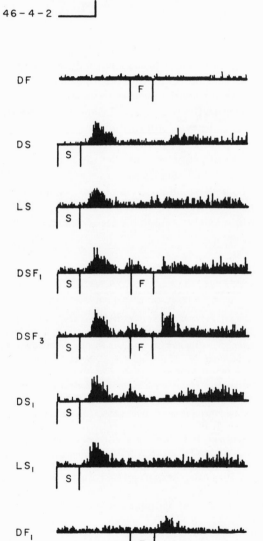

FIG. 9. PSTH's of a binocular cell. Same calibration as in Fig. 8.

would suggest a higher proportion of these cells in the monkey's LGD. A different consideration would indicate that these are more primitive and less differentiated cells and therefore should decrease in number in higher animals.

CONCLUSION

Although the integrative functioning of the geniculato-cortical system remains obscure, the present experiments contribute several guidelines toward its eventual revelation. Thus, in addition to the topographically organized anatomy with its overlap between parallel nerve pathways and the hierarchically organized physiology with its detecting functions of individual neurons, one has to take into account the redundancy of information transmission from the retina to the visual cortices, the possibility of neural reorganization at the LGD, and the existence of a system of plastic cells parallel to the majority of cells that rigidly connect to input-output circuits. Knowledge of how the cat's pattern vision could ultimately be understood in terms of these multiple factors depends not only on accumulating more experimental data, but also, more importantly, on generating insightful models to guide the search for the workings of this exquisitely organized machinery.

REFERENCES

Barris, R. W., Ingram, W. R., & Ransom, S. W. Optic connections of the diencephalon and midbrain of the cat. *Journal of Comparative Neurology,* 1935, **62,** 117-153.
Baumgartner, T., Brown, J. L., & Schutz, A. Responses of single units of the cat visual system to rectangular stimulus patterns. *Journal of Neurophysiology,* 1965, **28,** 1-18.
Bell, C., Sierra, G., Buendia, N., & Segundo, J. P. Sensory properties of neurons in the mesencephalic reticular formation. *Journal of Neurophysiology,* 1964, **27,** 729-739.
Bishop, P. O. Properties of afferent synapses and sensory neurons in the lateral geniculate nucleus. *International Review of Neurobiology,* 1964, **6,** 191-255.
Bishop, P. O. Central nervous system: Afferent mechanisms and perception. *Annual Review of Physiology,* 1967, **29,** 427-484.
Brindley, G. S., & Hamasaki, D. I. Histological evidence against the view that the cat's optic nerve contains centrifugal fibers. *Journal of Physiology,* 1966, **184,** 444-449.
Bureš, J., & Burešová, O. Plastic changes of unit activity based on the reinforcing properties of extracellular stimulation of single neurons. *Journal of Neurophysiology,* 1966, **30,** 98-113.
Chang, H. T. An analysis of fiber constitution of optic tract of cat. *Scientia Sinica,* 1961, **10,** 538-556.
Chow, K. L. Visual discriminations after extensive ablation of optic tract and visual cortex in cats. *Brain Research,* 1968, **9,** 363-366.
Chow, K. L., & Dewson, J. H. Numerical estimates of neurons and glia in lateral geniculate body during retrograde degeneration. *Journal of Comparative Neurology,* 1966, **128,** 63-74.

Chow, K. L., & Lindsley, D. F. Microelectrode study of residual neurons in the degenerated lateral geniculate nucleus of cat. *Journal of Neurophysiology,* 1969, **32**, 116-126.

Chow, K. L., Lindsley, D. F., & Gollender, M. Modification of response patterns of lateral geniculate neurons after paired stimulation of contralateral and ipsilateral eye. *Journal of Neurophysiology* 1968, **31**, 729-739.

Doty, R. W. Functional significance of the topographic aspects of the retino-cortical projection. In R. Jung and H. Kornhuber (Eds.), *The visual system: Neurophysiology and psychophysiology.* Berlin: Springer, 1961.

Galambos, R., Norton, T. T., & Frommer, G. P. Optic tract lesions sparing pattern vision in cats. *Experimental Neurology,* 1967, **18**, 8-25.

Gerbrandt, L. K., Skrebitsky, V. G., Buresova, O., & Bures, J. Plastic changes of unit activity induced by tactile stimuli followed by electrical stimulation of single hippocampal and reticular neurons. *Neuropsychologia,* 1968, **6**, 3-10.

Glees, P. The termination of optic fibers in the lateral geniculate body of the cat. *Journal of Anatomy,* 1941, **76**, 65-92.

Glickstein, M., King, R. A., Miller, J., & Berkley, M. Cortical projections from the dorsal lateral geniculate nucleus of cats. *Journal of Comparative Neurology,* 1967, **130**, 55-76.

Hayhow, W. R. The cytoarchitecture of the lateral geniculate body in the cat in relation to the distribution of crossed and uncrossed optic fibers. *Journal of Comparative Neurology,* 1958, **110**, 1-64.

Horn, G., & Hill, R. M. Habituation of the response to sensory stimuli of neurons in the brain stem of rabbits. *Nature,* 1964, **202**, 296-298.

Hubel, D. H., & Wiesel, T. N. Receptive fields of single neurons in the cat's striate cortex. *Journal of Physiology,* 1959, **148**, 574-591.

Hubel, D. H., & Wiesel, T. N. Integrative action in the cat's lateral geniculate body. *Journal of Physiology,* 1961, **155**, 385-398.

Hubel, D. H., & Wiesel, T. N. Receptive fields, binocular interaction, and functional architecture in the cat's visual cortex. *Journal of Physiology,* 1962, **160**, 106-154.

Hubel, D. H., & Wiesel, T. N. Receptive fields and functional architecture in two nonstriate visual areas (18 and 19) of the cat. *Journal of Neurophysiology,* 1965, **28**, 229-289.

Jung, R. Neuronal integration in the visual cortex and its significance for visual information. In W. Rosenblith (Ed.), *Sensory communication.* Cambridge, Massachusetts: M. I. T. Press, 1961.

Kamikawa, K., McIlwain, J. T., & Adey, W. R. Response patterns of thalamic neurons during classical conditioning. *Electroencephalography and Clinical Neurophysiology,* 1964, **17**, 485-496.

Kandel, E. R. & Spencer, W. A. Cellular neurophysiological approaches in the study of learning. *Physiological Reviews,* 1968, **48**, 65-134.

Kozak, W., Rodieck, R. W., & Bishop, P. O. Responses of single units in lateral geniculate nucleus of cat to moving visual patterns. *Journal of Neurophysiology,* 1965, **28**, 19-47.

Kuffler, S. W. Discharge patterns and functional organization of mammalian retina. *Journal of Neurophysiology,* 1953, **16**, 37-68.

Lashley, K. S. Thalamo-cortical connections of the rat's brain. *Journal of Comparative Neurology,* 1941, **75**, 67-121.

Laties, A. M., & Sprague, J. M. The projection of optic fibers to the visual centers in the cat. *Journal of Comparative Neurology,* 1966, **127**, 35-70.

Lindsley, D. F., Chow, K. L., & Gollender, M. Dichoptic interactions of lateral geniculate neurons of cats to contralateral and ipsilateral eye stimulation. *Journal of Neurophysiology,* 1967, **30**, 628-644.

Meikle, T. H., & Sprague, J. M. The neural organization of the visual pathway in the cat. *International Review of Neurobiology*, 1964, 6, 149-189.

Morrell, F. Electrical signs of sensory coding. In G. C. Quarton, T. Melnechuk, and F. O. Schmitt (Eds.), *The neurosciences: A study program*. New York: Rockefeller Univ. Press, 1967.

O'Leary, J. L. A structural analysis of the lateral geniculate of the cat. *Journal of Comparative Neurology*, 1940, 73, 405-430.

Otsuka, R., & Hassler, R. Uber Aufbau and Gliederung der corticalen Sehsphare bei der Katz. *Archiv. fur Psychiatrie und Nervenkrankheiten*, 1962, 203, 212-234.

Polyak, S. L. An experimental study of the association, callosal, and projection fibers of the cerebral cortex of the cat. *Journal of Comparative Neurology*, 1927, 44, 197-258.

Rodieck, R. W. Quantitative analysis of cat retinal ganglion cell response to visual stimuli. *Vision Research*, 1965, 5, 583-601.

Rodieck, R. W. Maintained activity of cat retinal ganglion cells. *Journal of Neurophysiology*, 1967, 30, 1043-1071.

Spinelli, D. N. Visual receptive fields in the cat's retina: Complications. *Science*, 1966, 152, 1768-1769.

Sprague, J. M. Visual, acoustic, and somesthetic deficits in the cat after cortical and midbrain lesions. In D. Purpura and M. Yahr (Eds.), *The thalamus*. New York: Columbia Univ. Press, 1966.

Stone, J. The Naso-temporal division of the cat's retina. *Journal of Comparative Neurology*, 1966, 126, 585-600.

Stone, J., & Hansen, S. M. The projection of the cat's retina on the lateral geniculate nucleus. *Journal of Comparative Neurology*, 1966, 126, 601-624.

Urbaitis, J. C., & Meikle, T. H. Relearning of a dark-light discrimination by cats after cortical and collicular lesions. *Experimental Neurology*, 1968, 20, 295-311.

Vinogradova, O. S., & Lindsley, D. F. Extinction of reactions to sensory stimuli in single neurons of visual cortex in unanesthetized rabbits. *Federation Proceedings*, 1964, 23, *Translation Supplement*, pp. T 241-246.

Weingarten, M., & Spinelli, D. N. Retinal receptive field changes produced by auditory and somatic stimulation. *Experimental Neurology*, 1966, 15, 363-376.

Winans, S. S. Visual form discrimination after removal of the visual cortex in cats. *Science*, 1967, 158, 944-946.

OCCAM:
A COMPUTER MODEL FOR A CONTENT ADDRESSABLE
MEMORY IN THE CENTRAL NERVOUS SYSTEM

D. N. SPINELLI

Stanford University
Stanford, California

It is a common observation that man and animals can learn to recognize new situations and objects, a faculty which has fascinated philosophers and scientists through the centuries. In modern times experimentation has supplemented theoretical thinking and the search for mechanisms capable of explaining how sensory patterns are processed and stored in the brain has become a major aspect in physiological and psychological research. The tremendous development of digital computers has influenced theory-making in the biological and psychological fields and has also allowed the possibility of checking theoretical models in actual operation by the simulation of hypothesized neuronal networks or by the use of programs that simply implement the logical operations believed to take place in the process being studied. Whatever the biochemical processes are by which a final mark is laid in the proteic structure of the brain, it is clear that the reading-in and the reading-out of memories has to be effected through the medium of neuronal activity. As the activity of nerve fibers and nerve cells is accompanied by electrical manifestations, it seems at least logically possible that one should be able, so to speak, to surprise memories while they are in the process of being recorded or played back. Efforts in this direction have been numerous; I will therefore refer to only a few that seem to indicate the general findings.

By training animals to differentiate between a 10 per second and a 6 per second flickering light and recording from different brain structures with electrodes, John & Killam (1959) were able to show that the frequency of the stimulus could be recorded in structures which are part of the specific visual pathway and also from structures which are part of the nonspecific system. Of their findings, the most dramatic one has to do with records obtained during stimulus generalization. The records from the visual cortex of a cat trained to press a bar to avoid a shock whenever a flicker of 4 cps was presented show 4-cps activity. If a flicker of 10 per second is now presented after learning, the animal still performs the avoidance response, but the records from visual cortex now show what look like a mixture of 10 per second and 4-cps activity. After differentiation to the 10 cycles, the activity in visual cortex is mostly represented by 10 cps. It would seem that when the animal is generalizing to the 10 cps, two kinds of activities are generated in the cat's visual cortex: The 10 per second is produced by the stimulus; the other one, the 4 per second, could conceivably be a playback of what the animal had previously learned. Because the animal was expecting 4 per second, he performed appropriately to the 10 per second. The real reason he performed appropriately to the 10 per second was because the previous memory, namely the 4 per second one, was being played back with the appropriate behavior attached to it. Recent work in our laboratory (Spinelli, 1967) also supports the idea that different stimuli generate different forms of electrical activity in the visual cortex of a monkey. Conceivably these different wave forms[1] could be learned by the cortex and played back during recognition. Accompanying wave forms (Pribram, Spinelli, & Kamback, 1967), signaling the presence or absence of reinforcement and the type of behavior that is going to be performed, have also been detected. Again it is conceivable that the total complex of wave forms might be stored by the brain. The representation of stimulus, behavior, and consequences of the behavior would then be available for further reference.

In a different vein, a similar result was also obtained by Morrell (1961) with his experiments on the mirror focus. It has been known for some time (Kopeloff, Barrera, & Kopeloff, 1942; Kopeloff, Chusid, & Kopeloff, 1954, 1955) that an epileptic focus situated in one hemisphere causes, after a period of time, the production of another epileptic focus in the opposite hemisphere at the mirror point. Morrell revived these experiments. Epileptic foci were produced in one hemisphere in rabbits by freezing the cortex. After a week or two, an epileptic focus developed in the opposite hemisphere. If the corpus callosum was sectioned at this time, the secondary focus ceased to exist, but if more time was allowed to pass, about a month or so, sectioning of the corpus callosum did not make the secondary focus disappear. In other words, the secondary focus had assumed a life of its own. The implication seems to be that the healthy tissue in the opposite hemisphere "learned" the pattern of activity that the mirror focus was sending through the collosal fibers. Morrell's result suggested the following experiment: A chronic stimulator was implanted in a cat and a point was stimu-

[1] Brain waves are here interpreted to be a more or less direct expression of neuronal processes so that while they may not be direct "carriers" or "codes" of the information transacted they must nevertheless be correlated with the activity of the neuronal networks, much as the noise of a mechanical calculator would be correlated to the operations being performed.

lated at 6 per second in the anterior part of the lateral gyrus. Records were taken from the mirror point. After activating the stimulator, activity in the mirror point was followed over a period of weeks and the stimulator turned off for a few minutes once every few days. Initially activity at 6 per second in the mirror point ceased the moment the stimulator was turned off, but after several weeks of continuous stimulation the 6 per second activity persisted, in bursts, even after the stimulation was discontinued. Again, the indication seems to be that the neural tissue of the cortex can learn a pattern of activity which is repeatedly induced into it and can then play this activity back when appropriately triggered. The question then is: What is the structure of the neuronal network that can so perform? Histological examination of the cortex shows such wealth of connections that it is probably beyond hope to expect to be able to follow fiber after fiber, neuron by neuron, until the whole network consisting of billions of cells is completely unraveled and known. The generation of a parsimonious model would seem therefore not only useful, but indispensable, to allow further experimentation. It is in the nature of a model to generate hypotheses and requirements. The model described in the following paragraphs has highly specific characteristics. Specific types of cells are described and will have to be found to attribute physiological significance to the model. If the elements necessary to the model cannot be identified physiologically, it would then be clear that the model would have to be changed or abandoned. The aim of this model is then to remain as faithful as possible to what is known from neurophysiological studies, but to provide specific assumptions where the data or the theoretical formulation from the physiological field are either incomplete or missing.

NERVE NET STRUCTURE

The speed and reliability with which we recognize spoken words or stimuli presented in any of the sensory modalities make one shy away from a memory model that requires sequential search of any kind among the items stored to identify the stimulus in the outside world. It is therefore assumed, and it would seem indeed desirable, that all memory networks be addressed in parallel by any stimulus entering the central nervous system. In computers an item of information is stored in and retrieved from locations in the core memory: i.e., to retrieve a given item one has to remember where it is stored; this is a memory within a memory requiring indexes and lists. It seems to be more economic to suggest that the basic structure of the memory system used by the brain is not addressed by location (location addressable) but by content (content addressable). What this means is that to retrieve a chunk of information all that is necessary is to provide the system with a fraction of the chunk, and the remainder will be played back. One such network is described here and can be visualized in Fig. 1.

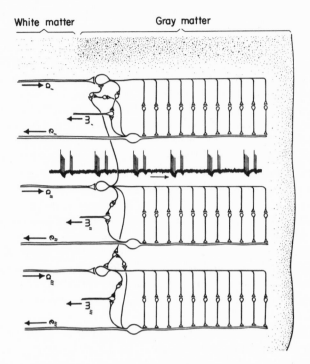

FIG. 1. A network of cells addressed in parallel.

An input fiber enters the cortex and connects itself to a receiving cell; this cell in turn gives origin to many branches that connect themselves to a number of interneurons. The number of interneurons is assumed to be rather great, possibly on the order of several hundreds. The interneurons, in turn, connect themselves to the dendritic ramifications of a further cell. This last cell generates an axon, which leaves the cortex and is therefore part of the output system, whereas the first fiber was part of the input system. Both the input cell and the output cell generate collaterals which connect themselves to a third cell called the Match cell. The Match cell in turn generates an output axon which is also part of the efferent system. This is the basic structure of one content addressable network. In addition, the input cells give rise to collaterals that inhibit laterally other input cells in the nearby networks. Match cells also have collaterals and these collaterals also inhibit input cells in nearby networks.

The Characteristics of Interneurons

It is now assumed that, either because of recovery (cycle-like) or different length in the branches of the input cell or both, the interneurons will be capable of being activated by the input activity only in a more or less sequential order. In other words, assuming that a pattern of activity is presented to the input cell, this pattern will activate those interneurons that have sufficiently recovered from previous activation, and in turn the interneurons will transmit the activity to the output cell. After a while these interneurons will become refractory or will enter a period of recovery and will be essentially unavailable for further stimulation. Other interneurons will then have sufficiently recovered from previous activity and will transmit subsequent portions of the pattern of stimulation and so on. The logical function performed by the interneurons then is that of a moving window or of a switching network. The final result is that different temporal segments of a pattern of activity will be transmitted by different interneurons. That this switching of activity through different fibers in a very regular temporal manner is achieved in the central nervous system has been shown, for example, in motor nerves, where individual fibers fire at frequencies that are less than 10 per second. Smooth contractions are obtained by regular phasing in and out of the different motor units. A further and crucial assumption to the model is that the synaptic connections formed between the interneurons and the output cell have the characteristic of plasticity. Very simply stated, this means that the more activity is put through one of these synaptic connections, the more open the connection itself will become. Conversely, the less the activity, the less conductive the junction will be. Precisely stated, the assumption is that the synaptic conductivity tends in the limit to be directly proportional to the activity which is going through the synaptic junction itself, so that if a given quantity of activity is presented to the same synapse over and over an asymptote will eventually be reached such that the conductivity will represent faithfully the amount of activity that produced it. The subsynaptic membrane is assumed to have a special characteristic. This characteristic is such that whenever a synaptic connection is activated, the amount of excitatory potential generated is proportional not to activity that generates it, but to the synaptic conductivity. To clarify the function of the interneuron/output cell junction, an analogy is in order.

It is known that muscles become hypertrophic and stronger with exercise, while lack of exercise results in a decrease in the strength and size of muscles. If we consider what is taking place in a single neuromuscular unit, we observe that given a single spike in the nerve fiber the strength of the contraction generated by a single muscle fiber is a function not of the neural spike but of the previous history of the muscle fiber. If the muscular fiber is hypertrophic, a single neural pulse will generate a strong contraction. If the muscular fiber is hypotrophic, a single neural spike generates a small contraction. Exercise, namely the amount of previous activity at the neuromuscular junction, determines the strength of contraction. This is exactly what is assumed to be the function of the synaptic connection between the interneurons and the output cell. To summarize it again, synaptic junctions between interneurons and the output cell have the characteristic of plasticity. Further, the excitatory postsynaptic potentials generated in the output cell by activation of one of these junctions is a function of the previous history of the junction itself rather than of the input activity at that time. The input activity at that time modifies the junction in the sense that postsynaptic activity tends, upon repeated presentations, to an asymptote which represents faithfully the amount of input activity repeated at the same junction.

Match Cell Characteristics

The Match cell receives collaterals both from the input cell and the output cell and the assumption here is that the Match cell fires only if coincident activity is received from both terminals. When activity in the input cell and in the output cell is identical, this cell will fire maximally. When activity in the input cell and the output cell is completely different, this cell will fire minimally or not at all.

NETWORK PARAMETERS

Lateral Inhibition and Redundancy of Storage[2]

Let us now assume the existence of a number of these networks. Let us say, about 50 of them, and let us say that a given wave form, for example, an evoked potential, is presented to all the networks in parallel to the input fibers over and over and over. The regular switching of the interneurons assures us that different portions of the wave form will be stored at different synaptic junctions in all the networks. Initially all the networks will begin to store the same input pattern, but eventually one of the networks will be just a little bit better than the neighboring ones in reproducing the input pattern through its output cell, so that the Match cell will be more active for this network than for the others. At this point, lateral inhibition will inhibit nearby networks and will prevent them from learning this particular pattern any further so that essentially the network that just by chance gets ahead first will draw the pattern to itself and will prevent the other networks from learning it. *The number of networks that learn the same pattern is thus determined by the extent of the lateral inhibition.* Without lateral inhibition all networks would learn the first pattern presented to them all. With an infinitely far reaching lateral inhibition, namely with an inhibition that reaches all the 50 networks, only one network will learn the pattern. If the lateral inhibition only reaches three or four networks away, five or more networks might learn the pattern and so on.

[2]The terminology of the following paragraphs has been freely borrowed from neurophysiology, psychology, and computer engineering. All terms have retained the correct meaning.

Afterdischarge and Learning Speed

A second important parameter in the input side of the net is the afterdischarge of the interneurons. It is assumed that each time a cell is activated, an afterdischarge ensues. The longer the afterdischarge, the more the synaptic conductivity will be changed. The shorter the afterdischarge, the less the synaptic conductivity will be modified, so that different times will be needed to reach the asymptote, i.e., different learning rates are possible.

Usage and Novelty

Let us assume that we have presented a waveform a number of times to the 50 networks and that the learning speed, namely the afterdischarge, was such that the waveform has been learned in about 50 or 60 presentations. If the lateral inhibition was sufficiently strong to inhibit the 50 networks on each side of the network that ended up learning the pattern, then only one representation of the waveform will be present in memory. Assume now that a second wave form is presented to the network. If this new wave form is totally different from the one that has already been learned, the Match cells will find no similarity between the input wave and what the net as a whole contains. The content of the net, of course, is of one wave form which we assume to be a meaningful string of signals and 49 sequences of completely random numbers. The chance is then one in fifty that the new pattern will overlay a preexisting memory, and thus destroy it. It seems clearly desirable that *new waveforms,* namely new strings of signals, should be stored *into networks that have not been previously used.*

In essence, it must be that networks that have been used in the past many times are *harder* for a new waveform to enter than are networks that have never been used or have been used fewer times. A simple way of achieving this is to endow the Match cell with some plasticity of its own but of a special kind. We can assume that the Match cell is initially linear in its responding to the number of matches between input and output waveform but that with further usage a nonlinearity begins to appear for low levels of match. In other words, low levels of match would not be signaled by a Match cell that has been activated many times in the past but higher levels of match would be signaled normally. The amount of nonlinearity would have to be proportional to the number of times that the network has been used previously. A new waveform entering the net would then produce in the Match cells a very limited amount of activity which would be due to chance matching between the unrelated content of the memory networks and the values characterizing the waveform. While all previously unused networks would signal chance level of match, previously used networks would signal a below chance level of match. The new waveform would then be stored in that one of the unused networks that by chance presents the highest level of match. This network naturally would inhibit all the other networks and prevent them from learning the second waveform.

Similarly, a third waveform would again generate a purely chance level of matches in all the unused networks and a below chance level of matches in the networks that have stored waveform number 1 and waveform number 2. If waveform number 1 is now again presented to all the input fibers of the network, it would be immediately recognized; namely the Match cell of the network that stored waveform number 1 originally would present the highest level of activity of all the Match cells. Presentation of only half of waveform number 1 would still produce a higher level of activity in the Match cell of the network containing waveform number 1. It can then be seen that such a complex of content addressable networks is not only capable of pattern recognition, but it is also capable of playing back the total pattern when it is presented with only a sufficient fraction of the pattern itself. This last form of behavior can be used in explaining the associative properties of such a memory network in the temporal or the spatial domain. It can also explain S-R behavior; namely, if an organism has had the repeated experience that pressing a red circle is followed by the appearance of a peanut, whereas pressing the green square is followed by the appearance of no peanut, then the appearance of the red circle could conceivably generate or cause the playback of the full sequence which involves appropriate behavior for obtaining the peanut.

Admittance and Generalization

A third parameter is the admittance of the Match cell. This parameter really defines the amount of variability admitted for each point to be detected by the Match cell. If the Match cell requires a very low degree of variability between *each point* of the input wave and *each point* of the output wave to be activated, then we could say that the admittance is very, very small. Conversely if the degree of variability allowed by the Match cell between the input and output is great, we could say that the degree of admittance is greater. In other words, this parameter has to do with the y dimension of the wave and determines the range over which y values will be *generalized,* i.e., considered to be the same.

Acceptable Match and Risk

The fourth parameter controlling the net is the acceptable match. This parameter, not to be confused with admittance, has to do with how many points between the input and the output waves were found to be matching by the Match cell, i.e., the x dimension of a waveform. If all the points were matching, then the match is, of course, 100%. If only half of them were matching, then the match is 50% and so on. It is clear that the total presentation of a pattern which has been learned before will provide 100% match and therefore full recognition.

But this condition is also the least informative. In other words, while there is no uncertainty about the pattern, there is also no extra information furnished by the recall of this pattern. A less than total presentation will provide the organism with some extra information, namely the stimulus from the environment will generate the playback of a sequence of signals which is longer than the sequence provided by the stimulus itself.

If wave forms in the brain represent stimuli, responses, and the consequences of responses as we have previously seen (Pribram *et al.*, 1967), then presentation of the stimulus will generate a playback of the whole sequence; that is to say: recognition of the stimulus, the appropriate behavior that went with the stimulus, followed by the expectation of the consequences of the behavior. The amount of extra information obtained by the network or by the organism is greater, the smaller the segment of the total input string. The amount of uncertainty, and therefore of risk for the organism in using the sequence itself becomes, on the other hand, correspondingly greater. An analogy in the auditory mode helps in understanding the significance of this parameter. The name of a song followed by the playing of the whole song will, of course, be recognized, if it has been heard before. The name of the song followed by half of the song will enable the listener to remember the remainder of the song. Ultimately, just the name of the song, or a few notes, will enable the listener to recall it entirely. But if the notes are too few, or if the name of the song is equivocal, then the level of match would be correspondingly very, very small and might not enable the recaller to identify which song we are referring to. It might be that the few notes provided are part of the beginning of many songs. Ideally then, the acceptable match parameter should be set for that minimum value which allows unequivocal recognition of the stimulus with recall of the associate behavior and consequences of behavior. It follows from the above paragraph that such a network is then capable not only of pattern recognition and of S-R behavior, it is also capable of being biased. Imagine a number of strings of signals recorded in memory having to do, for example, with feeding behavior. These strings would be located in visual memory for those parts of the feeding behavior that are directly connected to vision, for example, seeing an appropriate stimulus that when manipulated under visual control leads to availability of food which then can be taken to the mouth, be ingested, and produce subsequently the cessation of hunger. The assumption has to be that while visual memory contains most precisely and primarily visual strings, it also contains enough nonvisual information to allow the readdressing of the system by the visually triggered strings so that auditory, somatic, gustatory, etc., strings are subsequently called into play. The internal state which would be part of the string, for example, hunger and the disappearance of hunger, would activate or would facilitate all those memory strings that contain such information in themselves and therefore produce a partial level of match. This would then make available to the rest of the brain strings containing pertinent information about feeding behavior. If other parts of some strings are available in the environment, a higher level of match would be achieved for certain strings and the connected behavior could then be played back if the acceptable level of match is reached or exceeded.

An analogy at this point again might help in understanding the functions of a network containing, for example, 50 content addressable units. Imagine that we have 50 computers for average transients (CAT) and let us say that at zero time their memory cores contain nothing but random numbers. If we now present to the 50 CATS in parallel an input wave over and over, an average of the input wave will begin to be formed in all 50 of them. The one CAT computer that begins to show, ahead of the others, more points of match between the input wave and the output, can inhibit the remaining 49 and will prevent them from proceeding with the average, whereas it will continue to build up a more and more clear representation of the input in its own core memory. The decision on which CAT computer is ahead of the others is performed by the Match cells. Match cells, in other words, determine the degree of match between input and output for each memory network. The CAT computer analogy is also helpful in understanding that a small or medium amount of variability in the input waves will not upset the network but will still result in the learning of a waveform which is the representative average of the waveform presented.

COMPUTER IMPLEMENTATION OF AN OMNIUM-GATHERUM CORE CONTENT ADDRESSABLE MEMORY (OCCAM)

Simulation of the network described above was undertaken to verify that the hypotheses and assumptions made would indeed enable the network to perform the functions required. The simulation was performed on a small general purpose computer, the PDP-8. The core memory of this computer consists of 4096 twelve-bit words and is therefore too small to allow simulation of *all cell characteristics.* Only those functions of each cell that are involved specifically in the model have therefore been simulated. With respect to interneuron function, it is clear for example that the presence of the input cell is not really necessary and that a fiber branching onto the interneurons would do just as well, provided one is willing to accept presynaptic inhibition rather than postsynaptic into the system of lateral inhibition. Similarly the interneurons themselves are not really necessary, provided one is willing to assume that the ramifications of the input fiber, because of different length and diameters, act in effect as a switching network. The fundamental characteristic is the presence of lateral inhibition. Without it the network would only learn one pattern of activity regardless of the number of content addressable networks contained in the total net. As has already been said, the extent of lateral inhibition determines the amount of redundancy with which a pattern is stored in the net.

The second set of crucial elements in the neuronal model are the synaptic connections between the interneurons and the output cell, or alternatively between the ramifications of the input fiber and the output cell. It is this junction with its special plasticity and subsynaptic membrane characteristics that together with the characteristics of the Match cell make it possible for the model to perform.

What has therefore been simulated is the following: a switching network which breaks an input wave into fifty segments. Each segment then is directed to a "synaptic" junction. The special plastic characteristics of the junction are simulated. The postsynaptic junctional activity is adjusted each time by a small fraction so that if the input to it is repeated a number of times, it would eventually asymptote to it. The activity generated by the postsynaptic membrane in turn depends only on the past history. In other words, the average of all preceding activities at the synapse is generated every time the synapse is activated, irrespective of the amount of activity causing the activation.

Concerning the Match cell, the characteristics that have been simulated are the admittance, namely, the amount of similarity between each one of the 50 input values and the 50 output values that is required. In addition, a usage factor which determines output on the basis of the number of times the output cell was activated. Finally, the property of totalizing the number of matches detected has also to be simulated for this cell.

Of the parameters described for the neuronal model, four have to be given real values, for example: lateral inhibition, i.e., redundancy of storage, had to be set at one value or another and in the actual simulation it was set for a value of 50 which means that only one representation of each wave form would be formed. The afterdischarge and therefore the learning speed (namely, the number of times the same pattern afterdischarges within the networks) were set in such a way that learning would take place in 50 to 60 trials.

A Match cell usage parameter, as already noted, is the inverse measure of novelty. Admittance value, i.e., generalization, also has to be specified together with the parameter that controls the increasing nonlinearity. These two parameters together control the "tuning" with which a given network recognizes its own wave form. The fact that the networks which have been used many times are harder to enter gives this program not only the characteristics of a content addressable memory but also the characteristics of a push down list. Assuming that memory were ever to be filled, a new wave would be stored in the network that has been used the least of them all, which makes sense from an adaptive point of view because the least used string is, by definition, the least useful. The admittance parameter is crucial in determining the way in which a waveform is learned. If the parameter is too loosely set, if the admittance is very broad, then subsequent waveforms will overlay previously learned ones, because the tuning of the networks is not fine enough. At the other end of the spectrum, if the admittance parameter is too narrow, a given network will not be able to recognize on the second presentation of a waveform that it is the same waveform that it began storing on presentation number 1. Therefore a new network might take on the waveform at the second presentation, but because a very small amount of learning takes place from one presentation to the next, this second network might not recognize the waveform on the third presentation, so that a new network would come into play for each presentation. In other words, the net would be prevented from learning the waveform because it could not, by using a too rigid criterion, recognize it until it was fully learned, which would effectively make it incapable of learning.

One way out of this impasse would be to maintain a very narrow acceptance but increase the learning speed so that instead of 50 to 60 presentations, only two or three would be required. In this case after one presentation, learning would have proceeded so fast that there would be no question about recognizing the waveform on presentation number 2. This solution is far from ideal for a number of reasons; the first one being that slow learning imparts to the system *averaging* properties which seem to be a desirable feature. The second reason is somewhat connected to the averaging properties and would be that slightly different versions of the same waveform would be stored as two separate representations, namely the system would be unable to generate representative strings of signals rather than individual ones and therefore would store many representations of the same pattern.

The fifth parameter, namely, acceptable match, does not need a real value and can be set to zero. When this is done, Occam simply shows the best match it finds in its networks to whatever waveform is being presented to it. It is clear that in a real organism, the value of the acceptable match would therefore have to be defined by the software in some fashion.

Figure 2 shows this program, named Occam for Omnium-Gatherum Core Content Addressable Memory, in real operation. A waveform in A is presented to Occam repeatedly. From the top are subsequent responses, every 10 trials showing further and further improvement until after about 50 trials Occam generates a waveform which is practically identical to the input wave form. In Fig. 2b, Occam is presented with a second waveform which is also learned. Upon presentation of parts of waveform number 1 or waveform number 2, Occam retrieves the remainder of the waveform appropriately.

GENERAL COMMENTS

Reinforcers as Dissimilarizers of Memory Strings

It is evident from the model that Occam would have a hard time learning two different patterns which are very similar to each other. As a matter of fact, this

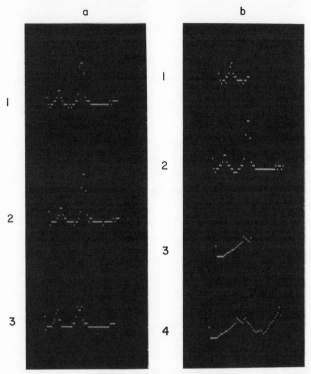

FIG. 2. An Occam program.

is an impossible task. This is because, if two patterns are very similar, presentation of one of them will produce a high level of match in the network that has stored the other one, so that the second pattern would always enter the network of the first one and interfere with it. A way to enable Occam to learn two very similar patterns would be to attach to one of the patterns a different ending signal. For example, we could follow one of the patterns with a series of oscillations at a given frequency whereas we could follow the other pattern with a series of zero levels or with a series of oscillations at a frequency different than the first one. The operation seems to be extremely similar to the one which is done usually in behavioral experiments when an animal is trained to discriminate between two patterns. One pattern is usually followed by a reinforcer whereas the other pattern is not. This serves as a pointer to notify the organism that two patterns which might have looked identical are really different, even though the difference might be small. Similar concepts have been expressed by Pribram (1963). The organism can then institute such procedures that it can look for differences and end up by storing the two patterns or enlarged versions of small sections of the two patterns.

Reinforcers as Controllers of Learning Speed and Redundancy

It is also possible to imagine that reinforcers act on the parameter of learning speed and lateral inhibition. If reinforcers would possibly decrease the extent of lateral inhibition and increase learning speed, this would enable an organism to learn faster and more redundantly strings of signals which are associated with information which is of survival value. It would seem at least at first glance that reinforcers are divisible into two classes. The first kind of reinforcer would be connected to pain, food, and the like. This particular system can be conceived as permanently wired-in so that whenever activated lateral inhibition and learning speed are appropriately affected. The second kind of reinforcer, having to do with social situations, psychological situations, and the like, would be acting on the memory only through the software, namely, as parts of existing programs or plans (Pribram, 1963).

To summarize, a computer simulation of a hypothetical neuronal network is provided. The network consists of many identical subunits which are all addressed in parallel and have the characteristic of content addressability. It would seem that the model furnished can explain pattern recognition and stimulus-response behavior.

REFERENCES

John, E. R., & Killam, K. F. Electrophysiological correlates of avoidance conditioning in the cat. *Journal of Pharmacology and Experimental Therapy,* 1959, **125**, 252-274.

Kopeloff, L. M., Barrera, S. E., & Kopeloff, N. Recurrent convulsive seizures in animals produced by immunologic and chemical means. *American Journal of Psychiatry,* 1942, 98, 881.

Kopeloff, L. M., Chusid, J. G., & Kopeloff, N. Chronic experimental epilepsy in *Macaca mulatta. Neurology,* 1954, **4**, 218.

Kopeloff, L. M., Chusid, J. G., & Kopeloff, N. *A.M.A. Archives of Neurology and Psychiatry,* 1955, **74**, 523.

Morrell, F. Lasting changes in synaptic organization produced by continuous neuronal bombardment. In J. F. Delafresnaye, A. Fessard, & J. Konorski (Eds.), *Symposium on brain mechanisms and learning.* Oxford: Blackwell, 1961. Pp. 375-392.

Pribram, K. H. Reinforcement revisited: A structural view. In M. Jones (Ed.), *Nebraska symposium on motivation.* Lincoln: University of Nebraska Press, 1963. Pp. 113-159.

Pribram, K. H., Spinelli, D. N., & Kamback, M. C. Electrocortical correlates of stimulus response and reinforcement. *Science,* 1967, **157**, 94-96.

Spinelli, D. N. Evoked responses to visual patterns in area 17 of the rhesus monkey. *Brain Research,* 1967, **5**, 511-514.

AUTHOR INDEX

Numbers in italics refer to the pages on which the complete references are listed.

SUBJECT INDEX

A

Acetoxycycloheximide, memory storage and, 58
Acetylcholine, brain and, differential experience and, 75, 76
Acetylcholinesterase, brain and,
  differential experience and, 75-77, 80, 84
  growth and, 82
  stress and, 80
Acquisition, 224, 228
  avoidance response and, 57
  cortical lesions and, 276
  drugs and, 58
  long-term memory and, 47
  motor skills and, 44
  plasticity and, 230-231
Activation, stimulus duration and, 194
Activity level, transfer of training and, 140-141, 145-147, 151-153
Adenine, 109
After discharge, neuronal networks and, 299, 303
After-effects,
  single neuron and, 175-189
  method of investigation of, 176-179
  modification of electric activity of, 179
  pacemaker and, 179, 181, 183-189, 193
  single stimulus presentation and, 193,

194, 196
  spike activity dependence on current intensity and, 184
  spike generation activation due to iontophoresis of positive ions, and, 181-183, 188, 189
  spike generation activation evoked or occurring spontaneously, 179-181
  spike generation sensitization and, 184-185
  spike generation suppression and, 183, 186, 188, 189
Amnesia,
  anterograde, 39
  global, 47
  retention and, 56
  retrograde, 36, 53
Amnestic syndrome, *see under* Temporal lobe lesions
Amygdala,
  lesions of, 30, 34, 36
  neuronal activity of, 214, 217
Anesthesia, *see* Sleep
Animals, memory storage in, 51-60
Antibiotics, behavior and, 112
Aplysia,
  abdominal ganglion of, cellular mechanisms in, 163, 166-168, 170-173
  pacemaker neurons of, 186-187
Apomorphine hydrochloride, avoidance training and, transfer of, 130, 154-156

313